T0339678

FROM CONFLICT TO CRISIS

FROM CONFLICT TO CRISIS

The Danger of U.S. Actions

JEANNE M. HASKIN

Algora Publishing
New York

Library of Congress Cataloging-in-Publication Data —

Haskin, Jeanne M., 1964-
   From conflict to crisis : the danger of U.S. actions / Jeanne M. Haskin.
   pages cm
   Includes bibliographical references and index.
      ISBN 978-0-87586-960-5 (pbk.: alk. paper)—ISBN 978-0-87586-961-2
(hbk.: alk. paper)—ISBN 978-0-87586-962-9 (ebook) 1. United States—Foreign
economic relations—Central America. 2. Central America—Foreign economic
relation—United States. 3. Neoliberalism—United States. 4. Business cycles—
United States. 5. Capitalism—United States. I. Title.
   HF1456.5.C4H37 2012
   337.730728–dc23
                              2012032091

Printed in the United States

This book is dedicated to Elizabeth Hull,
my long-time friend and fellow writer,
who shares my passion for humanitarian causes
and has always been the first to review and assist with my work.

I would like to thank my family and Algora Publishing for remaining committed to my research endeavors and making it possible for my work to become available to the world.

TABLE OF CONTENTS

Table of Contents

INTRODUCTION

This a book about moderation in the face of global dangers caused by constant recalibration of how narrowly economic benefits are shared at home and abroad. At many times in U.S. history, and in Central America perhaps even more clearly, miscalculation of the least common benefits required for pacification under greatly repressive systems led to violence, revolution, and retaliatory covert action until the countries were so damaged and their people so desperate, exhausted, and demoralized that defeat and political turnabouts were not only accepted but conducive to the application of neoliberalism.

Unlike classical liberalism, which was embraced during the Cold War to combat the spread of Communism and install the global cornerstones for extractive developmentalism, neoliberalism re-set and further lowered expectations for economic advancement once the Communist threat and the "third way" proved less viable than capitalism. The question then became how to push the U.S. government, its allies, and reformed enemies from conflict to crisis via debt leverage manipulated through monetarism. In this way, populations could be persuaded to suffer even more inequities and economic hardship while teetering on the tipping point between resistance and acceptance. The next step for minimalization strategists in contemporary politics is to disenfranchise parts of the populace that can't be co-opted, and this even applies to military governments, which are not overthrown for repression but to break their grip on resources.

This analysis will begin with how paths are created with the potential to produce crises, then examine U.S. policies with special focus on Central America, before returning to the present day and the neoliberal impact of more advanced and fully deliberate economic minimalization.

The point is not to add fuel to the fire for countries already in turmoil or to compromise U.S. security, but to argue for retrenchment, cohesion, and intelligent moderation before it is too late to pull back from crises of danger.

Preferred Paths and Ends

A conduit to crisis is a medium that facilitates, conducts or makes possible a path to anything controversial, including but not limited to legislation, research, lobbying, fundraising, diplomacy, disarmament, militarization and strategy, as well as unfair advantages in armaments and allies. Under inhibiting parameters that make negotiation difficult and compromise unlikely, a transition from conflict to crisis involves premeditated pressures designed to elicit pain and develop conduits toward preferred paths or ends.

A transition from conflict to crisis can be successfully avoided if the conflict in question is consistently non-harmful. When the issue was freeing gays in the military to express their sexual orientation without fear of discharge, the paths toward that end involved community action, group solidarity, support from high-profile figures, political contributions, lobbying, and inclusion of such individuals in the decision-making process through government participation. This engendered protest from some religious groups, homophobic communities, and political representatives, but, for the most part, measured responses, delays in implementation, the largely positive reception from the latest generation of service men and women,[1] and President Obama's insistence that "Don't Ask, Don't Tell"[2] should be repealed through Congress rather than by Executive Order, showed that this particular conflict, negotiated on a continuum, generated acceptance without escalating to violence.

---

1 Who grew up with non-controversial exposure to the LGBT community.
2 DADT was, in itself, incremental as an earlier measured compromise arranged under President Clinton.

On the other hand, the Internet is filled with pages of religious condemnation expressing the view that acceptance of the LGBT[3] community is consistent with Biblical Revelation as a sign of evil in the End Times, or the end of civilization. There is also a whole survivalist movement prepared to respond with violence against what it perceives as a New World Order and in defense of the Constitution. In this case, fear mongering even promotes the idea of a new constitution to protect what is perceived as "real" American values, dating back to the settlement of the New World and the American Revolution.

Lest we be tempted to think this is harmless, all resistance movements unearth the bones of their founders to defend a past that was either repressive or idealized as sacred. It is a ritual of purification against encroachment by other cultures, hostility toward their lifestyles, a perception of unfair advancement, and, first and foremost, anger toward their consumption of coveted resources.

Economic Scapegoating

Although the LGBT community may be the latest group to demand respect, acceptance, and benefits, the dying American dream spawns a backward-looking mentality that catalogues a long line of economic usurpers, from all manner of immigrants to blacks and nonconformists, until the term "liberal" loses its sense of tolerance and becomes an all-encompassing label for what's universally hated and patently wrong with America.

Those who were once made welcome, to fuel the growth of the nation, quickly became disposable under altered expectations. The greater the economic contraction, the "purer" must be the nation.

Learning from Yugoslavia

Pre-war Yugoslavia offers a useful comparison. Cultural assimilation, ethnic heterogeneity, participatory government, and economic wellbeing had made it resemble the United States and the beloved American dream. Its conduits to crisis began with the collapse of the social contract under economic reform, new constitutions that disempowered ethnic minorities, and rushed democratic reforms (under threat of U.S. penalization) that depended almost entirely on ethnic solidarity. From there it was only a short step to republican and ethnic secessionism, Serbian militarism, and vol-

---

3 Lesbian, Gay, Bisexual and Transgender community.

untary Bosnian disarmament, the outcome of which was genocide, wars over territory, and such bitter, enduring hatreds that the first thing school children learned in the war's aftermath was their status of victimhood.

Much of this is mirrored here in the United States. Just as the West denied further funding to former Yugoslavia and insisted on economic austerity, after the 2008 fiscal crisis conservatives in Congress have fought the President's stimulus spending as well as every one of his budgets and proposed revenue sources. Vermont has tried to secede from the Union and Californian Christian communities have sought secession within their state. Arizona made constitutional changes regarding immigration and the most nativist, bigoted document ever to hit *The Washington Post* was entitled "The Conservative Constitution of Real America," which appeared in 2011. The proposed "Conservative Constitution," said to have been making the rounds among Republican legislators, who signed on to the document, mandates forced Christian conversions as a condition of survival (like the Serbs in former Yugoslavia). But worse and even creepier, the results of the latest U.S. Census are available in detail, with information on race, profession and income for every identified household. In the same way that Bosnian Muslim professionals were assassinated on the basis of hit lists, all any "real American" needs to conduct assassinations is an Internet connection. The closure of U.S. military bases is similar to Bosnian disarmament, since it has left the Northeast coast largely dependent on Maine and, in the wake of 9/11, the Department of Homeland Security mandated contingency plans for vital operations to be moved to secret locations, presumably not in the North, thus securing important resources should there be a confrontation with the "liberal" Eastern establishment.

The Threat of "Balkanization"

People who hope for a conservative takeover, with economic austerity and deeper economic liberalization, find committed opposition in people who fear deeper stratification and economic deprivation, forcible Christian conversion, fundamentalist violence, and more corruption in Washington.

If it should ever come to secessionism, fundamentalists have an evangelical imperative to control people who oppose their values, and this coincides neatly with maintaining the federal union, unless fueling separatist sentiments makes it tempting to pursue expulsion or other forms of mistreatment.

The push–pull dynamic between federalism and separatism allows for one of three likely outcomes:

1. The government will continue as it always has in terms of inclusion and tolerance (in which case, rightwing radicalism and militarism can be expected to increase exponentially and induce a challenge sooner or later).

2. The government will become exclusivist and will institute repression (either in fear of radicalization or under its momentum).

3. There will be population movements and territorial divisions.

There's a Reason It's Called Scapegoating

Reform parameters championed by conservatives are precisely the harmful policies we've forced on other nations, as will be demonstrated in the analysis of Central America, though wreaking destruction at home was mostly taboo in the past. Two things changed the conservatives' minds: the collapse of the Soviet Union and the intellectual argument against the nation-state, which purports to offer the road to peace but can be distilled to a single point: that money owes no loyalty and should therefore have no home. In that sense, globalism is what the U.S. demonstrates in microcosm. Offloading the costs of government, while controlling its repressive machinery, has always been the goal of those who own almost everything.

The rich understand that capitalism is a game of musical chairs. It's systemic class warfare conducted on a grand scale to discourage broad solidarity across class lines that might otherwise threaten the system, and the Tea Party's rise was preemptive—with all its implied violence and "real" American theater—as the means to channel the electorate's anger into voting out Obama so reform might proceed unimpeded, with all its inherent dangers.

CHAPTER ONE: UNEARTHING THE BONES

In the United States, a great deal of study and energy goes into promoting respect for democracy, not just to keep it alive here but also to spread it around the world. It embraces the will of the majority, whether or not its main beneficiaries have more resources than other citizens do, as shown by the election of President Obama, who promised hope and change for the suffering majority, but did not sit long in office before being subjected to an economic vote of no-confidence. Those who claim we run a plutocracy (government for the rich by the rich) — or that we're victims of a conspiracy contrived by a shadow government — are right while being wrong. Our government is beyond the reach of ordinary American citizens in terms of economic power. However, the creation of a system to keep the majority of the populace at the losing end of a structure which neither promised nor delivered a state of financial equality was a predictable extension of the economic system the U.S. government was formed to protect.

The Start of a New World

In the war for liberation, Americans stood for economic freedom and imposed their idea of fairness by coercion, or force of arms. No one disputes this; in fact, we celebrate it, and scholars of American history are well-versed in the ideals embraced by our government's founders. Namely, that none shall take away any portion of what we earn and own without the consent of the citizenry, and then only for narrow purposes. So it makes perfect sense that current accusations of "Taxation Without Representation" should resonate deeply with Americans who feel threatened by an unsustainable national debt, uncertainties in the tax system, and programs of entitlement from which they feel they derive no gain. It was, and is, the most sacred underpinning of American government that we embrace capitalism. And capitalists have searched for, and settled on, democracy as that system of government which is most condu-cive to profit and the avoidance of war for any reason other than self-interest.

When the founders devised our government, they idealized a society where the laws applied equally but the course of a man's for-tunes were left to labor and ambition, talent and ingenuity. There was as yet a vast frontier where any man could carve out a living (if we ignore, for the moment, that the frontier was already occupied); and it's easy to imagine that men looked up to each other with re-spect for thrift and industry. Disparities in fortunes were probably inspiring rather than a source of envy because resources were too abundant to begrudge any man his due. Instead, they could all agree that keeping their world this way meant institutionalizing their values with a government that served them. And, in this, they had the guidance of their revolutionary experience, beginning with the conditions that made them leave Britain.

Separation of Church and State

British Puritans condemned the relationship between the church and the British Crown because the church was expected to foster compliant commoners versus the royals and the rich who purchased dispensations from sin. More bluntly, they paid the church to prop them on a pedestal, no matter what they did, while moralizing the commoners. This corrupt double standard led to in-creasing rebellion and, lest the Puritan movement spread, Britain sanctioned their move to the New World. The Puritans believed themselves God's faithful and set forth for the promised land, cer-tain it would be their reward.

The belief in an ability to interpret the Bible privately (without a required intermediary in the form of a priest) was consistent with the turn to rational thought during the Enlightenment. However, this was a freedom that trickled down from European philosophers, who debated the aspects of life and governance most conducive to wealth creation. When the monarchy and the church were a mutual source of legitimacy, it meant that anyone could be taxed by Divine Right for expenditures they didn't agree with at rates they couldn't protest. Therefore, revolutionists in the New World necessarily rejected the tag-team of church and state.

The New World offered freedom of worship to Quakers, Protestants, Puritans, and others who believed that faith and honest work would culminate in God's intended communities. At the same time, it housed opportunists for whom government legitimacy stemmed from the freedom to pursue economic self-interest. As a value held in common for overlapping reasons, the separation of church and state was enshrined in the Bill of Rights, which states in the First Amendment that "Congress shall make no law respecting an establishment of religion or prohibiting the free exercise thereof."

This does not mean our society has never reflected religious input. School children used to say the Pledge of Allegiance (to which the phrase "under God" was added in 1954), which then gave way to the Moment of Silence. The words "In God We Trust" are printed on U.S. currency. President Eisenhower once said he didn't care what god you believed in, so long as you believed there was a god. But when you insist that America was, or is, a nation of any religious denomination, whether you comprise a majority of citizens or merely possess the resources to shout the longest and loudest, what you actually seek is the tyranny we rejected as revolutionaries.

The Enlightenment of Self-Interest

It's not coincidental that the beliefs of our founding fathers reflect the philosophies attributed to the Enlightenment. Having already benefited under a system of mercantilism that favored the growth of manufacturing with monopolies, tariffs, labor controls, and the import of raw materials extracted from colonies, British industrialists extolled the benefits of capitalism because economic self-interest would allow them to produce greater wealth without government controls. The term laissez-faire, which means "leave it alone," quickly became inseparable from free market economics.

The challenge was to persuade the king that greater wealth for individuals would mean higher productivity and therefore increased revenues. So economic theories devised by intellectuals put forth arguments as to what kinds of taxes and ownership would interfere least with profits and revenues. Not surprisingly, men like David Ricardo targeted the cronies of royalty, who held land in monopoly and could raise rents against free market principles. Others, such as Adam Smith, trusted the landed nobility more than the up-and-coming industrialists, so taxation was hotly debated, along with development issues. Industrialists met in salons, cafés, and coffee houses, where discussions of the latest in philosophy eventually led to a hodge-podge re-interpretive approach as to what served them best.

As the man with the greatest influence on American capitalism, Adam Smith wrote *The Theory of Moral Sentiments* before he produced *An Inquiry into the Nature and Causes of the Wealth of Nations.* Interpretations of his work have attempted everything from honesty to aggrandizement, to negation, to self-serving piety, in ways not always consistent with what is known of his life. It has been said he believed capitalism was the gift of Providence and the natural order of things (in line with survival of the fittest and Social Darwinism), though, in the way of many rationalist philosophers, he wrote of the early superstition with which men attributed the causes of life to their gods and later proclaimed himself a deist (a believer in God but not Jesus Christ as the accepted son of God). In practice, he found common ground with atheist David Hume.

Not by any stretch does Smith promote modern practices of government intervention in economic schemes, but it's common to insist that his principles went forth and multiplied from the three sacred cows we adopted with more fervor than any known religion. No matter that one of them stemmed from Smith's musings and was not offered in the spirit of an Economic Commandment: heads will roll and fur will fly if we, the uninitiated in mathematics and economics (not to mention values), cast aspersions of doubt on the dogma of the "invisible hand," which has been distorted according to need, depending on who doesn't "get" what it does. One minute, it means something unintentionally fortuitous. The next, it's perceived as the most diffuse (and therefore successful) form of coercion ever to prevent people who lose their jobs, assets, and homes from lashing out in retaliation. (This illusion has been somewhat spoiled by the very visible paws of lobbyists, banks, and governments.)

Smith said that when you want something for society, you get it by talking to investors not about your needs but about their advantages. So presumably self-interest is the sole virtue required for economic sainthood.

Scientific Obfuscation

Like all exalted beings, economic saints will work in mysterious ways with no obligation to listen to others, much less explain the existence of evil. But as descendants of the same people who despised the Catholic Pope and objected to the use of Latin on the grounds that it kept the true meaning of religion from honest, ordinary folks, it's odd that they will *leap* to the defense of economic science and all its trappings of obfuscation.

Because, eschewing the math and jargon, I could sit my three-year-old niece in a sandbox with an abacus and have her reach the conclusion she'll cry if I take it away from her. Then I could turn to my fourteen-year-old niece and posit the following math problem, to be resolved with fifth-grade algebra, which she blew through years ago:

Three-year-old Elizabeth has an abacus, represented by x. If 5y represents her tendency to become a socialist revolutionary when Billy robs her of x, what will it cost to replace 5y with 10^4 power if 10^4 constitutes the amount Billy wants Elizabeth to pay *him* in appreciable gold bullion while cheering him on to the fourth power and incurring a 35% Value Added Tax for Billy to rob her of x?

Can you guess? Forty years of Cold War and the ultimate realization that abuse of the communist system and a hierarchy of privilege proved that system to be vulnerable to selfishness — in common with the triumphant capitalist countries.

Because any desired outcome can be written into an equation to exclude unwanted facts or inputs by holding some things constant while applying chosen variables that may not hold true under every historical circumstance, it's considered "falsifiable" and therefore "scientific." But only if it appeals to the right people and justifies a given political need will it become sacrosanct (until the next round of "progress").

In Adam Smith's Own Words

I'm not suggesting we throw the capitalist baby out with the manipulative bathwater, but if you believe that individuals acting in their self-interest have the power to self-regulate without the imposition of government, then you have to be self-critical before you can be self-regulating. So let's look at Smith's writings and the context in which he produced them.

To start:

> The annual labor of every nation is the fund which originally
> supplies it with all the necessaries and conveniences of life
> which it annually consumes, and which consist always either
> in the immediate produce of that labor, or in what is purchased
> with that produce from other nations.[4]

Smith cites labor (the input of human beings) in the production of goods for domestic use (consumption) or export (trade) as
the source of a nation's wealth. The combination of production for
home use and what's purchased with production through trade,
supplies a nation with its wants and necessities in proportion to
what they're worth. A nation not producing enough to provide for
its needs is either:

a) not using its labor efficiently; or
b) not employing a sufficient labor quantity.[5]

Otherwise, goods are abundant and opportunity exists for every
person to better his lot, regardless of relative wealth.

> Among civilized and thriving nations...though a great number of
> people do not labour at all, many of whom consume the produce
> of ten times, frequently of a hundred times more labour than the
> greater part of those who work; yet the produce of the whole
> labour of the society is so great, that all are often abundantly
> supplied, and a workman, even of the lowest and poorest order,
> if he is frugal and industrious, may enjoy a greater share of the
> necessaries and conveniencies of life than it is possible for any
> savage to acquire.[6]

The advantage of civilization over a hunter–gatherer society is
that it provides for all in common without periods of hardship and
starvation. However, the proportion of goods available depends on
more or less employment, which, in turn, is made possible through
investment in factories and equipment.

> Whatever be the actual state of the skill, dexterity, and judg-
> ment with which labour is applied in any nation, the abundance
> or scantiness of its annual supply must depend, during the con-
> tinuance of that state, upon the proportion between the num-
> ber of those who are annually employed in useful labour, and
> of those who are not so employed. The number of useful and
> productive labourers, it will hereafter appear, is every where in
> proportion to the quantity of capital stock which is employed

---

4 Smith, Adam, *An Inquiry into the Nature and Causes of the Wealth of Nations.*
  (New York: P.F. Collier & Son, 1909) Page 5.
5 Ibid.
6 Ibid., Page 6.

in setting them to work and to the particular way in which it is so employed.[7]

Smith's conclusion is that a nation's factory owners will employ labor and equipment in the most efficient combinations possible and favor domestic industry, not from loyalty to the state or concern for the public good, but from an interest in their own security, as if led by an "invisible hand" to produce a benevolent outcome they aren't aware of and never planned.

As every individual, therefore, endeavours as much as he can to employ his capital in the support of domestic industry, and so to direct that industry that its produce may be of the greatest value; every individual necessarily labours to render the annual revenue of the society as great as he can. He generally, indeed, neither intends to promote the public interest, nor knows how much he is promoting it. By preferring the support of domestic to that of foreign industry, he intends only his own security; and by directing that industry in such a manner as its produce may be of the greatest value, he intends only his own gain, and he is in this, as in many other cases, led by an invisible hand to promote an end which was no part of his intention. Nor is it always the worse for the society that it was no part of it. By pursuing his own interest he frequently promotes that of the society more effectually than when he really intends to promote it. I have never known much good done by those who affected to trade for the public good. It is an affectation, indeed, not very common among merchants, and very few words need be employed in dissuading them from it.[8]

From an equally rational perspective, Smith's argument for an efficiency orientation embraces the theory of comparative advantage long before economists coined the term. If it makes sense for industrialists to employ labor and machinery in the least expensive and most productive combinations possible, then no nation should waste its resources on producing what another nation can manufacture more cheaply.[9] Nor should government interfere with the decisions of individuals as to the manner of investment or mode of industry, since it possesses neither the necessary knowledge nor the right:

What is the species of domestic industry which his capital can employ, and of which the produce is likely to be of the greatest value, every individual, it is evident, can, in his local situation, judge much better than any statesman or lawgiver can do for

7 Ibid.
8 Ibid., Page 351.
9 Ibid., Page 352.

him. The statesman, who should attempt to direct private people in what manner they ought to employ their capitals, would
not only load himself with a most unnecessary attention, but assume an authority which could safely be trusted, not only to no
single person, but to no council or senate whatever, and which
would no-where be so dangerous as in the hands of a man who
had folly and presumption enough to fancy himself fit to exercise it.[10]

This does not mean Smith trusts businesses and producers not
to seek government favor to the detriment of society, but, returning to the "invisible hand" and the unintended benefits of individual self-interest, he perceives a natural incentive that will produce
business without it:

It is not from the benevolence of the butcher, the brewer, or the
baker, that we expect our dinner, but from their regard to their
own interest. We address ourselves, not to their humanity but
to their self-love, and never talk to them of our own necessities
but of their advantages.[11]

Importantly, Smith's *Theory of Moral Sentiments*, written before
The Wealth of Nations, proposed that men acted in society with a
need for sympathy from observers. Notice he didn't say men were
motivated to act toward others from sympathy (or even empathy)
with what wasn't their own predicament. In this way, he could
write *The Wealth of Nations* with no mention of the Scottish Tobacco
Lords who made their fortunes through slavery. However, Smith
declared that the gluttony of the rich was unproductive labor after
traveling to France near the time of the French Revolution.

Abusive Self-Interest

In 1764, twenty-five years before the embrace of Madame Guil-
lotine (when heads rolled literally to put the fear of the mob into
politics), contempt for the filth and poverty in which the French
commoners lived while the nobility gorged on luxury goods showed
how arrogant they were, not just in confidence that their offices
of entitlement were beyond reproach and unassailable, but that
mockery and insult in the face of deliberate deprivation would be
borne with obedience and humility.

It certainly affected Smith's outlook, since he wrote *The Wealth
of Nations* with a focus on self-interest rather than moral sentiments. And while this may be purely pragmatic, based on what

10 Ibid., Page 352.
11 Ibid., Page 20.

he witnessed, he also wrote about the potential for self-interest to become abusive, both in collusion with individuals and when combined with the power of government. Business interests could form cabals (groups of conspirators, plotting public harm) or monopolies (organizations with exclusive market control) to fix prices at their highest levels. A true laissez-faire economy would provide every incentive to conspire against consumers and attempt to influence budgets and legislation.

Smith's assertion that self-interest leads producers to favor domestic industry must also be understood in the context of the period. While it's true that the Enlightenment was a movement of rational philosophy radically opposed to secrecy, it's important to understand that this had to be done *respectfully,* insofar as all arguments were intended to impress the monarchy under circumstances where the king believed himself God-appointed and infallible, no matter his past or present policies, and matters were handled with delicacy. Yet, Smith's arguments are clear enough (and certainly courageous enough) to be understood in laymen's terms.

In an era when the very industry he's observing has been fostered by tariffs, monopolies, labor controls, and materials extracted from colonies, he did his best to balance observation with what he thought was best for society. It's not his fault we pick and choose our recipes for what we do and don't believe or where we think Smith might have gone had he been alive today.

The New Double Standard

The only practical way to resolve the contradiction between the existing beneficiaries of state favoritism in this period and Smith's aversion to it is to observe that the means to prevent competition and interference with the transition from one mode of commerce to another that enhances the strength of the favored or provides a new means to grow their wealth is to close the door of government intervention behind them and burn any bridges to it.

In psychological terms, the practice of "negative attribution" is to assume that identical behavior is justifiable for oneself but not another. It may not be inconsistent with a system of economics founded on self-interest, but it naturally begs a justification as to why it rules out everyone *else's* self-interest. The beauty of this system is that it will always have the same answer.

You may have guessed it.

Progress.

Reallocation of Assets

It was always understood that capitalism produces winners and losers. The art of economizing is to gain maximum benefit for minimum expenditure, which generally translates to asset consolidation and does not necessarily mean there is minimum sacrifice. There's an opportunity cost for everything, whether it's human, financial, environmental, or material. But the most important tenet of free market capitalism is that asset redistribution requires the U.S. government to go to DEFCON 1, unless assets are being reallocated for "higher productivity," in which case the entire universe is saved from the indefensible sin of lost opportunity.

Private property is sacred—up until an individual decides he can make more productive use of it and appeals to the courts for seizure under eminent domain or until the government decides it will increase national growth if owned by some other person or entity. In like manner, corporations can suffer hostile takeovers, just as deregulation facilitates predatory market behavior and cutthroat competition promotes an efficiency orientation that means fewer jobs and lower incomes, which result in private losses.

In the varying range of causes underlying the loss of assets, the common threat is progress—the "civilized" justification for depriving some other person or entity of their right to own property, presumably earned by the sweat of their brow, except their sweat doesn't have the same champion as someone who can wring more profit from it. The official explanation is that the government manages the "scarcity" of resources to benefit the world. This is also how we justify war, aggression, and genocide, though we don't always admit to that unless we mean to avoid it.

Perfectly Rational Genocide

History cooperates with the definition of Enlightenment if we imagine that thoughtfulness has something to do with genocide. In the context of American heritage, it has meant that when someone stands in the way of progress, his or her resources are "reallocated" to serve the pursuit of maximum profit, with or without consent. The war against Native Americans was one in which Americans either sought and participated in annihilation efforts or believed this end was inevitable. In the age of rational thought, meditation on the issue could lead from gratitude for the help early settlers received from Native Americans to the observation they didn't enclose their land and had no concept of private property, to the conviction they were unmotivated by profit and therefore irreconcilable savages. But it takes more than rational thought to mobilize one society to exterminate another.

The belief in manifest destiny—that God put the settlers in America for preordained and glorious purposes which gave them a right to everything—turned out to be just the ticket for a free people opposed to persecution and the tyranny of church and state.

Lest the irony elude you, economic freedom requires divorcing the state from religion, but God can be used to whip up the masses, distribute "It's Them or Us" cards, and send people out to die on behalf of intellectuals and investors who've rationalized their chosenness.

This is not to say that Native Americans didn't fight back, and refuting the fact of genocide (which simply means we killed enough people to threaten their nation's survival) can always be done by playing the numbers game. Author A says there were one million before the Europeans arrived. Author B says there were three, and Author C says there were twelve. Regardless of the fact that researchers relied on physical evidence to improve knowledge over time, it makes us all look like idiots because none of them says the same thing, therefore none of them must be right. Affirm a couple of minor things with the proper wince factor, then deny or gloss over the rest. Take pains to appear even-handed and, by all means, explain that these "vermin" really deserved to be called that. But, most importantly, state plainly for the reader that we weren't gassing Native Americans or burning them in ovens, because, despite the fact that genocide is not dependent on methodology, only European Jews, whom we saved (six million souls too late) have a legitimate right to pain.

In part, this is a backlash against researchers who draw deliberate comparisons to the Holocaust, which is, and always will be, a war crime like no other, and, in part, it's a self-serving mockery of what we swore we learned from it. To induce a state of denial, it's in the interest of instigators to jeer at the thought of genocide, particularly when it's one of the crimes in the UN Charter that urges collective intervention.

I was six years old when I watched "The World at War." I covered my mouth with my hands when the Nazis stripped the Jews to recycle their boots and clothing. Disbelieving, I stared at the fillings taken from their teeth. Black and white film clips of mass graves and death camps had me crying silent tears. It was my life's most formative moment to hear the words "Never Again," and think, Thank God, we saved them.

Today, I grieve that we knew and didn't feel a need to intervene until saving the survivors coincided with our self-interest. But I won't allow the uniquely sadistic crimes of the Nazis and the Jews' inconceivable suffering to be used to negate the experience of others who were, or are, targeted. Especially if we take into account that the October Revolution of 1917, which launched the birth of Communism, later allowed Stalin to kill between three million and some say as many as sixty million people through forced famine, purges, and collectivism.

It seems Stalin got the idea that they stood in the way of progress, which, in itself, is inevitable, so why not speed the process?

That's a thought you should hold onto. It's going to prove important.

CHAPTER TWO: INSTILLING THE ILLUSION OF CHOICE

Selfishness may be exalted as the root and branch of capitalism, but it doesn't make you look good to the party on the receiving end or those whose sympathy he earns. For that, you need a government prepared to do four things, which each have separate dictums based on study, theorization, and experience.

Coercion: Force is illegitimate only if you can't sell it.
Persuasion: How do I market thee? Let me count the ways.
Bargaining: If you won't scratch my back, then how about a piece of the pie?
Indoctrination: Because I said so. (And paid for the semantics.)

Predatory capitalism is the control and expropriation of land, labor, and natural resources by a foreign government via coercion, persuasion, bargaining, and indoctrination.

At the coercive stage, we can expect military and/or police intervention to repress the subject populace. The persuasive stage will be marked by clientelism, in which a small percentage of the populace will be rewarded for loyalty, often serving as the capitalists' administrators, tax collectors, and enforcers. At the bargaining stage, efforts will be made to include the populace, or a certain percentage of it, in the country's ruling system, and this is usually marked by steps toward democratic (or, more often, autocratic) governance.

At the fourth stage, the populace is educated by capitalists, such that they continue to maintain a relationship of dependency.

The Predatory Debt Link

In many cases, post-colonial states were forced to assume the debts of their colonizers. And where they did not, they were encouraged to become in debt to the West via loans that were issued through international institutions to ensure they did not fall prey to communism or pursue other economic policies that were inimical to the West. Debt is the tie that binds nation states to the geostrategic and economic interests of the West.

As such, the Cold War era was a time of easy credit, luring post-colonial states to undertake the construction of useless monoliths and monuments, and to even expropriate such loans through corruption and despotism, thereby making these independent rulers as predatory as colonizers. While some countries were wiser than others and did use the funds for infrastructural improvements, these were also things that benefited the West and particularly Western contractors. In his controversial work *Confessions of an Economic Hit Man,* John Perkins reveals that he was a consultant for an American firm (MAIN), whose job was to ensure that states became indebted beyond their means so they would remain loyal to their creditors, buying them votes within United Nations organizations, among other things.

Predatory capitalists demand export-orientations as the means to generate foreign currency with which to pay back debt. In the process, the state must privatize and drastically slash or eliminate any domestic subsidies which are aimed at helping native industry compete in the marketplace. Domestic consumption and imports must be radically contained, as shown by the exchange rate policies recommended by the IMF. The costs of obtaining domestic capital will be pushed beyond the reach of most native producers, while wages must be depressed to an absolute bare minimum. In short, the country's land, labor, and natural resources must be sold at bargain basement prices in order to make these goods competitive, in what one author has called "a spiraling race to the bottom," as countries producing predominantly the same goods engage in cutthroat competition whose benefactor is the West.

Under these circumstances, foreign investment is encouraged, but this, too, represents a loaded situation for countries that open their markets to financial liberalization. Since, in most cases, the

IMF does not allow restrictions on the conditions of capital inflows, it means that financial investors can literally dictate their terms. And since no country is invulnerable to attacks on its currency, which governments must try to keep at a favorable exchange rate, it means financial marauders can force any country to try to prop up its currency using vital reserves of foreign exchange which might have been used to pay their debt.

When such is the case, the IMF comes to the rescue with a so-called "bailout fund," that allows foreign investors to withdraw their funds intact, while the government reels from the effects of an IMF-imposed austerity plan, often resulting in severe recession the offshoot of which is bankruptcies by the thousands and plummeting employment.

In countries that experienced IMF bailouts due to attacks on their currencies, the effect was to reset the market so the only economic survivors were those who remained export-oriented and were strong enough to withstand the upheaval. This means they remained internationally competitive, which translates to low earnings of foreign exchange. At the same time that the country is being bled from the bottom up through mass unemployment, extremely low wages, and the "spiraling race to the bottom," it is in an even more unfavorable position concerning the payment of debt. The position is that debt slavery ensues, as much an engine of extraction as any colonial regime ever managed.

The Role of Indoctrination

The fact that it is sovereign governments overseeing the work of debt repression has much to do with education, which is the final phase of predatory capitalism, concluding in indoctrination. With the collapse of the Soviet Union, the lesson to the world was that socialism can't work, nor were there any remaining options for countries that pursued "the third way" other than capitalism. This produced a virulent strain of neoliberalism in which most people were, and are, being educated. The most high-ranking of civil servants have either been educated in the West or directly influenced by its thinking. And this status of acceptance and adherence finally constitutes indoctrination. The system is now self-sustaining, upheld by domestic agents.

While predatory capitalism can proceed along a smooth continuum from coercion to persuasion to bargaining to formal indoctrination, the West can regress to any of these steps at any point in time, given the perceived need to interfere with varying degrees of force in order to protect its interests.

Trojan Politics

Democracy is about having the power and flexibility to graft our system of government and predatory capitalism onto any target country, regardless of relative strength or conflicting ideologies. An entire productive industry has grown up using the tools of coercion, persuasion, bargaining, and formal indoctrination to maximize their impact in the arena of U.S. politics. Its actors know how to jerk the right strings, push the right buttons, and veer from a soft sell to a hard sell when resistance dictates war, whether it's with planes overhead and tanks on the ground or with massive capital flight that panics the whole world.

When the U.S. political economy goes into warp overdrive, its job proves far more valuable than anything ever made in the strict material sense because there's never been more at stake in terms of what it's trying to gain. It's the American idea machine made up of corporations, lobbyists, think tanks, foundations, universities, and consultants in every known discipline devoted to mass consumerism, and what they sell is illusory opportunity dressed in American principles. They embrace political candidates who'll play by elitist rules to preserve the fiction of choice, and, in this way, they maintain legitimacy, no matter what kind of "reallocation" is on the economic agenda.

The issue is not whether we'll question it, but who we'll applaud for administering it.

In the Information Age, perception management is king.

Chapter Three: Political Strategizing

If we start with perception management, we can challenge the Tea Party and even the Coffee Party with something as patently absurd as the Artificial Creamer Party.

Recognize any familiar tactics in the following campaign strategy?

1) We shall insist on the separation of milk and state, and bar any organization affiliated with milk from being eligible for public subsidies.

2) The rights of dairy farmers to marry, adopt children, and openly serve in the military shall be considered morally objectionable and debated at every opportunity.

3) In the event of an election, the multiple evils of milk shall be used to distract the public from questioning the candidates on anything.

4) Think tanks, foundations, and the political correctness police shall enforce the world's perception of Artificial Creamer as a "bridge to the future," "the salvation of the global village," "the right of the human family," "the key to sustainable development," and "the path to lasting peace."

5) Artificial Creamer will win a Nobel Prize, in light of everything it might do to fill the world with sparkle ponies.

See? Something for everyone. But that's just perception management. Here's the net effect.

The only ones to benefit will be the 0.13% who are lactose intolerant and the 7% who make megabucks. It won't create U.S. jobs because it will be made in Botswana at the emancipating wage of twenty-three cents a day so 40% of Americans can afford to buy it at Walmart. For the 50% who are destitute, the FDA will declare Artificial Creamer a food group so it can be purchased with WIC and Food Stamps, lest there be a riot against unfairness or Artificial Creamer should fail to cash in on its share of national social programs.

Aren't we ingenious? We might demand that great-grandpa bag groceries on an oxygen tank, thirty years into retirement, to afford his hypertension medicine, and reduce his Social Security if someone gives him a five dollar tip that puts him over the income limit.

But, by God, he can have Creamer—in any flavor he wants it. This is a land of choice and opportunity, damn it.

Which is all fine and good, but when Artificial Creamer doesn't prove to be everything it said it was, we'll go back to milk (again). And milk will get carried away in an orgy of self-indulgence until we return to Artificial Creamer (once more). Either way, we'll have the satisfaction and euphoria of empowerment.

Or something, anyway.

If you're confused about U.S. principles and who's supposed to benefit, you may not be to blame. We've responded to boom and bust cycles inherent to our development choices and other countries' criticisms with different programs and palliatives over decades of continuity.

But it doesn't take a genius to see that the tyranny of science is fighting to replace the tyranny of royalty-teamed-with-religion we rejected in the eighteenth century. Science is the power that buttresses democracy and capitalism, also in the name of "progress." Not that we won't play the God card when corruption is so glaring that it requires another support system which is conveniently available in the form of religious sanction.

It's a function of self-esteem to seek affirmation of our beliefs and share safety in numbers, but the existence of like-minded people who hold the same fears, hopes, values and disappointments is what makes them predictable targets and therefore most vulnerable to strategic manipulation. It's like handing over the remote control to your decision-making power or wearing a badge on your sleeve that says, "I'll buy anything you tell me, as long as you sell it this way."

The more pressure this puts on society, the more opportunity there is to distract and manipulate. However, it's easier than it ever was to counter perception management with a connection to the Internet, provided you're willing to acknowledge history that may make you uncomfortable, which we'll do later on to illustrate U.S. foreign policy and how it's found its way home to produce our current conflicts with the potential to turn into crises.

CHAPTER FOUR: BEHAVIORAL ECONOMICS

Absent ideology, mathematics is amoral. It's neither good nor bad but true, even if the existence of truth represents stability in the world. The equation of 2 + 2 = 4 will always have the same answer when it excludes wants and needs. But watch how we transform this with assets and human behavior.

John uses $2.00 worth of raw materials and $2.00 worth of labor to produce a product that costs $4.00, but if he sells it for $4.00, his profit will be zero. At what price will John balance profit incentive with the money a buyer is willing to pay? Can John expect more profit the greater the number of buyers? What if John isn't the only seller? What if the sellers band together? At what price will the sellers face new competition?

This type of rationalization is what prices assets based on human behavior. Where trade once relied on assessments of equal worth or superior value in exchange for what was offered, the system was crude and unreliable due to differing perspectives. The owner of a butter churn and the purveyor of four dozen rabbit skins had to dicker and reach a compromise or ultimately refuse to trade.

Merchants who dealt in exotic goods understood that rarity (or scarcity) increased their value. People would pay more for something they couldn't get locally, especially if the merchant was the only one providing it. Likewise, manufacturers favored by government understood they would lose their pricing advantages if faced with competition. Functions of price derived from scientific induction—observing something, forming a hypothesis, performing experiments to verify that hypothesis, then positing a theory based on all of this—produced the laws of supply and demand, which are like DNA to the body—an underlying code.

Economic Faith

The perceived "truth" of a theory is not what makes it useful in practice. It's whether the method of pricing can be imposed, sustained, and upheld under public scrutiny, since the whole system of prices, once you go beyond concrete inputs like intellectual property, labor, and materials, is based on human perception. It stems from anticipation and has always been artificial. Just because you can inflate a price by fulfilling a number of expectations, doesn't mean you've added value.

Unlike the laws of thermodynamics, the laws of supply and demand are profit rationalization, backed by observable auction behavior and passed into "law," lest the validity of the illusion be questioned.

Capitalist Hand-Waving

The story of "The Emperor's New Clothes" makes fun of how value conjured from nothing allows a tailor to charge the emperor for clothing him in his own nakedness by virtue of hand-waving. The emperor then parades himself proudly before the royal panderers and sycophants and people who fear to point out the obvious, so the illusion continues to work until someone with more common sense than reverence undoes the deception.

In the history of the U.S., we adhered to gold and silver standards, then gold alone, then paper backed by gold, and inevitably "I said so" notes. The appeal of capitalist hand-waving is that it can be applied to anything.

Money, Religion and Politics

Because the same justifications are periodically reinvented to produce similar outcomes, I'm going to condense the history of money in the form of another parody.

Let's say the Artificial Creamer Party is made up of sheep. The sheep live in fear of the wolves that run the Party of Milk, which uses coercion, persuasion, bargaining, and indoctrination to exploit the cows. Wolves have fangs and claws. Cows have hooves and greater mass. A single wolf could be trampled by a panicked herd, but a pack could isolate a cow and successfully make a kill. Before the birth of Observant Wolf the wolves didn't care whether they bagged a cow or a deer. Meat was meat. No big deal.

Then Wondering Cow was born to wonder why wolves fed on cows whereas cows fed on grass because *surely* this meant the existence of Evil in the world. Wolves and cows were both mammals who breastfed their young, but the wolves warred with themselves along with everyone else over dominance and territory, even though they didn't use the land for anything but room to hunt and...run around. It was common for one pack to steal from another's hunting grounds by invading and herding the cows, until Observant Wolf was born.

Observant Wolf observed that beggar-thy-neighbor raids meant they starved their own kind. Because if it stalked like a wolf and snarled like a wolf, it probably *was* a wolf.

Observant Wolf ran to Thoughtful Wolf and said, "We howl at the same moon!"

"Ah," said Thoughtful Wolf. "That's because we were made by the Moon and why I was born to speak for him."

"Really?" Observant Wolf asked.

"Yes," Thoughtful Wolf said. "Now go to Dominant Wolf and tell him he has been chosen by the Moon to form a Nation of Wolves."

Observant Wolf did as he was told, and soon enough Dominant Wolf came to Thoughtful Wolf. "How will I form this Nation?" he asked.

"Well," said Thoughtful Wolf, "you mark the pack's territory by pissing on plants and trees. What if we keep the cows inside and prevent them from moving on?"

"Hmm," said Dominant Wolf. "Then all the other packs will fight."

"That," said Thoughtful Wolf, "is why we'll cut a deal. Instead of starving in the winters, we'll provide for everyone all year and let the leaders control their packs, as long as they accept your authority and agree to worship the Moon."

Dominant Wolf said, "What will that accomplish?"

Thoughtful Wolf grinned. "If they pledge wolves to our defense, who do you suppose they'll send?"

Dominant Wolf nodded as understanding dawned. "Those who might grow strong enough to challenge their leadership of the packs."

"Right," said Thoughtful Wolf. "Because we're hierarchical beasts."

Then Dominant Wolf bound the cows to the land, and his supporters were rewarded in proportion to their loyalty. Pack leaders sent their challengers to serve Dominant Wolf and he grew stronger by the year. So did Moon worship, run by Thoughtful Wolf.

But some pack leaders starved their cows, which yielded too little meat. Others conserved their cows so only the privileged could gorge. A few learned to husband their cows and cultivate a herd.

Then it happened that Suffering Cow was born to Wondering Cow and, living in captivity, he wrote the Book of Woe.

Dominant Wolf realized that the more his army grew, the more it cost him in cows. He also heard that wolves were dying and there was fighting among the packs. Dominant Wolf couldn't send more cows, so he forced the packs to make do with less and redistributed the cows from those who were better off. He did away with the quota of wolves and accepted the pack leaders' promises to send wolves if he had a need. Then he whittled down his army to the wolves he wanted to keep and sent the rest back to their packs.

Once again, the cows were consumed according to the habits of the packs, and their leaders became disrespectful to varying degrees. There were accusations of favoritism, betrayal, and more war between the packs. Some dared to question Dominant Wolf's leadership, and this reached Thoughtful Wolf through the Moon priests who lived among the packs to stick up for Dominant Wolf and force the cows to accept their lot.

It was about this time that Suffering Cow added to the Book of Woe with the Book of Why Me?

Then Dominant Wolf realized he needed successful wolves. He wasn't opposed to using his army if the packs turned rebellious, but how dumb *was* he to send half his army back to the angry packs? And why did he have an army if not to accumulate cows?

The solution was to attack the Nation of Jackals, convert them to Moon worship and force them to share their cows. Then Reasonable Jackal proposed a reasonable distribution. He gave Dominant Wolf a chest full of stones, polished and made smooth by the ocean along the coast. Since Reasonable Jackal controlled their source, the stones conveyed an exclusive right to five cows per stone. Dominant Wolf was only asked to stagger their redemption, so as not to exhaust the supply of cows and make everyone starve.

So Dominant Wolf cashed in some stones for the first installment of cows. Then he went home happy because he possessed the power to purchase more cows, but none of the pack leaders knew. They would consume their allotments of cows according to their habits, and when famine threatened again, he would secretly redeem more stones. In fact, this was wise because pack leaders were bound to demand more consumption the more they knew he could buy.

Meanwhile, Thoughtful Wolf installed Moon priests inside the Nation of Jackals and, through their network, he learned that Reasonable Jackal's cows were fifty times more abundant than what Dominant Wolf could buy. By agreeing to stagger the use of his stones, Dominant Wolf allowed Reasonable Jackal to accumulate enough cows to pay Dominant Wolf, plus feed the jackals and form a growing surplus.

Then Dominant Wolf sent Thoughtful Wolf to Reasonable Jackal with the news he would make war unless Reasonable Jackal sent more stones to increase his share of the expanded stock of cows. So Reasonable Jackal sent him an additional stone for every hundred cows born in the waiting periods.

"This is ridiculous!" said Thoughtful Wolf. "You're the Moon-appointed leader and he agreed to worship the Moon. Just decree that all our stones are worth twenty times their value and he'll have to go along."

"So be it," Dominant Wolf agreed.

Well, Reasonable Jackal replied that this was the most *unreasonable* and arbitrary thing he'd ever heard.

"The heretic!" screamed Thoughtful Wolf.

"Why didn't he buy it?" asked Dominant Wolf.

"Because that will take the birth of Monetarist Wolf," Thoughtful Wolf said glumly.

Dominant Wolf shot him a look. "Okay, when will *that* be?"

"After the overthrow of Keynesian Sheep," Thoughtful Wolf pronounced.

"*Sheep!*" Dominant Wolf cried in alarm. "Who the hell are the *sheep?*"

Thoughtful Wolf sighed. "They come after Unfettered Free-Market Wolf."

"Damn it!" yelled Dominant Wolf. "How long before we take control?"

Thoughtful Wolf rubbed his jaw. "First there'll be Mercantilist Wolf, followed by Industrialist Wolf and Independent Currency Wolf. Then there'll be Capitalist Wolf."

Dominant Wolf threw up his hands in despair. "Fine. What about now?"

Thoughtful Wolf looked thoughtful. "It seems the cows are writing books we might be able to use..."

Putting It in Perspective

It doesn't really matter whether the parody above is based on the military quota system of the thirteenth century Ottoman Turks, the organization of medieval society, or the formation of the League of Nations (and later the United Nations) based on mutual business interests. Likewise, the value of "cows" could be human farm labor, which *was* bound to the land after the Black Death of the mid-fourteenth century killed thirty to sixty percent of Europe's population. It could equally pertain to slavery or the laws of forced labor supporting British industrialization.

By featuring wolves and herd beasts, it simply shows (among other things) that certain reliable tactics can prevent passive citizens from defensively mobbing and killing, even when the result is death and starvation. When the cows formed a competitive religion to deepen their sense of community, it could then be assimilated by the wolves to control the cows on their own terms.

Call them "dominant," "submissive," "aggressive," or "pacifistic," the point is that some people will fight for positions of leadership and some will consent to be led. A society that is reared on competition as the only source of sustenance or purpose of existence (in accordance with Social Darwinism, survival of the fittest, and the theory of Natural Selection) will have continual challenges to authority and fundamental instability if it doesn't set certain functions *outside* the arena of battle and preserve positions of privilege for those who would otherwise resort to *unacceptable* competition to topple and ruin the system.

In practice, all that matters—whether it involves hypocritical double standards, negative attribution, and reliance on loaded heuristics or flip-flopping, waffling, reinventing, and semantics—is what works for Dominant Wolf.

All he cares about is when the wolves can have it *all*.

Chapter Five: Favoring Old Money Over New

Like it or not, the U.S. has always been at war, even against itself. To understand, we must move past capitalist dogma to practical working knowledge of what the business cycle is and, in no way will this rely on outdated Marxism or any other competing system. The mechanics are simple, as is the logic for their retention. We can explain the business cycle without the presumptions that fill the academic timeline from as early as 1790 (when the National Bureau of Economic Research identified America's first recession) a year before Congress chartered the First Bank of the United States to perform the functions of central banking.[12]

The Boom–Bust Balance

The term "business cycle" refers to the regular alternation between "boom" and "bust" phases of economic behavior or, more simply, between times of success and failure.

It may be claimed that no one benefits from a period of failure. The typical characteristics of bankrupted businesses, high unemployment, low sales and plummeting prices, drastic budget cuts and reduced productivity are reliable indications that people on the losing end suffer hardship and sacrifice. The idea that this is unavoidable or inevitable has more to do with who benefits than any

---

12 List of Recessions in the United States http://en.wikipedia.org/w/index. php?title= List_of_recessions_in_the_United_States&printable=yes

so-called law of the economy, although ritualized business cycles and indoctrination on the subject have been unqualified successes in terms of public acceptance, not that the public has other options.

The linking of economic downturns to the political elective process demonstrates that their onset and timing are manipulative and deliberate. As noted in *Political Business Cycles: The Political Economy of Money, Inflation, and Unemployment*:

> The basic idea of the political business cycle literature is that because the typical lags in adjustment of inflation to changes in macroeconomic policy are longer than for unemployment, a carefully engineered economic expansion can give incumbent politicians the advantage of a booming economy just before an election, while most of the associated inflationary costs do not follow until the election is safely over. With less than full information and a short horizon on the part of the public, political incentives exist to destabilize the economy and in the process generate an inflationary bias.[13]

The most important aspect of American economics is the tension between "old money" and "new," because old money (representing an affluent minority, usually expressed as 2% or less of the U.S. population) benefits the most on the business cycle's downturn, whereas new money, along with new inventions and ideas, commonly grows to compete on the business cycle's upswing.

In an essay entitled, "The Myth of Old Money Liberalism: The Politics of the *Forbes* 400 Richest Americans," written and published by University of Oregon student Val Burris, he states that new money is more uniformly conservative than old.[14] Beginning with a summary of where the perception stems from, he writes:

> Arnold Rose (1967:91–92), in one of the defining statements of pluralism, cites the ideological antagonism between "old aristocrats" and "new businessmen" as one of several splits that render the propertied class incapable of political rule.

> Albert Szymanski, a Marxist, rejects the pluralist claim that capitalists are too fragmented to constitute a ruling class, but agrees that "new money is generally more right wing than old money" (Szymanski 1978:48). Thomas Dye, an institutional elite theorist, disputes both the pluralist thesis of fragmented power and the Marxist notion of a capitalist ruling class, but concurs

---

13 Willett, Thomas D., ed., *Political Business Cycles: The Political Economy of Money, Inflation, and Unemployment*, (Duke University Press: USA, 1988), p. 14.

14 Burris, Val, "The Myth of Old Money Liberalism: The Politics of the *Forbes* 400 Richest Americans," http://darkwing.uoregon.edu/~vburris/ oldmoney.pdf

on the difference between old money and new money: "Leadership for liberal reform has always come from America's upper social classes. This leadership is more likely to come from established 'old families,' rather than 'new rich'" (Dye 1995:196). The new rich, he explains, "do not fully share in the liberal, social welfarism of the dominant Eastern Establishment" (Dye 1995:204). Thus, despite fundamental disagreements on questions of class and power, social scientists from diverse perspectives affirm that old money is more liberal (or less conservative) than new money.[15]

Burris conducted a study of the contemporary rich and extrapolated conclusions from preexisting literature, which drew insight from older study data that is valid in the context of the French Revolution, Marxism, socialism and Communism, within which old money liberalism offered a pragmatic response to threats from below and was highly influential, both nationally and globally. It only became possible to abandon old money liberalism with the collapse of the U.S.S.R., when the disadvantage of alternative systems inspired the mistaken belief that authoritarian clientelism, practiced successfully in Latin America, Africa and the Middle East, could be sustained worldwide.[16] Then old money liberalism gave way to monetarism, defended by Milton Friedman.

---

15 Ibid.

16 This was obviously negated by uprisings in Tunisia, Egypt, Yemen and Syria, among other Middle Eastern and African countries, where authoritarian clientelism produced huge disparities in income and disadvantaged conditions for the greater part of the populace. The positive (albeit cautious) U.S. response to the uprising in Egypt (and marked determination to turn a blind eye elsewhere) came on the heels of the December 2010 bombing of a Coptic Christian church that was widely misrepresented in the American conservative media as an Egyptian Islamic threat to the whole of Christendom. This bombing of a Christian site, unaddressed by Egyptian leaders, appeared consistent with the onset of "Holy War." This was repeatedly stressed on TV by Sean Hannity, even though former UN Secretary General Boutros Boutros Ghali spoke on behalf of Egypt to allay those very fears, noting that Muslims and Christians have peacefully coexisted in Egypt throughout most of its history. Egypt, like Pakistan (where India's RAW and the Israeli Mossad are deliberately radicalizing the Muslim opposition) was pressured to respond widely and forcefully to the bombing, despite the fact that thousands of Egyptian Muslims rushed to protect the Coptic Christians by serving as human shields. U.S. diplomatic cables (obtained via WikiLeaks) revealed Israeli concern with Mubarak's physical and mental debilitation. Mubarak's head of

Monetarism conducts incremental inflation as the means to manipulate economic downturns and either dampen the effects of recession or implement recovery. What it achieves in practice when too much money chases after too few goods while interest rates are soaring is to restore higher commodity prices, making it more difficult during recession for those hit the hardest to afford basic staples.

Implicit Political Bargains

The business cycle's downturn is a political commitment to favoring old money because it raises the cost of borrowing from banking institutions[17] at a time when recession causes widespread disruption for businesses dependent on borrowing and induces bankruptcies, downsizing, business takeovers, sales and mergers.

Even under economic liberalism, old money is generous to a point. The imposition of business cycles limits the degree of economic expansion while ensuring that all significant growth depends on old money, whether it is through bank borrowing, investments or the issuance of stock. All three mediums serve as a vehicle for the conditional distribution, growth and protection of old money. Old money isn't adverse to new, as long as its own benefits outweigh new money's gains. The problem has always been to prevent liberal

---

security was seen, even then, as the Israeli preference to succeed Hosni Mubarak, and it was not a coincidence that Mubarak named him Vice President when the uprising began. Also, the organizer of the uprising, Wael Ghonim, is an executive of Google, which became overtly involved in politics when it teamed up with George Clooney to monitor the secession of South Sudan via satellite months before. Because Mubarak's health would have necessitated change anyway, observers should be skeptical of the order of events and world reaction, especially since the transition from political uprising to labor strikes now threatens the Egyptian military, which owns all of Egypt's industry. Under these conditions, the military may lose patience, especially if the real thrust of the strikes is to compromise their holdings and open them up to foreign ownership. In any case, the fragility of peace is apparent.

17 Not to be confused with the Federal Reserve, which controls the nation's money supply and services banks through its discount window. It also extended that privilege to industry by handling short-term paper for such economic giants as McDonalds and Harley Davidson during the massive capital flight of 2008–2009 when the banks refused to lend, even after recapitalization, in solidarity with conservatives who would obviously benefit from a more protracted recession and especially a failed recovery.

policies from uncontrollably translating into independent political or economic power, not to mention overthrow.

Under the French Revolution, the mob reacted brutally to economic repression, but then went on to demonstrate a lack of political savvy and intellectual cohesion that quickly restored power to those who formerly governed. This was not the case with the Sandinista overthrow of Somoza in Nicaragua, when the U.S. relied on economic sanctions and covert military action to destroy the revolutionaries, who had been broadly successful in promoting widespread higher incomes, health, and nearly universal literacy for the first time in their miserable history.

In contemporary politics, the run on U.S. banks (camouflaged in the media by the sub-prime mortgage meltdown),[18] was equally concerted and hostile. Between 2008 and 2009, America's most powerful financial institutions facilitated capital flight on an unprecedented scale, as the direct route for conservative people of means to cast a vote of no-confidence with the ultimate intent to remove President Obama from power. In retaliation, the President resorted to public funds to re-capitalize the banks, force management turnovers, and establish Ben Bernanke (Chairman of the Federal Reserve) as the equivalent of an economic central planner.

---

18 This was exacerbated by false S&P ratings performing the same function as maintaining a pegged exchange rate long after it ceased to be accurate in order for privileged investors to offload at higher prices before the bottom fell out of the market.

CHAPTER SIX: MAKING THE WORLD SAFE FOR FINANCE

Since the Civil War, U.S. peace has largely been bought with ritualized business cycles and tacit political favoritism toward old money over new. However, the affluent worldwide have always had the means to vote with their assets, even more so after the global reorganization conducted in the wake of World War II and the economic liberalism implemented by the International Monetary Fund (IMF) and World Bank during the Cold War years. Both policies fostered inescapable debt traps created by the West. Thus, the end of colonization did not result in true emancipation but rather a devolution of power.

Rulers of independent states remain subservient to Western interests, even though the most obvious colonial indicators (chains, slavery and genocidal policies) are often gone. In their place is a system of debt peonage under which national leaders are forced to accept responsibility for the impoverishment of their peoples, the perpetuation and spread of hunger, high levels of infant and child mortality, and internecine war. They act as siphoning agents of the country's wealth and national resources to the benefit of external creditors whose main purpose in lending was to allow national governments to develop the basic infrastructure for economic extraction while keeping them tethered to the West via varying levels of debt.

This process began with international planning for the post-World War II world, during which the West identified its political, economic and geo-strategic interests as encompassing a broad range of countries, including the British Empire, the Far East and the entire Western hemisphere.[19] This was because the United States had grown accustomed to producing for World War II, but was also forward-looking and desired to expand. The need for raw materials and external markets was central to post-war planning.

Those countries most important to the West were required to grow and prosper to purchase U.S. exports. Countries on the periphery were less important, but they too became areas of international contestation due to the spread of communism and fear of its deeper infiltration. Thus, post-World War II rebuilding focused on those countries within the "Grand Area" prospectus.

The West hoped to avoid more wars on a world scale, so it created two organizations whose aim was to stabilize global finance, particularly balance-of-payment problems (a disequilibrium between imports and exports), which earlier resulted in competitive devaluations, restrictive import conditions and beggar-thy-neighbor politics. To that end, the IMF (International Monetary Fund) was created, along with its sister organization, the IBRD (International Bank for Reconstruction and Development). Named after the conference which produced them, the Bank and the Fund are known as the Bretton Woods Institutions.

After World War II, the spread of communism provoked U.S. military interference in Vietnam and elsewhere, but the failure of military intervention against a motivated and deeply entrenched population soon gave rise to a policy of liberal containment. This meant attacking the roots of communism and rebellion against Western policies, which were viewed as extreme poverty and a general lack of advancement.

Robert Strange McNamara (the former Secretary of Defense during the Vietnam war) was chosen to head the World Bank at this juncture, and changes had also been made to accommodate the new focus on poverty alleviation. These included the establishment of the IDA (International Development Association), which, unlike the IBRD, whose loans contain a five-year grace period, after which debtor governments have fifteen to twenty years to repay them at prevailing rates of interest, loans instead in credits, offered at a ¾

19 Shoup, Laurence H. and William Minter, "Shaping a New World Order: the Council on Foreign Relations' Blueprint for World Hegemony," *Trilateralism: The Trilateral Commission and Elite Planning for World Management*, ed. Holly Sklar (Boston, MA: South End Press, 1980) 138.

percent rate of interest with a grace period of ten years, after which repayment takes place over the next forty years.[20]

Together, the IBRD and the IDA make up the World Bank, although there are two other organizations included in the World Bank group. These are the International Finance Corporation (IFC), which makes loans exclusively for private enterprise in Bank borrowing countries, and the Multilateral Investment Guarantee Agency (MIGA), whose purpose is also to encourage direct foreign investment within developing countries.[21]

American Hegemony Within the Bretton Woods Institutions

As Margaret P. Karns and Karen A. Mingst point out, parameters for country programs were largely determined by the U.S. during the IMF's early years. Although the managing director of the Fund is by tradition a European, the U.S. had a great deal of influence in appointing people of its own preference. The deputy managing director has historically been a "Treasury man," further attesting to the close ties between the U.S. and the Fund, and Americans were pervasive in the staff of the organization.[22] Under the system of weighted voting, which was based on economic influence and a pattern of special majorities that empowered a U.S. veto, the United States was preponderant in the Fund's operations.

The same was also true of the World Bank, whose president is always an American. In the post-Vietnam era, under Robert McNamara, the World Bank began loaning expansively to countries whose loyalty was important to the West. And so determined was McNamara to "lift the world from poverty" that World Bank consultants traveled to these countries to seek out projects the World Bank could underwrite. They suggested improvements in basic infrastructure, such as roads, bridges and dams, investments in energy production and improvement of the country's agricultural systems, among the range of projects the Bank was willing to fund.

While some of these projects materialized in practice, more often investments benefited only the export sector and the country's

---

20 George, Susan and Fabrizio Sabelli, *Faith and Credit: The World Bank's Secular Empire*, 1st ed. (Boulder, CO: Westview Press, 1994) 12.

21 Ibid.

22 Karns, Margaret P. and Karen A. Mingst, eds., *The United States and Multilateral Institutions: Patterns of Changing Instrumentality and Influence* (London: Routledge, 1992) 94.

privileged classes, making it possible to coordinate the extraction of primary goods and natural resources. This was in marked contrast to the style of development pursued in countries of the "Grand Area," where governments worked to restore or build markets that were balanced and fully diversified, depending more on industrialization than primary goods and agriculture.

The World Bank looked the other way when authoritarian rulers pocketed their loans to enrich themselves and their cronies. They were also equally blind to widespread repression. While money remained unavailable for education, health care and housing, the salaries of the military and police were expected and never questioned.

Targeted lending persisted into the 1970s. On or about that time, economic decline and the advancement of other nations caused a shift in the U.S. position. By then, the U.S. weighted share within the IMF had sunk from 38 to 20 percent, forcing it to rely more on special majorities in order to enforce its decisions. By the same means, Europeans and the group of developing nations could impose their decisions. Thus, the IMF and World Bank became more autonomous, and this was reflected in a new pattern of lending designed to last for the long term.

The IMF Takes Up Long-Term Lending

The breakdown of the international fixed rate regime the Fund was supposed to police prior to the 1970s, produced less reliance on the Fund and more interest in having the private sector finance balance-of-payment problems. It was believed that countries experiencing shortfalls should rely on the market for help rather than multilateral institutions. Because nation states could also adopt their own exchange rate systems, the IMF's role seemed limited to financing poorer members who could not afford private credit and approving policy changes to reassure private creditors.

Changes had begun to blur the lines between the IMF as an emergency provider of temporary credit and the World Bank, which was a development bank and lender of long-term loans from the beginning. This began in the 1970s with the creation of the Extended Fund Facility (EFF), which recognized that balance-of-payments deficits could be of a structural nature, such as having an underdeveloped market that required long-term lending. In the 1980s, the Fund introduced the Structural Adjustment Facility (SAF) and the Enhanced Structural Adjustment Facility (ESAF), which produced significant overlap between the programs of the Fund and the World Bank.

Both the SAF and the ESAF were designed to help struggling governments pay the costs of economic restructuring at the heart of their balance-of-payment problems. Their structural conditionality focuses on the following:

1. Increasing the role of markets and private enterprises relative to the public sector, and improving incentive structures;
2. Improving the efficiency of the public sector; and
3. Mobilizing additional domestic resources.[23]

Since these are mainly problems for less developed countries, the pattern of IMF lending became increasingly skewed toward low-income countries.

Implementing Conditionality

During the early years, the World Bank's policies were so closely tied to the preferences of the U.S. that it was often seen as serving the United States. But participation by the U.S. and other member states allowed the Bank to lend at lower than commercial interest rates, making Bank loans attractive even when the Bank imposed conditions.

The World Bank introduced its own programs for structural adjustment during the 1980s, including Structural Adjustment Loans (SALs) and Sectoral Adjustment Loans (SECALs), whose strict conditionality was linked to balance-of-payments deficits. Although this was formerly the province of the IMF, the World Bank became concerned with economic restructuring in the countries that it loaned to.

This was consistent with a focus on liberalization. The World Bank, as yet, was not prejudicial of the private sector; it continued to fund many projects owned by the public sector. These included government-owned utilities, mining enterprises and other productive facilities.

Many countries preferred to borrow from private sector banks in order to avoid the conditionality attached to IMF and World Bank loans. These states were typically ruled by nationalist leaders who chose protectionism for their markets, such as high tariffs on imports and the nationalization of their resources, and also lobbied fiercely for a redistribution of global wealth through participation

---

23 Killick, Tony, *IMF Programs in Developing Countries: Design and Impact* (New York: Routledge, 1995) 25.

in the Non-Aligned Movement and the Group of 77 (G-77). In numerous Latin American and African states, attempts were made to form cartels for the production of bauxite, tin and other natural resources, as well as primary goods. Occurring in the wake of OPEC shocks, this display of solidarity between members of the underdeveloped South did not prove successful, but it did alarm the West and create a new agenda to "discipline" the South—a thing that would be achieved during the Reagan years.[24]

The Neoliberal Shift

Even though the 1970s saw a decline in U.S. influence, where other developed countries assumed more of the financial burden, this did not mean the U.S. was unimportant. Its policies were compatible with those of other Western states, and its influence was directly felt in the shift toward neoliberal economics during the Reagan years.

During its first year in office, the Reagan administration opposed an increase in the national IMF quotas, even though the world was in the midst of a debt crisis. The latter occurred because private banks had overextended while loaning out petrodollars and governments proved incapable of defending their exchange rate systems. This came at a time when President Reagan and Margaret Thatcher increased the level of interest tied to loans denominated in dollars so the resulting carrying costs became too expensive for most governments to shoulder.

The solution, according to Reagan, was not increased funding through the IMF. It was less lending and sharper adjustment in countries that had borrowed beyond their means. Reagan did not agree with the conversion of the IMF to a long-term lending facility and argued it must be concerned with privatization and free markets. As David Stockman, Director of the Office of Management and Budget, complained: "The IDA has supported state planning efforts to some countries in recent years and has placed a major emphasis on programs fostering income redistribution." After making the case that state planning and egalitarianism were not in the spirit of free markets, he went on to point out that: "The IDA has not been vigorous in using the leverage inherent in its large lending

---

24 Bello, Walden, "2 Global Economic Counterrevolution: How Northern Economic Warfare Devastates the South," *50 Years is Enough: The Case Against the World Bank and the International Monetary Fund*, ed. Kevin Danaher (Boston: South End Press, 1994) 15.

---

program to press recipients to redirect their economies toward a market-orientation."[25]

To revolutionize the system, Reagan rescued the bankers. During Reagan's second term, Treasury Secretary James Baker announced the Baker Plan, which revolved around a stronger role for the IMF in providing debt relief. At the same time that the IMF moved in, the private banks withdrew, leaving debtor states with new loans from the IMF whose even stricter conditionality they were powerless to prevent.

This marked the onset of the Structural Adjustment Program (SAP), which forced governments to focus on an export orientation, deeper liberalization and austerity measures as the means of siphoning wealth from the country. Thus, the IMF and the World Bank became the taskmasters and overseers of foreign debt repayment.

Coinciding with the collapse of the Soviet Union, the dissolution of communism served to embolden the West, to the point where it no longer cares that its domination of poor countries is painfully obvious. Tethered by foreign debt, these states were allowed to operate somewhat independently during the Cold War, only to be reeled in by the West now that they've reached the end of their proverbial ropes. These ostensibly sovereign states are curtailed from any action that might interfere with the repatriation of wealth to the West.

The Subtlety of Multilateral Aid

The tired and worn excuse of the so-called "invisible hand" by which the market operates has always had its limits, particularly when we look at the very visible paws of national governments behind the decisions and investments of the World Bank and IMF. Quoting, Margaret Karns and Karen Mingst:

> The logic of multilateral aid is rather subtle. On purely altruistic grounds, it makes sense to permit a country to receive aid unencumbered by the political interest of the donor or, at least, to reduce the politically motivated leverage of any given donor. But why should the donor forego the opportunity to pursue its own interests? There are three possible practical rationales. The first is to induce other donors to contribute in much the same way in order to increase the volume of aid devoted to approved purposes. As long as the multilateral institution does what a particular donor endorses, that donor can enjoy the magnifica-

---

25 Karns, Margaret P. and Karen A. Mingst, eds., 122.

tion of its own desired aid impact. Collective aid also reduces the scope of other countries' pursuit of political interests via their aid. The second rationale is to influence the policies of the aid recipient in the desired directions but without incurring the costs that often arise from direct and heavy-handed attempts at influence. Here, too, the utility of influence via multilateral aid obviously diminishes as the multilateral institution's initiatives depart from the preferences of the donor government. The third rationale is to allow for a "division of labor" between bilateral and multilateral targets or objectives.[26]

Using multilateral, rather than bilateral, aid allows governments to pretend they are not attaching conditions, but when multilateral institutions do impose conditions, they are acting in accordance with the wishes of their donors. In that event, who do indebted countries blame for conditionality? The IMF is comprised of numerous member states, including the debtor countries, whose access to World Bank loans was contingent on IMF membership. Supposedly, they belong to an institution in which their viewpoints are included and are therefore part of the system which now basically rules them.

To be sure, underdeveloped governments are responsible for the debt. Some borrowed unwisely and were despotic or corrupt, but their own people have never had any input on the paths they pursued or where the money went. Under the Cold War plan for liberal containment, many democratic elections produced autocratic leaders and the West preferred this turn of events. Reagan chose Jeanne Kirkpatrick to join his closest staff based on a paper she wrote which argued that authoritarian rulers were more malleable to U.S. interests and should be supported.

As a result, the beneficiaries of economic assistance were limited to national leaders and the elite in several countries. This was a reversion to clientelism, one of the four stages in the progression of neocolonialism (known as coercion, persuasion, bargaining and indoctrination). Now, to mute the protests arising from this arrangement, the West must turn to a new series of bargains.

Back to Bargaining

U.S. support for democratic reforms will ideally promote the belief that people control their states. But, this, they must do within the confines of neoliberal constraints and debt peonage. While it might buy social peace (for a while) and be the best means toward

---

26 Ibid., 134.

that end, it still does not alter the fact that futures are already mortgaged. In short, these countries will have few real choices. To see that even democratically elected governments may face troubled waters, we need only look at the effects of neoliberal reforms. Serving, as they do, to increase stratification through their subservience to free-market forces which tend to weed out smaller producers and formerly subsidized industries in favor of businesses that are able to rely on internal capital and compete favorably in exports, neoliberal reforms increase the chances for protest and social unrest at a time when new fledgling democracies come into hopeful existence. That governments may have to resort to repression in order to honor their debt commitments, is an obvious implication.

"Softening" Reform

As the author of *Dark Victory: The United States, Structural Adjustment and Global Poverty*, Walden Bello is a staunch critic of neoliberalism. In the following passage, he summarizes the criticism that led to a "softening" of IMF reforms:

> Latin Americans regard the reverse financial flow from their continent as the "worst plunder since Cortez" and refer to the 1980s as the "lost decade." Per capita income in 1990 was at virtually the same level as ten years earlier. Severe malnutrition stalks the countryside, paving the way for the return of cholera, which people thought had been eradicated. Technocrats at the World Bank and the IMF view this social devastation as the "bitter medicine" Southern countries must swallow to regain economic health. But after more than a decade of structural adjustment programs, the technocrats still haven't come up with an unqualified success story. They sometimes point to Chile as a model, but change the topic when conversation turns to the hunger and malnutrition pervasive in that land, where wages have declined by over 40 percent in real terms since the early 1970s. At other times, World Bank types wax eloquent over Mexico's resumption of growth, but become evasive when they have to explain why more than 50 percent of the population is now unemployed or underemployed, and why the real purchasing power of the minimum wage is about two thirds of what it was in 1970.[27]

Other critics, like UNICEF, have focused on the detrimental effects to the health of children, prompting the IMF and the World Bank to give their programs a "human face" by requiring that Policy Framework Papers prepared in connection with SAF/ESAF programs should "identify measures that can help cushion the possible

---

27 Bello, Walden, *Dark Victory: The United States, Structural Adjustment and Global Poverty* (London: Pluto Press, 1994) 18.

adverse effects of certain policies on vulnerable groups...in ways consistent with the program's macroeconomic framework."[28]

In this way, the IMF and the World Bank absolve themselves of responsibility for the poor, making it a government commitment that must somehow be achieved within the fiscal and monetary parameters the institutions assign to the country. In some cases, governments are helped by bilateral aid and microeconomic programs involving poverty reduction schemes. This is helpful, but governmental access to IMF/World Bank funds will continue to be contingent on progress with neoliberal reforms. In that sense, poverty reduction schemes and implemented reforms will work at cross purposes. Due to lost jobs, lower wages and landlessness, even sincere governments will face disappointing results.

The most positive development in IMF-debtor relations was an offer of debt forgiveness predicated on progress with neoliberal reforms. Thus far, the IMF has offered 100% debt relief to nineteen severely indebted countries, including Nicaragua and Honduras, which we will look at in this volume. It has also offered debt relief through the HIPC program (for Highly Indebted Poor Countries). These programs, arranged in conjunction with Strategic Poverty Reduction Strategies (SPRSs), which will entail billions of dollars in new IMF loans, are designed to place governments on a new footing, where the restructuring of their economies is subsidized by the West. Ostensibly, the SPRSs will ensure a more equitable income distribution while the economic restructuring makes the new loans affordable.

If we look critically at this program, it is based upon the same export-orientation demanded by Structural Adjustment and is intended to further liberalization in countries with histories of socialism or internal insurgencies. It is therefore a program to undercut the demands of the left while pursuing the goals of the right. The countries' goods will be made cheaper while an influx of Western imports under new free trade agreements deepens the persistence of balance-of-payments problems. It will also prevent the development of strong internal markets. Hence, the dependency relationship will be even further cemented. Debt, under these circumstances, will be like a merry-go-round these countries can never get off.

The Focus on Free Trade

As John Gershman puts it:

---

28 Killick, Tony, 23.

The free traders claim that they will create a "ladder" of comparative advantage, with the U.S. at the top, specializing in high-wage, high-tech goods. Mexico, Chile and Brazil would be a notch below, specializing in labor-intensive and some capital-intensive goods, while the rest of the region would be at the bottom, producing raw materials and doing basic assembly operations. As the U.S. moves into more and more high-tech and information-intensive industries, other countries would take over those industries left behind, moving up the ladder, so to speak. This rhetoric disguises some unpleasant realities. What the "ladder" actually provides is the institutional infrastructure for TNCs [Transnational Corporations] to develop integrated production facilities using the entire western hemisphere as their area of operations. TNCs have already located some high-tech operations in Mexico, for example, where they can get world-class quality and productivity at one tenth of U.S. wages. The ladder quickly becomes a slippery slope for workers, small farmers and small businesses.[29]

J.W. Smith reminds us that the heart of the GATT-Bretton Woods System is what is known as MFN—most favored nation. By this standard, GATT, NAFTA and the WTO basically determine "which nations will industrialize and which nations will remain as providers of resources for imperial-centers-of-capital. Those needed as allies and permitted to industrialize will accumulate capital and those reserved to provide natural resources to feed those industrial nations will remain poor and in debt."[30]

These decisions are implemented through the technocratic advice that the IMF and World Bank afford their customers. The IMF and World Bank have now extended their budgets to provide more hands-on advisors to countries of the Third World. It's also true that government cabinet members and economic advisors have been educated in the West, and they, too, are interested in promulgating what they learned.

That they are among the privileged, who do not experience the effects of their policies, need not be said. But, as Susan George observed, "[T]he [Third World] crisis is not necessarily a crisis for everyone. While the topmost layers of Third World societies remain largely insulated from debt distress, ordinary people in the South

29 Gershman, John, "4 The Free Trade Connection," *50 Years is Enough: The Case Against the World Bank and the International Monetary Fund*, ed. Kevin Danaher (Boston: South End Press, 1994) 27.

30 Smith, J.W., "Economic Democracy: The Political Struggle for the 21st Century (4th Edition, 2005), The Institute for Economic Democracy, http://www.ied.info/books/ed/unequaltrade.html.

sacrifice to pay back loans they never asked for, or that they even fought against, and from which they derive no gain."[31]

Gershman offers the following:

> If the goal of managers in the official institutions that rule over Third World debt were to squeeze the debtors dry, to transfer enormous resources from South to North and to wage undeclared war on the poor continents and their people, then their policies have been an unqualified success. If, however, their strategies were intended—as the official institutions always claim—to promote development beneficial to all members of society, to preserve the planet's unique environment and gradually to reduce the debt burden itself, then their failure is colossal. The most obvious aspect of this failure—or success, depending on your point of view—is financial. Every single month, from the outset of the debt crisis in 1982 until the end of 1990, debtor countries in the South remitted to their creditors in the North an average $6.5 billion in interest payments alone. If payments of the principal are included, then debtor countries have paid creditors at a rate of almost $12.5 billion per month...[32]

While it is true that debtor states were helped to join the modern world, the provision of electricity, telephones and roads were infrastructural improvements needed for resource extraction. They also benefited the privileged while most rural areas remained severely underdeveloped.

Now that the "free ride" is over, economic stratification, desperate competition and the pressures of debt repayment deepen deprivation while the countries that we subverted still struggle to recover.

To understand what we did (and still have the potential to do), we'll look closely at Central America, before and after our influence, to see how much of our foreign policy is coming home to roost.

---

31 George, Susan, "The Debt Boomerang," *50 Years is Enough: The Case Against the World Bank and the International Monetary Fund*, ed. Kevin Danaher (Boston: South End Press, 1994) 31.

32 Gershman, John, 27.

Chapter Seven: The Colonial History of Belize

The history of Belize is unique to Central America because IMF recommendations have been cushioned by prior adherence to free-market precepts. From the colonial period onward, the Belizean economy has been highly import-dependent, causing fiscal deficits and balance-of-payments problems. This is, in part, due to the nature of the Belizean economy, which is still an engine of extraction for natural resources and primary goods and, in part, due to the historic habits and customs of Belizeans, who look down on diversification as something that's beneath them, displaying a preference for imported goods and also fueling the manipulation of the domestic market to favor those who maintain control over the distribution and prices of imports.

Belize has problems, but decades of international aid prove it's been treated with care and concern for development, as well as the alleviation of poverty, even if it's reached the limits of creditors' reprieve.

The First English Settlers

From the outset, Belize was controlled by Englishmen (called Baymen) who started as buccaneers, pirates and adventurers seeking to plunder Spanish ships during England's wars with Spain. Once they settled the Bay area, the Baymen exploited the forests of logwood (from which dye is made) and extracted mass quantities for export back to England.

The Baymen were subject to Spanish reprisals for occupying the land that Spain had earlier claimed, although the Spaniards did not settle Belize because they preferred to travel inland to countries with precious metals and native populations that could be readily enslaved. Spain harassed the English settlers, despite English diplomacy aimed at securing rights for the Baymen.

During the seventeenth century, England did not yet plan to colonize Belize. The country was loosely controlled by Sir Thomas Modyford, the Governor of Jamaica. A treaty signed with Spain on May 23, 1667 gave Britain the right of trade in exchange for suppressing piracy. This was Spain's first concession, but was followed by another. The Treaty of Godolphin (also called the Treaty of Madrid) granted Great Britain:

> ...sovereignty, dominion, possession, and propriety in all the lands, regions, islands, colonies, and places whatsoever, being or situated in the West Indies, or any part of America, which the said King of Great Britain and his subjects do at present hold and possess.[33]

Although this language appeared to grant Britain *de facto* possession of Belize, the rights of the Baymen were still frequently challenged.

With the Treaty of Utrecht in 1713, Spain granted Britain an *Asiento*, which reiterated Spanish lordship while delivering trading rights to the British, prompting the creation of the British South Sea Company. The South Sea Company supplied African slaves to the Spanish colonies in addition to shipping logwood and exporting other goods.

The Introduction of Slavery

Before the Spaniards discovered Belize, the area was occupied by Mayans whose intricate, sophisticated society made great strides in the natural arts and sciences. In addition to having their own religion, writing system and hierarchical politics, the Mayans were skilled in astronomy and produced an accurate calendar.

The Spaniards found that the Mayans had abandoned the coastal areas, resulting in scattered inland settlements whose occupants could not be easily adapted to the *encomienda* system that later pre-

---

33 Setzekorn, William David, *Formerly British Honduras: A Profile of the New Nation of Belize* (Chicago: Ohio University Press, 1981) 134.

vailed in much of Latin America. Preferring to pursue mineral excavation, the Spaniards never settled the Bay area. However, even this limited contact between the Spaniards and the Mayans resulted in an 86 percent population decrease due to European diseases.[34]

The Baymen relied on their own labor for the harvesting of logwood, using the coastal rivers to transport their harvests, until deforestation forced them further inland, where they began to war with the Mayans. The Baymen burned homes and fields in an effort to starve the Mayans, but found they could not be subjugated, even if they could be pushed off the land. It was then that the Baymen solicited slaves in large numbers, through a triangular route of trade whereby the British imported African captives from their ports in Jamaica, exchanged them for goods and money in Belize, then exported those goods to Britain. Between 15 and 20 million Africans were imported to the Americas during the 300-year period preceding the end of slavery in Belize in 1838.[35]

A census in 1790 revealed that three-fourths of the Belizean population consisted of African slaves, whereas only one-tenth were white, with the remaining population consisting of free blacks and mixed whites. Over the next 25 years, the slave population declined to less than one-half while free blacks and mixed races increased to one-half, with whites at 10 percent.[36] The reasons for fewer slaves were not increased intermarriage and race-mingling, but rather high death rates, low birth rates, disease, malnutrition, overwork, accidents and suicides. With a ratio of 2-3 men per woman, the slaves had less reproductive capacity, and one author notes that abortion was common, as slave women refused to bear children in bondage.[37]

Author William David Setzekorn paints a placid picture of English–African relations, stating that:

> [T]hey worked shoulder to shoulder with their masters and fought the Spaniard with equal zeal. They proved to be courageous and loyal allies and the sense of comradeship shared between the British settlers and the newcomers, unique in American history, has lasted to the present day in Belize...[38]

William Arlington Donohoe echoes much the same:

34 Naturalight Productions, Ltd., *A History of Belize: A Nation in the Making,* http://www.belizenet.com/history/chap3.html.

35 Setzekorn, William David, 140.

36 Naturalight Productions, Ltd., http://www.belizenet.com/history/chap5.html.

37 Ibid.

38 Setzekorn, William David, 140.

The worst features of slavery, however, did not exist. The first settlers being too few in number for adequate protection of the settlement from the Spaniards, armed the negro. The slaves proved their loyalty and courage. They fought and worked side by side with the master, sharing with him the unrestricted life of the lumber camp—their machetes always by their sides.[39]

These accounts are questioned by researchers for whom the record of slave revolts and instances where they fled proves opposition to their lot and treatment during these years.[40] Under the conditions of harvest (a small group of slaves acting almost independently of supervision), opportunities for escape were frequent enough that Superintendent Hunter lamented in 1970:

Slaves, in this Settlement, being so by choice only; for the Vicinage of the Spanish Out Posts and the encouragement held out to seek freedom, by embracing the Roman Catholic Religion, afford them temptation to elope from their Owners. Many of the Settlers of this Country have been entirely ruined by these circumstances, and all experience frequent and heavy losses.[41]

There were also four recorded slave revolts. Occurring in 1765, 1768, 1773 and 1820, the last was the worst, resulting in a declaration of martial law.[42]

The Evolution of Belize Under the British

British rights to trade and settle in Belize were contested in the wars of 1718, 1727 and 1739. During the last, British ships were withdrawn from Belize for the war overseas, leaving the country vulnerable to attacks from the Spanish Crown. The Baymen then requested British colonial status and protection from Spain. But, even with the truce of 1748, Britain was reluctant to colonize Belize. It merely sought rights of trade while Spain continued efforts to forcibly expel the Baymen. Under the Treaty of Paris (1763), Britain gained the right to harvest logwood and build on the land of Belize. However, Spain retained sovereignty and the right of periodic inspection to ensure the prevention of English military fortifications.

39 Donohoe, William Arlington, *A History of British Honduras* (Montreal: Provincial Publishing Co., Ltd., 1946) 29.

40 "Belize Slavery in the Settlement, 1794-1838," http://workmall.com/ wfb2001/belize/belize_hisotry_slavery_in_the_settlement_1794_1838.

41 Bolland, O. Nigel, *Colonialism and Resistance in Belize: Essays in Historical Sociology* (Barbados: University of the West Indies Press, 2003) 28.

42 Naturalight Productions, Ltd., http://www/belizenet.com/history/ chap5.html.

Both France and Spain declared war on Britain as soon as it was preoccupied with the American Revolution. The Baymen in Belize survived only through the chance arrival of British warships just as the governor in Yucatan, Don Roberto Rivas Vetancur, ousted the Baymen from St. George's Cay and destroyed the settlement there. The British saved Belize City and the Baymen remained in Belize.

With the Treaty of Versailles in 1783, Britain's right to harvest logwood and build within Belize was restored under Spanish sovereignty. The settlers, by then, had overrun their boundaries, leading to renewed negotiations in 1786, the settlement of which allowed the Baymen to build on, and harvest from, the lands as far as the Silbun River. Farming was permitted, but not on a "plantation basis," and two commissioners were appointed (one from each of the governments) to ensure the treaty terms were kept.

The appointment of Colonel Marcus Despard to the position of Britain's Superintendent of Belize in 1786 was seen as the first step in seizing control of Belize. Yet, deeply disliked from the start, Despard was replaced by Colonel Peter Hunter, while Britain maintained in relations with Spain that it had no intention of colonization.

In October, 1796, Spain attempted to subdue the Baymen by force but was repelled. This marked the last battle between the colonizers and Spain, and is celebrated in Belize as a national holiday. Britain then established a British Supreme Court and criminal court to replace the local courts of settlement and declared that appointments to the Superintendency of Belize would be through Royal Letters Patent.

Weakened by the Napoleonic Wars, Spain began to lose control of the Spanish Americas. It lost Mexico in 1821 and, in 1823, the Central American Federation was formed. Patterned after the U.S. government with Guatemala as its nucleus, the National Assembly of the Federation adopted the position that Belize was a province of the new Federation of Central America. In response, Britain assigned Minister Frederick Chatfield to represent her rights until the Central American Federation dissolved in 1839.

The Early Government System

The first constitution of Belize, called Burnaby's Code after its founder, was established in 1765. It provided a punishment system for infractions and misbehaviors in accordance with the customs that had grown up at the time. The basic system of government revolved around the Public Meeting, at which only land owners and slave owners were politically represented.[43]

In 1790, 20 large estates owned more than half Belize's slaves. By the early nineteenth century, a quarter of the slaves were owned by 5 estates,[44] and this was consistent with land concentration. The country's productive acreage was held in very few hands (about 12 families in all).

The effect of such narrow representation was to ensure there was:

> ...a very "arbitrary aristocracy" who attempted to monopolize the mahogany business. [They are] almost our sole importers, exporters, and retailers, too; and they had the equity to import, just what served themselves; and their private purposes of keeping the people poor and totally dependent upon them; for they not only set their own price upon their goods, but also upon the logwood and mahogany which they received in payment of them.[45]

Despite the Public Meetings, through which a small, landed elite controlled the country's business, some Crown Superintendents were more heavy-handed than others. In 1814, Superintendent George Arthur declared that all unclaimed lands and those south of the Silbun River belonged to the British Crown. In 1833, Superintendent Colonel Alexander MacDonald assumed power to legislate by proclamation, took control of the nation's treasury, and decreed he had power to punish anyone.

By 1851, landowners became disappointed with the Public Meetings, overseen by a Crown-appointed Superintendent who selected his own magistrates. In 1854, Superintendent Colonel Wodehouse undertook to establish a Legislative Council which consisted of the Superintendent, plus eighteen popularly-elected and three Crown-appointed members. The prerequisite for membership was property holdings in excess of £400 until 1981.[46]

The People, Education, and Religion

In addition to hosting the English Baymen, Mayans, African slaves and Creoles (persons of European descent born in the New World), Belize saw an influx of Mexicans during the Caste War of the Yucatan Peninsula in 1847-48. This was followed by a second

---

43 Bolland, O. Nigel, 37.
44 Ibid.
45 Ibid., 38.
46 Setzekorn, William David, 174.

Mestizo migration in 1980, with thousands of people fleeing as refugees from Guatemala and El Salvador. There are also Caribs present (people native to the Caribbean), and the Garifuna are the descendants of the Africans and Caribs. The remainder of the population consists of Chinese, East Indian and North American peoples, who all came to Belize seeking economic opportunity.[47]

Nearly all of the English Baymen were Protestants. The Church of England was built in Belize City in 1777, followed by the establishment of St. John's Cathedral in 1812. Until the 1820s, Christianity remained the "white man's" religion, with British human rights activists pressing for conciliatory treatment of slaves. Their efforts produced new slave codes which prohibited physical mistreatment of slaves, the separate sale of parents and children and encouraged Christian marriage.[48]

With the coming of Protestant, Baptist and Methodist missionaries, the natives and slaves of Belize were afforded their first schools. Catholicism (which today affects 60 percent of the population) did not arrive in Belize until the mid-nineteenth century.

Missionary schools were the sole Belizean educators until 1930. Until then, the government saw no need to educate the natives and indeed felt threatened by them. For lack of training institutions, student teachers were chosen from those who completed primary school and were fourteen years or older.

The 1880s brought secondary schools and, in 1932, the British instituted a tax levy to pay for standardized education. This came on the heels of a devastating hurricane, after which the Crown took over Belize's treasury as the price for reconstruction loans. Thenceforth, a Superintendent of Schools was appointed, education was made compulsory for children under fourteen, and the Crown provided scholarships for secondary schooling.

The End of Slavery in Belize

In a secret, surprise move that startled the English Baymen, the new Central American Federation decreed the end of slavery in April 1823. This was protested by loggers, who had the most invested in slaves, until the British abolished slavery throughout the West Indies in 1834. Then the loggers side-stepped the issue by making all slaves free "apprentices," which effectively kept them in bondage.

---

47 Wikipedia, http://en.widipedia.org/wiki/Belize.
48 Ibid., 37.

Under the apprenticeship system, all former slaves aged 6 and over were forced to work without pay within the logging camps. Although paid a year in advance, apprentices were expected to re-pay their wages and were fined for being tardy, absent or inefficient. They were also charged exorbitant prices for goods at the company stores they couldn't do without. This system of debt-peonage proved unbeatable. The freedmen were always behind in payments and forced to re-sign their contracts with each successive Christ-mas. Finally, the freedmen were prohibited from owning land. The British Colonial Secretary discontinued land grants as soon as the slaves were freed, stating that the procedure would not "discourage labor for wages."[49]

Without land of their own, the freedmen were reliant on the Baymen who controlled the country's imports. Those who had land and resources also discouraged agriculture, lest it interfere with im-ports and profits. As such, there was little or no land under native cultivation. The system was wholly extractive, exporting logwood and mahogany timbers, with annual budget deficits to cover the cost of imports, whose prices were inflated.

The Guatemalan Dispute

Following the creation of the Central American Federation, Guatemala claimed Belize as an extension of its territory while Mexico, too, laid claim to Belize based on its inheritance of Span-ish sovereignty. On April 30, 1859, Rafael Carrera (the President of Guatemala), his negotiator Don Pedro de Aycinena, and British rep-resentative Charles Lennox Wyke held a convention to establish the boundaries between Belize and Guatemala. The result was the Boundary Convention of 1959, in which Guatemala won the con-struction of a trade road between Guatemala and Belize in exchange for recognition of British claims in Belize. British failure to follow through with constructing the route led to continued conflict.

By 1861, the Belize Legislative Council requested colonial rec-ognition. The British government capitulated on May 12, 1862. Be-lize was named British Honduras and a Lieutenant Governor ap-pointed. Guatemala continued pursuing its claims until 1884, when it insisted that the treaty of 1859 must be carried out.

Mexico announced in 1930 that any change in Belize's status would trigger Mexican claims to all territory north of the Silbun

---

49 Naturalight Productions, Ltd., http://www.belizenet.com/history/chap5.html.

River. Guatemala sent Britain two proposals to settle the dispute in September, 1936, one of which would transfer Belize to Guatemala at a cost of £400,000. The other requested that Britain pay this sum and cede Guatemala a strip of land to provide it with a sea route in order for Britain to own the country. When matters remained unresolved by 1939, Guatemala agreed to suspend its claims until after World War II.

The Economy

Logwood, the primary export, was replaced by mahogany until 1865, when the world market declined and British Honduras was threatened with deforestation.[50] This prompted the extraction of *chicle*, a latex sap drawn from sapodilla trees and used to make chewing gum. But the export of chicle declined (by nearly 40 percent), when it faced competition from synthetic formulations and oriental varieties after World War II.

To compensate, British Honduras increased re-export trade with Mexico after 1949. Revenue from this source rose from $77,000 to $209,000 in 1952, $713,000 in 1954, and $1,000,000 between 1956 and 1958. However, the total of British Honduran imports regularly exceeded exports by over 50 percent, with that imbalance rising to 100 percent between 1958 and 1959.[51] The country's deficit and balance-of-payments gap had to be redressed through colonial development grants and welfare schemes, as well as foreign investment.

British Honduras received Crown assistance from 1931, due to hurricane reconstruction and widespread economic depression. Its average annual assistance of $150,000 climbed to $380,000 in 1950. Although the country balanced its budget by 1951 and was released from Treasury control, large grants continued from colonial development and welfare funds, particularly after 1957 when the Crown wanted to increase salaries and expand the colony's administrative and social services. Then aid increased to $1,250,000 and arrangements were made to continue assistance until 1963.[52]

While the country's local funding stemmed from import duties, income tax, excise and entry tax, export duties and land taxes, colo-

---

50 Bott, Uwe, "Chapter 8 – Belize: The Economy, *A Country Study: Belize* (Washington, DC: Library of Congress Country Studies) http://lcweb2.loc.gov/cgi-bin/query/r?frd/cstdy:@field (DOCID+bz0049).

51 Waddell, D.A.G., *British Honduras: A Historical and Contemporary Survey* (London: Oxford University Press, 1961) 96.

52 Ibid., 101.

nial development and welfare schemes were intended to restructure the economy from dependency on lumber to diversified agriculture. Waddell describes the plan's two-fold purpose:

> ...to remedy the forest supply situation , by inducing large-scale regeneration, by improving communications so as to expand the area of exploitable forest, and by attempting to market further varieties of timber, and to broaden the base of the economy by developing the agricultural sector, which calls for communications, soil surveys, crop experiments, stock trials, the provision of credit and land-clearing facilities, and the education of the farming population.[53]

In line with diversification, the British promoted sugar, bananas, coconuts, plantains, rubber and cocoa. The land and climate also suited rice, coffee, cotton and tobacco, all of which were encouraged as new export products. Plantations were rejected, however, by natives who drew their expectations from heavily-exploited Jamaicans. Logging was more socially respectable so, at first, there was little interest in crop diversification.

Because communications improvements could not be economically justified via population statistics, the British toyed with an immigration scheme in 1959. This was never implemented from fear that the local Mestizos and Amerindians would be displaced by cheaper labor. Even though labor was scarce, this was not reflected in wages. Public Works laborers earned $2.00 per day and the wages of store clerks ranged from $7.00 to $15.00 per week.[54] Price controls, imposed during World War II, still remained in place, and many goods were rationed.

After 1961, over one-fifth of productive acreage belonged to the British Honduras Company, which became the Belize Estate and Produce Company (BEC). The BEC controlled Belize's development for the next hundred years. Like the oligarchy of landowners formed by the early settlers, the BEC offloaded the country's expenses onto the British Honduran government through low taxes, non-contribution to development costs and undervaluation of exports.

Since 1867, the BEC had been destroying Mayan villages. It eliminated Indian villages at San Jose and Yalbac during the 1930s. The subsistence farmers expelled by the BEC were left homeless and rightless.

---

53 Ibid., 103.
54 Setzekorn, 212.

By 1971, 3 percent of the landowners held 95 percent of the land, with 90 percent of that total in foreign hands. The remaining 1 percent formed small plots on which 91 percent of the populace was expected to subsist.[55]

Yet, land distribution did not contribute to the quest for independence. The desire came instead from conversion of the British Honduran dollar to parity with the pound. Prior to 1949, British Honduran currency was pegged to the American dollar, and that was the will of the people, as most of Belize's imports originated in the U.S. The devaluation of the British Honduran dollar resulted in increased trade with Britain, but it also made U.S. imports expensive, with the result that everyday commodities was priced out of reach for average citizens.[56]

The Politics of Independence

Although small labor unions existed before 1939, large-scale organization began with the formation of the General Workers Union (GWU). Its membership rose from "2,000 in 1947-50 to over 5,000 in 1951, 8,500 in 1952, 9,500 in 1953, 10,500 in 1954, and 12,000 in 1955."[57] Then a break-away faction of the GWU established the British Honduras Development Union in 1950. The GWU launched political organization in 1950, forming the People's United Party (PUP). Its foremost agitator, George Cadle Price, proposed the end of colonial rule and opposition to a British plan for a West Indian Federation, winning control of the Belize City Council in 1950. The PUP platform protested underdevelopment and proposed consumer/producer cooperatives.

Due to the grassroots agitation inspired by the PUP, British Honduras acquired a new constitution in 1954. Britain conferred the right of suffrage on all literate adults and established a Legislative Assembly to which nine members were to be popularly elected and six nominated by the Colonial Government. However, the control of the Governor was still absolute within the Executive Council and his reserve powers retained.[58]

In response to accusations that the PUP was infiltrated by communism, PUP spokesmen maintained they opposed communism as

55 Naturalight Productions, Ltd., http://www.belizenet.com/history/chap9.html.

56 Waddell, D.A.G., 109.

57 Ibid., 99.

58 Setzekorn, William David, 217.

a "world conspiracy against freedom, democracy and religion, and no solution to economic problems."[59] They especially denied Guatemalan influence when claims upon British Honduras were still a matter of conflict.

In the following election, Baymen loyal to the Crown were represented by the National Party (NP), which believed it would easily win. They were surprised when the PUP garnered eight of the nine elective seats in the Legislative Assembly.

Immediately, a divide in the PUP resulted in the establishment of the Honduran Independence Party (HIP). The HIP supported a British plan for a federation of former British colonies within the Caribbean, whereas Price of the PUP condemned the arrangement, fearing domination by Jamaica or Barbados. As an alternative, Price suggested an arrangement with the Central American republics and, in 1957, Price again led a sweep of the ballot, with the PUP winning all nine of the elective seats in the Legislative Assembly.

Further constitutional changes made by Britain in 1960 created a new Legislative Assembly of eighteen elected members, five nominated members and two ex-officio members. The new Executive Council consisted of a First Minister (the leader of the winning party), five Ministers (chosen by the Assembly from their ranks) and two ex-officio Ministers. The Governor chaired the Assembly.

In 1961, Price became the country's first Minister and the PUP gained all eighteen of the Assembly's elective seats. This led to another constitutional conference at which the British conceded to full internal self-government. Thenceforth, a bicameral legislature was divided between the House of Representatives and the Senate. The judiciary became independent, while the British Governor retained responsibility for foreign affairs, national defense, internal security and employment in the civil service.

As one of his first actions, Price demanded a settlement of the "Guatemala question." Two years of deliberations, led by U.S. attorney Bethuel M. Webster, resulted in the Webster Plan, proposing an "association" of Belize and Guatemala in which Belize would "consult" with Guatemala on all foreign affairs. As Belize's "big brother," Guatemala would "cooperate with Belize in the areas of defense, communications and economic development, leading to limited Belizean independence by 1971 with close ties to Guatemala."[60]

---

59 Ibid., 218.
60 Ibid., 228.

This was tantamount to proposing Belize's annexation and was overwhelmingly protested. Britain renounced the plan, and the U.S. concluded it had no further obligation to try to resolve the issue.

Meanwhile, Price was busy with a 7-year plan to lift the country out of economic underdevelopment and end its budget deficits. To that end, he lobbied for inclusion in the Organization of American States and the Central American Common Market.

Opposed by NIP candidate Philip Goldson in the 1969 elections, Price was again elected. The PUP won 17 of the seats in the House of Representatives, with the remaining seat occupied by a NIP-PDM (People's Democratic Movement) candidate.

Belize then became preoccupied with the construction of its new capital, Belmopan. This was due to the destruction of Belize City by hurricane, with an estimated project cost of US $13.75 million, of which $11.25 million was financed by the British Ministry of Overseas Development. Price also allocated 75 percent of the 1968 national budget to pay for the construction of Belmopan.[61]

In 1966, Britain surrendered control of the Belizean treasury and placed economic development squarely in Price's hands. Price hoped to promote tourism, light industry, and agriculture, but Belize was struggling with budget deficits because imports exceeded exports.

As incentives for development, Price sold government lands in small lots (20–50 acres), with purchase and repayment to take place over five years. This became a freehold if the purchaser acceptably developed it. Parcels of government land exceeding 50 acres were to be conveyed through leasehold, with eventual acquisition possible. Price also passed the Development Incentives Ordinance of 1960, which afforded tax holidays and protection from duties and tariffs to foreign and domestic investors. Finally, Price created an Agricultural Credits Fund and a Small Farmers Loan Fund, as well as a Government Marketing Board to buy farmers' surpluses.

Price was reelected in 1970, and Belize became a member of CARIFTA (the Caribbean Free Trade Area) in 1971. In entry negotiations, Belize was classified as a "Less Developed" country, allowing its tariffs to be lowered more slowly. The Belizean dollar was taken off the pound standard to re-achieve U.S. dollar parity.

Between 1979–1981, the trade deficit diminished. This was due to government financing and lending, which also resulted in foreign borrowing. The net foreign position in lending was $9.8 million,

---

61 Ibid., 230.

and Belize received an additional $70 million from the Caribbean Development Bank. At the time, the government's recurrent revenue was $64 million against recurrent expenditures of $54 million. This placed Belize in a favorable position for foreign lending, even though Belize's continued dependence on Britain was demonstrated by relatively high indebtedness.

A standing national army was formed on January 1, 1978. This was judged necessary due to the Guatemalan border dispute, and it freed Britain of responsibility for Belize's security. This was the final step leading to Belize's independence in 1981.

CHAPTER EIGHT: BELIZE — PARTY POLITICS AND DEBT

Constitutionally, Belize is a monarchy, which recognizes Queen Elizabeth II as sovereign. Below this, it acts as a parliamentary democracy, with its National Assembly consisting of a House of Representatives and a Senate. The 29 members of the House are popularly elected to a maximum 5-year term, whereas appointments to the Senate are controlled by the governor general (12), the Prime Minister (6), the leader of the opposition (3), and one each on the advice of the Belize Council of Churches and Evangelical Association of Churches, the Belize Chamber of Commerce and Industry, the Belize Better Business Bureau, the National Trade Union Congress and the Civil Society Steering Committee. The Executive branch contains the cabinet, led by the Prime Minister.[62]

For administrative purposes, the country is divided into six districts. These are: Belize, Corozal, Orange Walk, Cayo, Stann Creek, and Toledo. With the exception of Belize, all are administered by commissioners, and District Town Boards are largely concerned with municipal affairs.[63]

Although those who monitor Belize externally (like the U.S. and NGOs) report that the country's politics are democratic and fairly open, the government has come under increased criticism due

---

62 CIA – The World Factbook – Belize, http://www.travlang.com/gactbook/print/bh.html.
63 Setzekorn, William David., 10.

to its autocratic ruling style. This extends, in retrospect, to its first Minister, George Cadle Price, who is accused of being an "autocratic [ruler] with bully boys and the works."[64]

A publication by the Belize Development Trust states that:

> Things [in] those decades were rough mostly because nobody local had any experience with democracy, different opinions, open debate and all that. So those who opposed, or disagreed were brutally in many cases victimized...by PUP party adherents in the local rural rank and file. Most went into self exile, or were forced by circumstances to leave. Price followed in the steps of Huey Long in Louisiana...Huey Long was not noted for his democracy either, nor where his state police. Nor was the British Honduras police, or later the Belize National police. They took sides, often with brutality and a vengeance...a politically controlled police.[65]

On May 13, 1993, Britain announced it would remove most of its troops within a year. Price was then so confident that he called on the governor general to dissolve the National Assembly on June 30 and hold elections the following day. Opposing him were Manuel Esquivel, the leader of the United Democratic Party (UDP), and Philip Goldson, leader of the newly formed National Alliance for Belizean Rights. The environment turned ugly as Price accused Esquivel of corruption and a desire to devalue the Belizean dollar, while Esquivel, in turn, accused Price of making too many concessions to Guatemala. The result was a surprise victory for the UDP. On July 1, 1993, the UDP took 16 of the 29 seats in the National Assembly and Esquivel became the new prime minister on July 5th.[66]

Esquivel, unlike Price, allowed opposition and dissent. However, his first term in office resulted in little economic development. He was removed by the PUP, which then lost the next election to Esquivel due to corruption and political abuse. Seen as the lesser of two evils, Esquivel reigned for one more term. He was replaced again by the PUP in 1998.

Ironically, what restored the PUP was UDP corruption. The PUP political platform read:

> Corruption in public life has become pervasive. Citizens feel that politicians and public officials use their public office for

---

64 Belize Project.com, Report #37 March 1999, "Historical Evaluations of Political Party Government in Belize for First 35 Years," Belize Development Trust, http://belize1.com/BzLibrary/trust55.html.

65 Ibid.

66 "Belize-Introduction," http://workmall.com/wfb2001/belize/belize_history_introduction.html.

personal enrichment, and they demand immediate and practical solutions to restore integrity in government.[67]

Elected in 1998, Prime Minister Said Musa proposed introducing participatory mechanisms and government by consensus. His Referendum Act would have allowed challenges to village and district councils via petitions by 5 percent of villages and districts. Nationally, 2 percent of the voters in the country's last election would have been able to challenge national issues. In the end, only the government and its "rubber stamp" legislature were empowered to call referendums.[68]

This prompted the Belize Development Trust to write:

> It was amazing that the media didn't follow up on the debate, or lack of debate. Nobody expected the Opposition to do so. It has been their evowed declaration through Esquivel, that they do not want democracy for Belize, but wish to keep the autocratic elected dictatorship with all its advantages for personal enrichment.[69]

Personal enrichment is what the government of Belize is all about. It starts with an agreement between the PUP and the UDP to compensate each other richly for the rotation of parties in government. After the 1998 election, it was reported that the following people received tax free severance pay and annual pensions totaling well over BZ $1 million:

	Severance	Pension
Henry Young	$60,000	$14,400
Melvin Hulse	$45,000	$10,800
Ruben Campos	$60,000	$14,400
Salvador Fernandez	$60,000	$14,400
Manuel Esquivel	$65,725	$15,774
Dennis Usher	$32,022	
Joseph Cayetano	$35,382	
Russel Garcia	$35,382	

---

67 San Pedro Sun, "PUP Announces Political Reform Package," http://www.sandpedrosun.net/old/46pupreform.html.

68 Belize Project.com, Report #53 March 1999, "Referendum Act and the PUP Mystery?" Belize Development Trust, http://belizel.com/BzLibrary/trust53.html.

69 Ibid.

Faith	$32,574	
Aragon	$60,000	$14,400

Still to be paid were former UDP legislators Hubert Elrington and Elito Urbina, who anticipated severance of BZ $32,179 and BZ $26,279. UDP Representative Michael Finnegan was anxious for all his defeated colleagues to collect their severance pay and pensions exceeding BZ $700,000.[70]

By 2004, the PUP government faced financial crisis, due to recurrent fiscal deficits and repeated foreign borrowing. It was forced to turn to the IMF, but this did not stop the PUP from spending BZ $2 million that year for personal new vehicles.[71]

The Cash Cow of Government

The sum of salaries, perks and pensions paid to competing officials is not the most extreme measure of political abuses. The government is also a cash cow for prominent business interests via tax cuts, financing through the Belizean DFC (Development Finance Corporation), and government contracts for provisions and services, for which party members collected significant kickbacks.

Information on government schemes exists on Belizean blogs and web sites, where each new scandal tends to be viewed as a drop in the bucket drowning Belize in debt. According to FreeBelize. org, the government launched a scheme to buy printers from Yasser Musa's jointly-owned company under an annual contract award of BZ $2.5 million, to be paid quarterly in advance. It also sanctioned a land purchase at BZ $10.00 per acre by Deputy Prime Minister Johnny Briceno, which was then converted to a BZ $999,990 sale to its new foreign owners.[72]

While the government denied acting as loan guarantor for Glenn Godfrey's company Intelco, the proposed sale of Intelco to BTL exposed the involvement of ministers Ralph Fonseca and Said Musa. According to a letter to Ronald Sander from Glenn Godfrey, the government-secured debt was US $49,894,844 (a whopping BZ $100 million). But the corruption did not end there. The total

---

70 Belize Project.com, Report #80 June 1999, "The New Belize Growth Industry – Politics," Belize Development Trust, http://belize1.com/BzLibrary/trust80.html.

71 FreeBelize.org, http://www.freebelize.org/index.html.

72 Ibid.

debt secured by Social Security was US $21.1 million dollars. And the 5,000 computers for the Schools Wide Area Network that were supposed to be free from Intelco in exchange for its 15 year government contract were listed on the GOB budget as a US $1.5 million dollar bill owed to Glenn Godfrey.[73]

The Belizean Development Finance Corporation (DFC) issued numerous business loans that were neither researched nor collateralized. Recommending liquidation of the DFC in 2003, the IMF noted BZ $56.6 million in net irrecoverable costs for infrastructure and housing kits, and a need to write off BZ $25.3 million in bad loans. There were also four troubled businesses indebted to the DFC.

The largest debtor was Novelo's Limited (a transportation outfit), then in receivership and behind on scheduled payments. The total loans to Novelo were BZ $35 million, representing 10 percent of the DFC's loan portfolio as well as 100% of the DFC's total capital. According to FreeBelize.org, a European firm expressed interest in buying Novelo, after which Novelo acquired loans to purchase other transportation firms, with the help of Prime Minister Musa and his colleagues, believing the final sale would compensate all involved.[74] The deal fell through, and Belize became stuck with the loans. In a letter dated November 4, 2004 from Kevin Castillo to Mrs. Garcia of Social Security, Castillo acknowledged that Novelo's Bus Line Limited owed a payment of BZ $70,993, prompting this from FreeBelize.org:

> The truth of the matter is that this should have been paid by the previous owners a long time ago, however, like every other crony, special privileges were given and the Social Security Board could afford to give a "line of credit" to the Novelo's Group.

Glenn Godfrey's law firm then received BZ $2,915,430 from the DFC for filing suit against Novelo.[75]

Another important DFC debtor was Universal Health Services, which borrowed BZ $12 million to complete construction on a Belize City hospital. To complement the loan, the company acquired an additional BZ $17 million from local Belizean banks, which were guaranteed by the DFC. The DFC's total exposure was BZ $30 million (over 80% of the DFC's net worth).[76]

---

73 Ibid.
74 Ibid.
75 Ibid.
76 Ibid.

Overall, the DFC compromised BZ $134 million in its equity and loan position (four times its capital worth) to merit liquidation. But even liquidation required these commitments, listed by FreeBelize. org:

> 1. Belize Mortgage Company (2001–2002): A non-callable bond with a remaining principal balance of approximately US $38 million. Liquidation would accelerate payment or refinancing of the bond. In either case, preliminary checks show an additional payout fee of approximately US $11 million plus insurance premium payments of approximately US $13 million. Arrangement fees of approximately US $1 million for the refinancing would also be an additional cost.

> 2. An additional pool of loans will be required to substitute non performing loans. The estimated cost of administering this pool of loans is 5% of BZ $91.0 million or BZ $4.5 million per annum, for the next 7 years. The investor will need to approve the new servicing agent.

> 3. A severance payment to DFC employees of approximately BZ $3 million.

> 4. The Ministry of Education and the Ministry of Housing will need to increase their capacity to manage education and housing loans of BZ $50.0 million and BZ $18.0 million respectively. A rule of thumb of 3% is used in calculating a management fee of BZ $2.0 million per annum.

> 5. During the liquidation process, there will be a cost associated with the management of DFC until it is sold (1 year). This cost is estimated at 3% per annum or BZ $5.2 million.

> 6. Guarantees of BZ $20 million with the Belize Bank for UHS and Novelo, allows the bank to call on its guarantee and demand payment from liquidation proceeds.

> 7. Disbursement of loans currently under implementation, estimated at BZ $2 million will have to be continued under liquidation. Additionally, ongoing programs such as the CARD project and the EIB/CGA citrus replanting program would be terminated. Thus, the poverty alleviation and productivity/efficiency objectives of the respective programs would not be achieved. [77]

According to FreeBelize.org, the DFC planned to sell its real estate and mortgage financing packages valued at BZ $146,584,050 for half their value. This included the Soy Bean Project, which was created with a loan of US $17 million, and, according to its prospectus, would be sold for BZ $2,445,686. [78]

---

77 Ibid.
78 Ibid.

Costly Government Incentives

Belize's investment incentives are Tax Holidays and Duty Exemptions, combined with perks and privileges offered in the Export Processing Zones (EPZs) and Commercial Free Zone (CFZ).[79]

Tax Holidays:	The tax holiday period is normally for 5 years, accruing from the date of production. However there is a provision that the Minister of Economic Development can review the company's operations and renew the tax holiday period for a further term that is not to exceed ten years. In addition, there is an exception which states that in the case of a company which is engaged in agriculture, agro-industrial products, mariculture, etc. and the operation is strictly for export and highly labor intensive, the tax holiday may be for a maximum period of 25 years. Incentives under this clause also allow exemption from income tax, including the repatriation of profits and dividends.
Duty Exemptions:	The Act allows duty exemptions to every company which has been granted an Approved Enterprise Order (Development Concession) to import into Belize, free of import duty, and revenue placement duty. Duty exemption privileges begin on the date of signing of the Approved Enterprise Order, and the duty exception period shall be more than 15 years duration. However, the same can be reviewed by the Minister for a further period not exceeding ten years.
Export Processing Zones:	The EPZ program has been considered advantageous to investors as Belize has a preferential market access to the CARICOM under the treaty of Chaguaramas, the European Union under the Lome Convention, Canada under the CARIBCAN, and the USA under the Caribbean Basin Initiative (CBI) and the Generalized System of Preferences (GSP). Various incentives to investors under the EPZ Act include: • Full import and export duty exemptions; • Exemptions from capital gains, property and land tax, excise, sales, and consumption tax, trade turnovers, foreign exchange, and transfer tax; • A guaranteed income holiday of 20 years with an option to extend and deduct losses from profits following the tax holiday period;

---

79 Belize Investment Guide, "Investment Incentives Schemes," http://www.belize.org/html/big/ivsch.html.

- Divided tax exemption in perpetuity;
- Opportunity to sell, lease or transfer items, goods and services within an EPZ;
- Work permits at no cost for all professionals and technical staff;
- No raw material import restrictions;
- No import or export-licensing requirement;
- No trade licensing for business to operate;
- No licensing requirement for domestic suppliers who sell to EPZ business.

Commercial Free Zone:	The Commercial Free Zone was established at Corozal to attract foreign investment. And it contains its own list of Duty and Tax exemptions.
Duty Exemptions:	All merchandise, articles, or goods entering a CFZ for commercial purposes shall be exempt from import duties, stamp duties and revenue replacement duties; All fuel and goods required for the proper functioning of a CFZ business shall likewise be exempt from all duties and taxes; Nearly all imports and exports of a CFZ to or from whatever destination shall be exempt from all custom duties, consumption taxes, excise taxes, and export duties.
Tax Exemptions:	A tax credit of 1% of taxable income for employment of 10 to 30 Belizean workers; A tax credit of 1.5% of taxable income for employment of over 30 and up to 50 Belizean workers; A tax credit of 2% of taxable income for employment of over 50 Belizean workers; During the first 5 years of operation, a CFZ business shall be exempt from income tax or capital gains tax or any new corporate tax levied, and any dividends paid by a CFZ business shall be exempt from such tax for the first twenty years of operation; Where a CFZ business incurs a total net loss over the fire year tax holiday, that loss may be carried forward and deducted against profits in the three years following the tax holiday period; Any proceeds from the sale or stock or other partial or complete ownership interest in a CFZ business shall be exempt from tax levied under this section

As the IMF concluded in its 2005 Country Study, these expansive, far-reaching incentives are, in part, responsible for the sizable budget deficits the government sustains each year. They provide further examples of how the government caters to the private sector at the expense of the public domain.

Although tax incentives encourage foreign investment (ranging from US $19 million in 1998 to US $56 million in 1999 to US $27.6 million in 2000 to US $34.2 million in 2001),[80] the arrangement is parasitic and forces the government to rely on increasingly expensive foreign loans.

The Viewpoint of the IMF

The IMF analysis of Belizean lending and securitization omits mention of government corruption (even though Belize scored 3.7 on a negative scale of corruption and 5.5 on a positive),[81] focusing instead on schemes undertaken in 2000–2001 to boost the Belizean economy, including securities sales to the Royal Merchant Bank of Trinidad and Tobago (RMBTT) totaling US $100 million, for which Belize pledged an income stream from its domestic loan portfolio. The underlying credit risk remained with the DFC and the BSSB (Social Security Board) since their assets were not sold but used as collateral. In the event the pledged collateral became nonperforming, the institutions agreed to swap it for performing collateral. The government also provided a subsidiary guarantee and the central bank guaranteed convertibility into U.S. dollars.[82]

Belize made two bond placements during 2000, totaling 11 percent of GDP, to finance hurricane reconstruction and government expenditure. Then, in 2002, it launched the North American securitization scheme, in which Belize Mortgage Company, a subsidiary of the DFC, was created to buy mortgages from the DFC and the BSSB and sell bonds collateralized by these mortgages through the Bank of New York. The bond sales raised US $45 million, but the government also borrowed from foreign banks to finance construction of low-income housing and new schools. In promoting loans to the economy's productive sectors and also to cover home mortgages, the government relied on guaranteed receivables securitiza-

---

80 Encyclopedia of the Nations, "Belize Foreign Investment," http:www.nationsencyclopedia.com/Americas/Belize-FOREIGN-INVESTMENT.html.

81 2005 Transparency International Corruption Perceptions Index, http://www.infoplease.com/ipa/A0781359.html and http://www.nationmaster.com/country/bh/Government Belize.

82 International Monetary Fund, "Belize: Selected Issues," IMF Country Report 05/353, September 2005.

tion, on-lending from the central bank of external loans, and project loans by the Caribbean Development Bank (CDB). The Social Security Board participated in the receivables securitization and provided funding to credit unions.[83]

The DFC's net foreign indebtedness increased rapidly in 2001 reaching a peak in 2002 of 18 percent of GDP.[84] The government overextended the DFC, so that even its liquidation resulted in high costs, but government mismanagement transcended domestic abuse with the magnitude of foreign loans it contracted and guaranteed.

Belize's Foreign Debt

The DFC's inability to pay debt service required the government to refinance in 2004. It then had to address the securitized loans granted by the RMBTT via US $75.6 million in new notes to the RMBTT. By then, the government had also guaranteed US $30 million of the DFC's external debt in the North American securitization scheme and had issued guarantees of about US $70 million for debt owed due to the privatization of water, electricity and Belize's port facilities.[85]

In November, 2004, the IMF notes:

> The central government borrowed US $79 million through Capital Markets Financial Services (CMFS) acting as an intermediary for over 40 individual noteholders. Proceeds together with US $18 million from international reserves of the CBB were used to refinance US $95 million in maturing debt to the International Bank of Miami. New notes have a seven-year maturity and bear an interest rate of 9.25 percent. They also contain a put option provision that allows noteholders to sell them back to the government at specified dates beginning in November 2005 at a price that rises from par in 2005 to 124 percent of par at maturity in 2011. Noteholders also have right to request that proceeds from new external debt by the government and the sale of the government's shares in Belize Telecommunications Limited be used to prepay the CMFS notes. Fees for the CMFS transactions totaled US $2.4 million, including a 1.75 percent financial advisory fee and a 1 percent placement fee.[86]

Belize was forced to offer greater incentives to lending as it became more indebted. Rolling debt from one organization to another

---

83 Ibid.
84 Ibid.
85 Ibid.
86 Ibid.

resulted in fees of critical proportions to the economy of Belize. While the country's credit rating declined from B+ to CCC- , additional fees and options mounted with respect to later lending:

> The government issued US $137 million in two bonds in March 2005, consisting of a US $65 million ten-year bond and a US $71 million five year bond. Both bonds are amortizing with the former carrying a two year grace period. Net proceeds available to the government were US $94 million after subtracting upfront fees, insurance premiums, and contributions to reserve accounts totaling US $43 million. The government is obliged to maintain an international insurance coverage guaranteeing 95 percent of payments to bondholders while a reserve account was established to cover 180 days of debt service and to insure the 5 percent of the principal not covered by the international insurance company. Taking these costs into account, the effective interest rate for Belize is estimated at about 11 percent.[87]

As of June, 2005, the IMF wrote the following:

> Most of the commercial external debt consists of uninsured bonds issued through Bear Stearns in 2002 and 2003 and maturing in 2012 and 2015 respectively; two insured bonds issued through Bear Stearns in 2005, with one maturing in 2010 and the other in 2015, and bank debt to Citicorp, the International Bank of Miami, and the Royal Merchant Bank of Trinidad and Tobago (RMBTT). [As] of June 2005, the largest creditor is the Inter-American Development Bank (US $70 million) followed by the CDB (US $46 million) and the IBRD (US $32 million). Most bilateral debt is owed to Taiwan Province of China (US $111 million or 82 percent of the bilateral debt as of June 2005), followed by Kuwait (US $10 million), the UK (US $5 million), Mexico (US 4 million), and the U.S. (US $3 million).[88]

The country's principal payments (excluding interest) were scheduled to rise from US $50 million in 2006 to US $56 million in 2007 and US $58 million in 2008.[89]

The Predatory State

The democratically-elected elite have mismanaged Belize to the extent that their grandchildren's grandchildren will be burdened with foreign debt. In the process, the elite have benefited financially along with prominent business interests, both foreign and domestic. But does this make Belize a predatory state?

Quoting one of its domestic institutions:

87 Ibid.
88 Ibid.
89 Ibid.

Belize has always fitted from Colonial days through to the present, the outlines of a predatory state. Without popular control over the economic realm, democracy is at best limited in scope and incapable of reducing the vast inequities generated by a class ruler system. Whether this is represented by Colonial officers from a foreign power, or an elected clique that controls the machinery of a political party. The purpose of the predatory state is to provide the minimal means of government services, while using the status of exclusive government controls, to extract income from the rest of the constituents [for] a favored few, or business group, or new class of society. Whatever the legislation passed, the intent and purpose is to maximize the revenue of the group members, regardless of the impact on the wealth of the society...[90]

Coming from Belizeans, these are strong words to describe the ruling methodology. The PUP *has* spent money on education and healthcare, as well as low-cost housing and affordable mortgages. Further, Belize was granted reprieve from paying its debt service to Britain on condition that it improved the education and health care systems. The money slated for debt service was channeled into these sectors, representing 23 percent of expenditures for education and BZ $20 million for healthcare.

The government's choice, however, was to cater to the business community with conservative free-market policies that ultimately saddled Belize with BZ $2 billion in debt. Accordingly, it shaped their society in ways you might predict.

"Forty Years of Police Abuse"

Crime is not new to Belize, but has surged over the years. It affects tourists and travelers as well as Belizeans and occurs in any town or district at any time of day. Most troubling is the degree of human trafficking, with refugees from Guatemala and other Central American countries being forced into prostitution and exploited for child pornography.[91]

The police have posed their own problem, as a citizen attests:

The police are essentially autonomous. They operate under their own bosses and are national in scope. When public complaints arise in the villages and towns, if they are big enough and outra-

---

90 Belize Project.com, Report #58 April 1999, "Comparative Politics and the Predatory State Government!" http://belize1.com/BzLibrary/trust58.html.

91 U.S. State Department, "Belize," http://www.state.gov/g/drl/rls/hrrpt/2003/27886.htm.

---

geous enough, to affect the political party...that has current 5 year ownership of the country and everything in it; the party in power will attempt to bring the police to heel. Or at least put on a show of scolding the Police Commissioner in the capital and both will promise never ending promises of reform. Nothing though, ever changes! The police are useful the elite political party bosses have found out. They can be used to harass political opponents, bring false charges, imprison and physically abuse opposition political supporters. So the political elites keep this unruly, gang of thieves in uniform, because of the political advantages when they need them. Otherwise, the politicians leave the police to their own autonomous devices. There are some good officers, probably in the majority, but new recruits soon become disillusioned with the corruption within the force from older heads.[92]

Other reports of police abuse include false or arbitrary fines and detention without explanation. These accounts are supported by Amnesty International, which investigated ill-treatment and torture, fatal shootings and other human rights violations, including poor prison conditions.

In 1999, the Human Rights Commission of Belize documented more than 30 cases of police brutality. Between August and November 1999, Belize's Ombudsman reported separately that he received 25 allegations of excessive use of force.[93]

Reformers suggest popular election of Police Commissioners to create a bond with local citizens and prevent subservience to the government. However, chances of this are slim now that the government has its back to the wall over the issue of foreign debt. Too, it increased repression to combat the drug trade in accordance with U.S. demands.

As noted by Alma H. Young:

> According to the U.S. Drug Enforcement Administration (USDEA) Belize has rapidly become the most important center of narcotics trafficking in Central America, and the fourth largest supplier of marijuana to the United States (behind Colombia, Mexico, and Jamaica). There is also the potential for rapid expansion: the marijuana acreage has increased six-fold since 1982, and net production in 1984 was 1,100 metric tons. Marijuana is not the DEA's major concern; there are fears that if the drug

---

92 Belize Project.com, Report #107 September 1999, "40 Years of Police Abuse in Belize!" Belize Development Trust, http://belize1.com/BZLibrary/trust107.html.

93 Amnesty International, Belize: Government Commitments and Human Rights, http://www.amnestyusa.org/countries/belize/document.do?id=8BCDFD3938E87CAE802.

industry were allowed to flourish in Belize, the country could become an entrepôt for cocaine traffic en route from South America.[94]

Because the U.S. threatened to cut bilateral aid to countries that wouldn't fight drugs, Belize's security forces undertake search-and-destroy missions and engage in chemical warfare, spraying thousands of acres of fields. The country also strengthened anti-drug laws, allowing trials without juries in the case of drug convictions, for the first time in Belizean history.

In November 1987, Belize created the Security and Intelligence Service (SIS) for protection from "espionage, sabotage, subversion and terrorism both from internal and external sources."[95] The SIS tracks Central American refugees who become involved in the drug trade after their work permits expire, but Belizeans fear the SIS will increase political repression.

In 1987, the government required loyalty assessments of all civil servants. Large numbers of unproductive, part-time spies were empowered to carry guns and employed throughout the country." [96] Belize also banned the importation of any printed, audio or visual media which are, in the opinion of the Minister, contrary to the public interest.[97]

The PUP and the Public

Until the last half of this decade, Belize's strategy to reduce poverty through increased public spending on infrastructure and housing was matched by decreases in taxes. However, reliance on foreign lending meant the government's publicly guaranteed debt rose from 30 percent in 1990 to 48 percent in 1999 to 100 percent by the end of 2004.[98] After 2004, the government continued to borrow, even with downgraded credit that allowed foreign lenders to charge fees and insurance premiums for all further lending. This led

---

94 Young, Alma H., "6 The Territorial Dimension of Caribbean Security: The Case of Belize," *Strategy and Security in the Caribbean*, ed. Ivelaw L. Griffith (New York: Praeger Publishers, 1991) 142.

95 Ibid.

96 Goodman, Louis W. , William M. LeoGrande, and Johanna Mendelson Forman, eds., *Political Parties and Democracy in Central America* (Boulder, CO: Westview Press, 1992) 132.

97 Ibid.

98 International Monetary Fund, "Belize: Selected Issues," IMF Country Report 05/353, September 2005.

to higher borrowing with lower net loan disbursements, which increased the budget deficit and merited crisis measures.

On November 2, 2004, a meeting was held between the Prime Minister, the Belize National Teachers Union (BNTU) and the Public Service Union (PSU). Also present were members of the government's National Economic Council, made up of eight Cabinet Ministers plus a technical team from the Central Bank and the Ministry of Finance. A proposal to increase the retirement age of Public Officers from the 55 to 60 was opposed by the BNTU. More shocking were the government's honest revelations, put forth as follows:

- A projected budget deficit for Fiscal Year 2004/05 of at least BZ $100 million.
- A GDP growth at constant prices of about 3% of projected GDP.
- Foreign debt of about BZ $2 billion, of which the government needed to pay up to $139 million by March, 2005.
- Declining foreign reserves with the Central Bank of only about BZ $77 million (just 1/3 of standard requirements).[99]

On January 13, 2005, the government announced an 11 percent increase of the real estate tax, a 5 percent tax increase for financial institutions, an 8 percent increase of tax on tobacco, and a 100 percent tax increase on rum. Because these taxes affected everyone, a response was swift in coming.

There were protests at the National Assembly on January 15, 2005, involving clashes between police and demonstrators. This was followed by a call from the business community and labor unions for a nationwide 2-day strike, which commenced on January 20th. Some protestors set up roadblocks during the strike and burned government buildings. Others threw stones and broken bottles at unpopular government ministers. It was the first major unrest to occur since the 1980s (when a proposition was made for annexation to Guatemala), and the police dispersed the crowds with rubber bullets and tear gas, physically dragging off union members.[100]

By February 5, 2005, a strike of teachers and public officers entered its twelfth day and provoked a solidarity march of 7,000

99 FreeBelize.org, http://www.freebelize.org/index.html.

100 Wikipedia,"2005 Belize Unrest," http://en.wikipedia.org/w/index. php?title+2005_Belize_unrest&printable=yes.

protesters. The government threatened to dock the pay of the demonstrators in order to quell the disturbance.[101]

In May 2005, the authorities announced a voluntary adjustment program involving sharp cuts to reduce the FY 2005/06 deficit to less than 4 percent of GDP, more tax hikes, and the curtailment of capital expenditure and civil service employment. The Central Bank boosted interest rates and tightened monetary policy to contain credit expansion.[102]

Austerity and Sacrifice

Gone are the days when the government could spend money on poverty alleviation. The Central Bank's tight-money policy will ensure higher interest rates for people who couldn't have accessed credit markets without government help. (As of 1999, the local lending rate was already between 16 and 18 percent.)[103] As the crisis worsens, there will be a wave of bank foreclosures and paychecks issued through banks so debts can be easily serviced will shrink in line with wages or disappear through layoffs.

In 2005, Belize's labor force consisted of 96,000 people, with unemployment at 13 percent. Wage-growth was slow (the minimum wage was BZ $2.25),[104] but past government spending did help to create jobs, as Belize's exports grew strongly over the last 10 years. Sugar increased by 21 percent from 1995-2004, bananas by 82 percent, citrus products by 126 percent, and marine products by 690 percent. Arrivals of cruise ship passengers grew by 100 percent from 1998–2004. During the same period, unit prices of sugar declined by 30 percent from 1995–2004, bananas by 34 percent, citrus by 40 percent and marine products by 51 percent, explaining the limitation on wages.[105] More downward pressure is naturally forthcoming.

---

101 Belizean-The Belize News Blog, http://www.belizean.com/mt-static/archives/2005/02/protests_contin.html.

102 International Monetary Fund, "IMF Executive Board Concludes 2005 Article IV Consultation with Belize, September 30, 2005, http://www.imf.org/external/np/sec/pn/2005/pn05136.htm.

103 Belize Project.com, Report #62 April 1999, "5 Facts About the Belize Economy," Belize Development Trust, http://belize1.com/BzLibrary/trust 62.html.

104 U.S. Department of State, "Belize," http://www.state.gov/g/drl/rls/hrrpt/2003/27886.htm.

105 International Monetary Fund, "Belize: Selected Issues," IMF Country Report 05/353, September 2005.

Because Belize's export base remains undiversified, it competes with other countries for the same product markets. The protections and guarantees it had through the Lome Convention with Britain and the U.S.-sponsored Caribbean Basin Initiative (CBI) are now supplanted by free trade.

The EU Sugar Protocol provided African, Caribbean and Pacific countries with quotas and set prices 3–4 times higher than market prices, until the EU announced in June 2005 that the guaranteed sale price would be cut by 39 percent. [106] To help its trade partners prepare for financial changes, the EU promoted modernization by financing improvements in the cane-delivery system and drainage/ irrigation systems for banana cultivation. The adoption of CAFTA (the Central American Free Trade Agreement) further eroded stability.

To earn the same currency expected before these changes, Belizeans will have to stimulate higher volume transactions. This signals a need for labor, but at much lower wages. The more pertinent question is whether growers and producers will even survive the market.

Previously, Belize encouraged citrus-growers to use pesticides in hopes of increasing their growth yield, but many farmers downsized because they had no help with the costs. Faced with market upheaval that leads to consolidation, more owners and producers will become landless laborers. [107]

In terms of free-market methodology, Belize did all the "right" things to encourage foreign investment. Now more than 90 percent of the country is owned by foreign interests and the onset of debt peonage means ordinary Belizeans are slaves in their own land.

---

106 Ibid.

107 Belize Project.com, Report #50 February 1999, "The Politics of Efficiency or Free Trade Seek to Makea New Slave/Serf Class in the British Caribbean," Belize Development Trust, http://belize1.com/ BzLibrary/trust50.html.

CHAPTER NINE: BELIZE — RECOMMENDATIONS OF THE IMF

While preparing to meet the IMF, Prime Minister Musa punished members of his Cabinet for Belize's financial troubles. He sacked Mark Espat, Cordel Hyde and Eamon Courtney (whom he later rehired), while increasing the responsibilities of Ralph Fonseca by adding Commercial Free Zones and Export Processing Zones to his portfolio. This wasn't done to fight corruption, but was rather politically motivated, as these members of the so-called G-7 had fought to have Fonseca ousted. And, this, they did because Prime Minister Musa and Ralph Fonseca were responsible for the Social Security scandal in which that organization made and secured loans for financially nonviable enterprises.[108]

Musa's public comment regarding the IMF was, "We are not looking for any kind of Structural Program." Instead, he was interested in an IMF vetting process so Belize could continue to restructure and refinance its loans. To that end, Musa undertook voluntary budget-cutting and levying tax increases, as already noted above.

For the most part, the IMF offered a favorable report at the conclusion of its executive meeting:

> [T]he Directors welcomed Belize's low inflationary environment and continued strong growth performance. [However,] they expressed concern that Belize's fiscal and external current

---

108 Ibid.

account deficits remain unsustainably high, resulting in sub-
stantial increases in the external public debt and a serious ero-
sion of domestic and international confidence. Directors under-
scored the urgency of addressing these imbalances to safeguard
the country's international reserves and ensure the sustainability of the pegged exchange rate system. They encouraged the
authorities to mount a campaign to educate the public on the
benefits of reform and the growing risks of inaction.[109]

As it pertained to the steps Musa already took, the IMF suggested that Musa's procrastination, combined with delays in implementation, would prevent significant impact on the 2005/06
budget. Even if Belize met its targets, there would be an external
financing gap in 2006. The directors called for stronger measures
to "reduce domestic demand, close the remaining financing gap,
and restore confidence and Belize's creditworthiness" through increases in fiscal revenue and reduced expenditures. This would require reductions of tax holidays and exemptions, as well as cuts in
purchases (excluding essential social services), and more monetary
tightening.[110] The IMF recommended a Fund-supported program to
underpin Belize's efforts to bolster investor confidence and secure
agreements with external creditors.

This is a mild list of demands because most of the terms of
Structural Adjustment have already been applied. As listed by
Anup Shah, these are:

1. Cut backs and "liberalization" of the economy to create
resource extraction/export-oriented open markets.

2. The reduction of regulations and standards to induce
foreign investment.

3. The encouragement of privatization as well as reduced
protection of domestic industries.

4. The minimization of the role of the state.

5. Currency devaluation, increased interest rates, "flexibility"
of the labor market, and the elimination of subsidies such as food
subsidies.[111]

---

109 International Monetary Fund, "IMF executive Board Concludes 2005
Article IV Consultation with Belize, September 30, 2005, http://www.
imf.org/external/np/sec/pn/2005/pn05136.htm.

110 Ibid.

111 Shah, Anup, "Causes of Poverty: Structural Adjustment—A Major
Cause of Poverty," November 20, 2005, http://www.globalissues.org/
TradeRelated/SAP.asp.

With very few exceptions, Belize has followed the IMF prescription, and this explains why Belize was allowed to become so indebted.

Because it remained export-oriented from the colonial period onward and was friendly to foreign investment through tax holidays, exemptions, special export zones and the generous extension of government-guaranteed loans, Belize's debt was tolerated as the cost of doing business. The only remaining task is to minimize the role of the state within the economic sphere. Instead of being a business guarantor, the state will recede from this role to focus on debt repayment.

It will need to cut spending deeply and accept that the IMF definition of "essential social services" involves economic liberalization rather than social assistance. Construction of low-income housing will cease, as will the contract for public service wages which formerly guaranteed salary increases. Jobs will be lost in the public sector and, within the private sector, the IMF will expect wages to be "flexible" so the country's export prices will be internationally competitive.

How this is going to happen when 50 percent of the labor force earns less than BZ $720 dollars a month and another 25 percent earns less than BZ $120 a week, is a matter of concern.[112] In some areas, citizens earn as little BZ $634 a year. A poverty assessment conducted in 2002 revealed that over 31 percent of the young are living below the poverty level, as is 27 percent of the elderly population.[113]

The gap between achievement and the PUP's stated goals underscores the fact that Belizeans are in no position to endure more sacrifice. Relying on wages of little more than a dollar an hour, they have no room for "flexibility." Government retrenchment at a time of widespread poverty means Belize is careening toward uncertainty with little reason for optimism. The government may find it can no longer "buy" social peace, with Belizeans joining the citizens of other developing countries in political insurrection that leads to labor strikes.

In that event, the government will increase repression (with tacit Western consent), or take steps to make government more inclusive on the surface. It may pursue a combination of both. The

---

112 Belizean – The Belizean News Blog, "PUP Reps Reject New Budget," January 26, 2005, http://www.belizean.com/mt-static/archives/2005/01/pup_reps_reject.html.

113 Cornerstone's Hunger Appeal, "The Challenges of Poverty," http://www.peacecorner.org/hungerbz2.htm.

new support for democratic reform, now that Belize's leaders have saddled the economy with BZ $2 billion in debt, means the Belizean people will have little or no power to effect significant change. They'll be subjected to external discipline and severe limitations, with the added expectation that they maintain social peace now that they have "a say" in the country's ruling system. While this may be touted as a "deepening of democracy," its effects will be cosmetic, ensuring, as ever, that the people have no input on economic decisions.

Anup Shah lists many of the problems facing developing countries:

1. *Poor countries must export more* in order to raise enough money to pay off their debts in a timely manner.

2. Because there are so many nations being asked or forced into the global market place—before they are economically and socially stable and ready—and told to concentrate on similar cash crops and commodities as others, it is like *a huge price war.*

3. The *resources then become even cheaper* from the poorer regions (which favors consumers in the West).

4. Governments then need to *increase exports* just to keep their currencies stable (which may not be sustainable, either) and earn foreign exchange with which to help pay off debts.

5. Governments therefore must:
   - spend less
   - reduce consumption
   - remove or decrease financial regulations
   - and so on

6. Over time then:
   - The value of labor *decreases*
   - Capital flows become more *volatile*
   - And we get into a *spiraling race to the bottom*
   - *Social unrest* is often one result leading to "IMF riots" and protests around the world.

7. These nations are then told to peg their currencies to the dollar. But keeping the exchange rate stable is costly due to measures such as increased interest rates, etc.
   - Investors obviously concerned about their assets and interests can then pull out very easily if things get tough.
   - In worst cases *capital flight can lead to economic collapses* like we have seen in the Asian/global financial crisis of 1997/98/99, Mexico, Brazil and many other places.

8. When IMF donors keep the exchange rates in their favor, it often means that the poor nations remain poor, or get even poorer.

- *Millions of children end up dying each year.* [114]

A loss of investor confidence could also produce a run on the Belizean currency, in which case the IMF prescription is to maintain the exchange rate peg by spending crucial foreign reserves. Instead of inhibiting disinvestment, the IMF facilitates capital flight, then recommends devaluation and offers emergency funds for economic stabilization.

Devaluation limits domestic consumption while making exports competitive, and these may be seen as good things, but they will lower the standard of living and earnings of foreign exchange. Even as people are being beggared, the country will have less potential than ever to service and pay off debt.

As to what happens, Robin Hahnel describes the process:

> What may [be] the greatest asset swindle of all time works like this: International investors lose confidence in a developing world economy, dumping its currency, bonds, and stocks. At the insistence of the IMF, the central bank in the developing country tightens the money supply to boost domestic interest rates to prevent further capital outflow in an unsuccessful attempt to protect the currency. Even healthy domestic companies can no longer obtain or afford loans so they join the ranks of bankrupted domestic businesses available for purchase. As a precondition for receiving the IMF bailout the government abolishes any remaining restrictions on foreign ownership of corporations, banks, and land. With a depreciated currency and a long list of bankrupt local businesses, the economy is ready for the acquisition experts from Western multinational corporations and banks who came to the fire sale with a thick wad of almighty dollars in their pockets. [115]

In short, Belize's remaining native industries will be transferred to foreign hands at bargain basement prices for repatriated profits. Excluded from owning natural resources and the country's means of production, debt slavery ensues.

Post-colonial governments that maintained dependency through export-oriented economies and costly investment incentives, which reduced their earnings and promoted unsustainable debt, have led to activist associations seeking debt relief. One such

---

114 Shah, Anup.
115 Smith, J.W.

is the Latin America Solidarity Coalition (LASC), whose web site asserts the following:

- The environment of Latin America and the Caribbean is being destroyed as a result of the economy of colonialism which includes clearing large tracts of natural forest to create large export-production plantations and the export of natural resources. The destruction of the environment has been perpetuated by post-colonial capitalist trading relationships with former imperial powers.

- As a result of the colonial economy many Latin American and Caribbean countries' own economies are export-oriented and focused on the sale of natural resources such as tropical produce, oil, etc.

- Colonialism and neo-colonialism created a South–North economic dependency that forces Latin America and Caribbean countries to accept loans from bilateral and multilateral funding sources in order to be able to compete in an increasingly global economy with declining terms of trade.[116]

Under "Understanding the Illegitimacy of Debt," the LASC explains:

- Much of the debt of Latin America and the Caribbean was contracted by private corporations and passed on to governments, and in many of these cases, the funds were pocketed or wasted.

- The debts have actually been paid many times over by people in the Caribbean and Latin America. In financial and economic terms, the interest accumulated on debt has inflated the amount paid and owned by countries to well beyond the original value of the loans themselves. The peoples of Latin America and the Caribbean have also paid the debt in human, social and environmental terms.

- Debt was often contracted secretly without civil society scrutiny.

- Debt has often undermined the consolidation of the national democratic process.

---

116 LASC (Latin American Solidarity Coalition), "Globalization/Debt Strategy Paper," http://www.lasolidarity.org/papers/globalization. htm.

- Debt has endangered the national capacities of food security and sustainability in Latin America and the Caribbean.
- The payment on debts have provoked human rights violations. [117]

The LASC can then be quoted in part as describing the "Direct and Indirect Effects of Debt":

- Debt and SAPs are the leading cause of the degradation of health, nutrition, food security, education, and the environment. SAPs require national governments to prioritize debt payments over human needs. In addition, SAP conditions follow a basic neoliberal model which does not consider the uniqueness of any country and often has deleterious effects on the economy, labor rights, and the national standard of living.
- By promoting economic programs that prioritize adhesion to a neoliberal economic model over human needs, debt and SAPs aggravate unemployment, ecological degradation, and regional conflict. On a grassroots level, these programs also contribute to the disintegration of families, which leads to juvenile delinquency and prostitution, and the worsening of women's socioeconomic conditions and daily life.
- Debt is used as a mechanism of oppression.
- Debt eliminates the national sovereignty of the countries in Latin America and the Caribbean while increasing the political and economic subordination of the international financial institutions and the transnational corporations. [118]

To quote J.W. Smith, "The IMF has repeatedly stated that it is not, and was never intended to be, a *development* institution." Its fundamental goal is to create markets for the goods of industrialized countries (a pattern that is maintained when underdeveloped and developing countries focus solely on an export orientation, thereby keeping them dependent on imports from other countries). At the same time, the developed world needs these countries to foster repetitive export markets so the cost of their goods to the developed world will be depressed to an absolute minimum. This allows developed countries to rework these goods with minimal

---

117 Ibid.
118 Ibid.

investment and sate labor in the developed world with abundant, low-cost goods so attempts can made to depress their wages also.

As one author notes, "It is really the old colonial plantation system that once produced for Europe, restructured on a massive scale to produce for the industrialized world."[119]

Quoting Joseph Stiglitz, the operations of the IMF are hardly inspiring of the term "democratic":

> The IMF likes to go about its business without outsiders asking too many questions. In theory, the fund supports democratic institutions in the nations it assists. In practice, it undermines the democratic process by imposing policies. Officially, of course, the IMF doesn't "impose" anything. It "negotiates" the conditions for receiving aid. But all the power in the negotiations is on one side—the IMF's—and the fund rarely allows sufficient time for broad consensus-building or even widespread consultations with either parliaments or civil society. Sometimes the IMF dispenses with the pretense of openness altogether and negotiates secret covenants.[120]

Stiglitz, a winner of the Nobel Prize for achievement in economics, was ousted from the World Bank due to confrontation over the management and objectives of international lending.

In the underdeveloped world, there's a chance that "democratic deepening" could destroy the parties in power by inspiring local cohesion and the growth of new political movements, but any party that comes to power will have to follow the Western script. Failure to maintain dependency and/or support Western reform will be met with the elimination of credit and the collapse of the economy or, depending on the circumstances, more forceful intervention.

Now we'll turn to Nicaragua to see what happened there.

---

119 Smith, J.W.

120 Stiglitz, Joseph, "What I learned at the world economic crisis. The Insider," *The New Republic*, April 17, 2000.

Chapter Ten: Nicaragua 1522–1939

Before Europeans arrived, Nicaragua was known as the Intermediate Area, located between the lands of the Aztec and the Maya to the north and the Inca Empire to the south. West of the central highlands, pre-Columbian peoples lived in centralized societies, which maintained a division between their elites (who were rulers, nobles and priests) and the commoners (who carried out most economic activities). To the east of the central highlands, there were mainly tribal societies, consisting of extended families.

Although British explorers chose not to settle the east, they introduced a trading system with the indigenous population that allowed one local group to gain supremacy over the rest through the acquisition of firearms. This group became associated with escaped slaves in the area, and the result of their intermingling was a people first known as the Zambo and later the Miskito Indians. The people they subordinated, or successfully drove from the land, were called the Sumo (or Sumu).[121]

Western Spanish settlements decimated the indigenous populace via European diseases. The first expedition, led by Gil Gonzalez Davila (who claimed he baptized 50,000 Indians, including a chieftain named Nicaragua) was followed by the arrival of Hernandez de

---

121 Millett, Richard L., "Nicaragua: Chapter 1A. Historical Setting," *Countries of the World*, http://www.highbeam.com/library/doc3.asp?DO CID=1P1:28385584&num=3&ctrlInfo=R.

Cordoba in 1524. De Cordoba established the cities of Granada and Leon, which became important colonial centers.

Indigenous Depopulation

When Pedrarias Davila, governor of Panama, exerted control over the region, the conquistadores were fighting over Indian goods and slaves. Davila, too, became a competitor, and arrested then executed Hernandez de Cordoba.

In 1527, the governor of Honduras, Diego Lopez de Salcedo, moved in to join the contest. Salcedo's looting and enslavement produced an Indian revolt and also intensified indigenous depopulation. From 1528-1540, an estimated 400,000–500,000 Indian slaves were shipped to Panama and Peru.[122] This trade required five full-time ships to service southern demand. Eighty-five percent of Indian slaves died during transport.[123]

To combat abuse of the natives, the Spanish Crown appointed priest Diego Alvarez Osorio as Protector and Defender of the Indians in Nicaragua. But by 1548, the Pacific coast population declined more than 92 percent. In Managua, where 40,000 people had lived, only 265 tributary natives remained. In Granada, the population dropped from 8,000 to a few hundred. By 1578, Bishop Antonio de Zayas estimated a remaining Pacific population of eight thousand—a decline of 97.5 percent.[124] Genetically, socially and culturally, the Indians were being obliterated.

After Pedrarias Davila died in 1531, Governor Castaneda expressed concern for the Indians but was unable to curb the slave trade. The next governor, Rodrigo de Contreras, proved to be as avaricious and brutal as Davila.

In opposition to Contreras, Catholic friar Bartolome de las Casas catalogued the brutality against the natives:

> They sent fifty men on horseback to put the lance to a whole province...which left neither man nor woman nor old person nor child alive, for some very trivial reason, like for not having come quickly enough at their call, or not having brought them enough corn...or enough Indians to serve them...And since the land was

---

122 Walker, Thomas W., *Nicaragua, the Land of Sandino* (Boulder, CO: Westview Press, 1981) 11.

123 Whisnant, David E., *Rascally Signs in Sacred Places: The Politics of Culture in Nicaragua* (Chapel Hill, NC: University of North Carolina Press, 1995) 19.

124 Ibid., 20

flat, no one could flee from the horses, nor from the infernal ire of the Spanish.[125]

"The most horrible pestilence," las Casas said, was enslavement. To induce the Indians to bring them slaves, the Spaniards burned their prisoners alive or fed them to hungry dogs.

Those who escaped slavery were subjected to forced labor and often died at the mines, forests, shipyards and indigo plantations. Nearly 200 natives died in a single mining incident of 1533. Whisnant notes, "It was possible to tell the way to the mines by the skeletons of Indians along the roadside."[126] Life was equally hard for workers in the shipyards, and the production of indigo dye exposed the natives to harmful vapors and skin-burning liquids. Other forms of forced labor included the *encomienda* and *repartimiento* systems.

Encomienda and Repartimiento

In 1503, the Spanish Laws of Burgos allocated native labor and the Spaniards took advantage of native tribute systems. The laws required a colonial official to ensure humane treatment and fair levels of tribute, but this happened every three years and abuse was rife in the meantime. Villages had to pay tribute on Indians who died, and harsh measures (such as burning homes) were taken to discourage flight. In the face of excessive demands, any failure to pay (even at times of poor harvest) resulted in whipping or jail.[127]

Due to depopulation exacerbated by slavery, competition for *encomienda* labor was fierce. It resulted in a few, large *encomenderos*, possessed of fabulous wealth. These were: Governor Francisco de Castaneda, Governor Rodrigo de Contreras, Pedro de los Rios, Benito Diaz, and Yseo de Santiago (the widow of Mateo de Lezcano). Between them, they subjugated the natives, and forcibly extracted labor in addition to payment of tribute.

Through the *repartimiento* system, those outside *encomenderos* were converted to wage slavery, where the degree of required labor became ever greater. Nor were their tasks dissimilar from those in *encomiendas*. Wage-slaves worked in the fields and mines, spun yarn, wove cloth and grew food that sold for a pittance. Sometimes they were paid with goods or currency. More frequently, the Spaniards withheld compensation.

---

125 Ibid.
126 Ibid.
127 Ibid., 25.

Conflict with the Church

Due to the activism of las Casas and the reports he submitted of indigenous abuse, Spain passed the New Laws (Leyes Nuevas) in 1542, which gradually abolished *encomiendas* and outlawed slavery.[128] Spain subjected Nicaragua to centralized control, in opposition to the *encomenderos*, who desired a semi-feudal system.

In 1543, Antonio de Valdivieso was appointed bishop of Leon. Noting that abuse of the natives continued, Valdivieso complained to the Crown and placed himself in conflict with governor Rodrigo de Contreras. Contreras took his case to the Council of the Indies, which favored Valdivieso, after which Contreras' sons assassinated Valdivieso and looted the city of Leon. Spain quelled the rebellion and imposed colonial laws.

Considered part of Panama in 1538, Nicaragua was transferred to the Viceroyalty of New Spain when Spain divided into two viceroyalties in 1543. With Leon as its capital, Nicaragua became part of the Captaincy General of Guatemala, or what was sometimes called the Kingdom of Guatemala.[129] By 1548, a Spanish census of Nicaragua revealed that the native Western populace had declined to 11,137.[130] The only thriving cities were Granada and Leon.[131]

Harassment by the British

Battles between families, who fought for power and land, continued into the 17th century and did not begin to decline until an economic downturn. Then indigo replaced slaves and gold as the colony's major export, together with small amounts of cacao, tobacco and pitch. Labor shortages threatened, and the colony was harassed by British pirates and adventurers who settled the Atlantic coast, making shipping difficult and causing other problems.

The British sacked Granada twice (first in 1665, then in 1685) despite the hasty construction of Spanish protective forts. Recruiting Miskito Indians helped the British claim possession of the Nicaraguan coast, which remained in British hands at the end of Spanish rule.

---

128 Foroohar, Manzar, *The Catholic Church and Social Change in Nicaragua* (Albany, NY: State University of New York Press, 1989) 2.

129 "Nicaragua – Colonial Rule," Library of Congress, http://countrystudies.us/nicaragua/6.htm.

130 Millett, Richard L.

131 "Nicaragua COLONIAL PERIOD," http://workmall.com/wfb2001/nicaragua/nicaragua_history_colonial_period_1522_1820.html.

The indigenous population made a slow recovery, with its total more than doubling between 1684 and 1778. But, during this same period, the non-native populace multiplied twenty-two times over, from 1,663 to 35,726.[132] Many non-natives were ladinos (Mestizos of mixed Spanish and Amerindian descent). The ladinos, unlike the natives, were uninvolved in tribute, but the Spaniards pressed the ladinos into military service. In clashes with the British and the Miskito Indians, the poorly armed and paid ladino infantry cleared the way for the elite Spanish cavalry.

The Liberal–Conservative Divide

The War of Spanish Succession (1701–1714) replaced the Hapsburgs with the Bourbons, and Bourbon policy toward the colony involved liberal free-trade. The factions that benefited (crop growers, merchants and exporters) came to be known as liberals, whereas those who lost under Bourbon policy came to be known as conservatives. Conservatism later aligned with the Roman Catholic Church and the city of Granada became its power base. The city of Leon was central to the liberals.

Competition over influence became tumultuous and violent as Granada and Leon each developed armies. Between 1824 and 1842, they fought seventeen major battles.[133] In time:

> [T]he hatred and violence between the two cities and the two factions became institutionalized, and often the original ideological difference was forgotten. Independence in the next century only exacerbated the struggle as it eliminated Spain as a referee. The violent rivalry between liberals and conservatives was one of the most important and destructive aspects of Nicaraguan history, a characteristic that would last until well into the twentieth century. Politicians frequently chose party loyalty over national interest, and, particularly in the 1800s, the nation was often the loser in interparty strife.[134]

Nicaragua's inclusion in the Guatemalan *audiencia*, explains why similar divides between liberals and conservatives occurred in every other province, such that liberals and conservatives often crossed provincial lines to support each other's causes. This became more of a problem once Nicaragua gained independence.

---

132 Whisnant, David E., 42.

133 Foroohar, Manzar, 6.

134 "Nicaragua – Colonial Rule."

Nicaraguan Independence

The push toward independence began in 1811 and, on this, the church divided. Father Jose Antonio Monino (a Franciscan friar) and Father Benito Miguelena (of the Merced order) opposed Spanish-born officials, taxes, monopolies, slavery and political imprisonment in a movement that spread to Granada, Chontales and Segovia. Bishop Garcia Jerez (a Spanish monarchist) agreed to meet their demands, but he proposed that each barrio elect its own deputies to form a ruling junta. Since Jerez controlled the deputy priests, he then dissolved the junta, proclaimed himself governor and instituted the death penalty for rebellion.[135]

When another uprising began in Granada on December 22, 1811, the point was to remove Spanish-born officials in favor of the Creoles. Bishop Jerez sent troops from Leon, but his men turned out to be Creoles who sympathized with Granada. This prompted Bustamante y Guerra, the Captain General of Guatemala, to crush the rebellion by 1813. However, small merchants, lower army officers, lower public workers and priests continued anti-colonial activism until they were jailed.

In 1821, Mexico became an independent empire and Central Americans everywhere moved to separate from Spain. Granada and Leon were divided over becoming part of an independent Central America or accepting annexation to Augustin de Iturbide's Mexican empire. Leon welcomed Mexico's takeover while Granada resisted it. The collapse of the Mexican Empire involved Nicaragua in the Federation of Central America until 1837, when attempted centralization resulted in civil war.

In the early 1840s, Nicaragua tried to reunite the Federation, but the union was rejected by Guatemala and Costa Rica. From 1842-1845, Nicaragua formed the United Provinces of Central America in a loose federation with Honduras and El Salvador.[136]

Between 1839 and 1855, conflict was rife between Granada and Leon, and certain families rose to power. The Sacasas dominated the liberals in Leon. The Chamorros led the conservatives in Granada. They argued for years over moving the capital to Managua, but this was not achieved until 1857. Nicaragua declared its independence from the United Provinces of Central America on April 30, 1838.[137]

---

135 Foroohar, Manzar, 3.

136 "Millet, Richard L.

137 "Nicaragua – National Independence," Library of Congress, http://countrystudies.us/nicaragua/7.htm.

Taking Land from the Indigenous Peoples

Through the church, Spain tried to Europeanize the Indians by teaching them reading, writing and arithmetic. By fostering docile workers and patriotic citizens, Spain hoped to defend elite prerogatives and promote agro-exports. At issue was rebellion over the massive intended theft of remaining native lands.

The Nicaraguan constitutions of 1826 and 1832 guaranteed indigenous peoples the right to hold lands in common. However, these rights were attacked in 1838, and expropriations for the nation's first coffee plantations were achieved by the mid-1840s.[138]

Encroaching further on native rights, two laws in 1852 required all lands to be surveyed, with the government announcing it would sell "vacant" lands and adjust communal holdings during the following year. A desire to force native labor on expropriated lands inspired vagrancy laws and prohibitions against subsistence farming.[139] As many natives fled, they sought refuge in mountains and cities, and throughout the Atlantic coast.

The Canal Treaty

The British held onto the Atlantic coast, seizing San Juan del Norte (Greytown) in 1841. The construction of military fortifications forced Nicaragua to recognize British sovereignty, and this raised alarm within the United States. President Polk invoked the Monroe Doctrine while Nicaragua asked for U.S. protection from British colonial interests. In 1849, the result was a treaty between Nicaragua and the United Sates, which gave the U.S. the right to fortify and utilize the transit route across Nicaragua in exchange for protection of Nicaragua's territorial sovereignty (excluding British claims).

Cornelius Vanderbilt won the right to build a canal across the isthmus and fortify installations along the land-and-water transit route. In 1850, however, the British blocked the route, resulting in the Clayton-Bulwer Treaty. The U.S. and Britain agreed that Central America and any future canal would remain free of claims to exclusive rights.[140] Nicaragua expected to benefit from the trans-

---

138 Ibid., 59.

139 Booth, John A. and Thomas W. Walker, *Understanding Central America*, 3rd ed. (Boulder, CO: Westview Press, 1999) 35.

140 "Nicaragua – Foreign Intervention, 1850-68," Library of Congress, http://countrystudies.us/nicaragua/8.htm.

isthmian transit route, but, from then on, control over the operation was in American and British hands.

William Walker

In 1853, conservative General Fruto Chamorro took over Nicaragua and exiled his liberal opponents. His opponents returned to fight a bloody war, allied with the liberal government of Honduras. The conservative government of Guatemala then invaded Honduras to end its support for Nicaraguan liberals. The liberals went on to seek American aid. In 1855, they offered adventurer William Walker a huge grant if he would overthrow the conservatives.

Walker, who was backed by Vanderbilt's rival, arrived with fifty-seven other Americans to install President Patricio Rivas as the head of a puppet regime approved by the U.S. But Walker did not stop there. Receiving additional help from New York and San Francisco, Walker's army grew to 2,500 men. This allowed him to stage a Nicaraguan "election" in June of 1856, which made him president.[141]

Walker was supported by the Church of Granada, even though his plans included a scheme to re-introduce slavery and rule all of Central America. The church donated both money and valuable jewels toward the purchase of war materiel, and Walker rewarded Father Agustin Vigil by naming him the Nicaraguan Minister to the U.S.

It was the British who armed the other Central American countries with the help of Vanderbilt's agents. Walker was defeated in the National War (1856-57), after which he returned to the United States. When he attempted to revisit Central America no less than four times after, he was finally killed by a Honduran firing squad on September 12, 1861.[142]

Conservatives versus Liberals

The battle against Walker brought Nicaraguan liberals and conservatives together. To avoid further competition between Granada and Leon, the capital was moved to Managua in 1857. President Patricio Rivas was allowed to serve for a third term, after which liberal General Maximo Jerez and conservative General Tomas Martinez assumed a bipartisan presidency. The Assembly convened in

141 Foroohar, Manzar, 6.
142 Weaver, Frederick Stirton, *Inside the Volcano: The History and Political Economy of Central America* (Boulder, CO: Westview Press, 1994) 62.

November of 1857 to name General Martinez as the president from 1858 to 1867.[143]

Conservatives remained in power until 1893, a period that is called the "Thirty Years" for the peace and prosperity it engendered. During this time, expanded export markets for coffee and bananas created a boom economy. Roads and telegraph lines were extended, and a railway was built from western Nicaragua to the Corinto port on the Pacific coast. Peace was marred, however, by the War of the Comuneros, an indigenous rebellion against expropriation of native communal lands by wealthy coffee growers in 1881. Several thousand natives were victims.

The succession of President Roberto Sacasa, a conservative from Leon[144] (rather than Granada) prompted a divide within the ruling conservative party. Sacasa tried to retain power, but a revolt broke out in April 1893. A coalition of liberals and conservatives placed another conservative in power. Then the coalition collapsed and liberal General Jose Santos Zelayas' followers resigned from the government to launch another revolt. Zelaya became president at a new constitutional convention. His autocratic rule endured until 1909.[145]

Zelaya's new constitution nullified the Concordat signed with the Holy See in 1862 and destroyed the hegemony of the Roman Catholic Church. Zelaya secularized cemeteries and marriage ceremonies. He also passed a law in May 1899 to confiscate church properties. Real estate, livestock and furniture passed into the hands of local governments for the purpose of development. Zelaya exiled Catholic nuns and priests, while opening the country to other religious denominations, finally resulting in his excommunication by Bishop Pereira y Castellon.[146]

Isaac Joslin Cox describes Zelaya's rule as one that:

> ...fostered monopolies, disposed of concessions with little regard for public interests, and in the later years of his administration burdened the country with reckless loans and issues of irredeemable paper money. Personal property rights were shamelessly violated. His opponents were frequently subjected

143 "Nicaragua – Foreign Intervention, 1850-68."

144 Walker, Thomas W., *Nicaragua, The Land of Sandino*, 14.

145 "Nicaragua – Conservative and Liberal Regimes, 1858-1909," Library of Congress, http://countrystudies.us/nicaragua/9.htm.

146 Foroohar, Manzar, 11.

to confiscation of goods, to imprisonment, and even to atrocious torture.[147]

Meanwhile, Vanderbilt's plans for a trans-isthmian canal were halted by the construction of the canal in Panama. This signaled a downturn in Nicaragua's fortunes, but Zelaya adopted other measures to promote internal development and modernize the country. He sanctioned new roads and seaport facilities, railroad lines and schools. He also allowed foreign investment and permitted U.S. firms to control production of coffee, bananas, gold and lumber by the early 1900s. With the help of U.S. mediation, Zelaya even gained control of the Mosquito Coast (formerly held by the British).

Although Zelaya was friendly to foreign interests, his regional aspirations were expressed at the Conference of Amapala in 1895. There, Nicaragua, Honduras and El Salvador formed a confederation called the Republica Mayor (the Greater Republic), for which a constitution was written in 1898. Before it could take effect, the government of El Salvador was overthrown. It then withdrew from the confederation and Zelaya let the Conference collapse. Zelaya could have imposed the confederation by force (he had already invaded Honduras twice), but he let the matter rest. He also applied arbitration to Nicaragua's boundary disputes.[148]

Zelaya earned the enmity of Americans and the British by soliciting German and Japanese interest in resurrected plans for a trans-isthmian canal. The U.S. and Britain sided with the rebels during conservative rebellions in 1903 and 1909. In the latter event, British funding and U.S. Marines drove Zelaya from power.[149] Also instrumental was U.S. private capital, which contributed $1 million to the rebellion, including $200,000 from the house of Joseph W. Beers and $150,000 from the house of Samuel Well.[150]

Following Zelaya's overthrow, the rebels looted the national treasury. Each person received a land grant of fifty hectares (about 123 acres), and vast sums were awarded to conservatives who suffered confiscation, forced loans, or "moral" injuries under Zelaya's rule.[151] This, combined with corruption and a spree of printed money, bankrupted the country, upon which conservatives turned to

---

147 Cox, Isaac Joslin, *Nicaragua and the United States, 1909-1927* (Boston: World Peace foundation, 1927) 705.

148 Walker, Thomas W., *Nicaragua, The Land of Sandino*, 17.

149 Foroohar, Manzar, 11.

150 Ibid., 12.

151 Ibid.

the U.S. An American agent was given charge of customs to ensure the repayment of loans made by U.S. banks.

President Jose Madriz, who was appointed by the Nicaraguan Congress following the ouster of Zelaya, resigned in favor of conservative General Juan Estrada, whom the U.S. agreed to support, provided the Assembly developed a new constitution. This, Estrada agreed to, but he then suspended payments on Nicaragua's foreign debt and canceled former concessions. Those who were affected sought reparations.

On the recommendation of Washington, Estrada submitted the government to a full investigation, after which a treaty was signed on June 6, 1911 between the U.S. and Nicaragua, providing for a loan of $15,000,000 from American bankers. The proceeds were used to pay claims against the government, consolidate the debt, stabilize the currency and build a railroad to the eastern coast. Customs were controlled by a collector-general, approved by the U.S. State Department.[152] The Knox-Castillo Treaty created a national bank. Controlling interests in the bank and National Railway were held as security by New York bankers and the U.S. undertook collection of Nicaragua's internal taxes. The American Congress, however, refused to ratify the treaty and other events suspended negotiations.

At the insistence of General Luis Mena, Estrada resigned in favor of conservative Adolfo Diaz. Mena then persuaded the Assembly to name him successor to Diaz when his term expired in 1913, which the U.S. refused to acknowledge.

Mena led a revolt, assisted by a force under the control of liberal Benjamin Zeledon. Diaz turned to the United States, which landed 2,700 marines to counter the revolt. As one U.S. observer noted:

> The U.S. could hardly permit the overthrow of the Conservative authorities. [If the rebels won] all of the efforts of the State Department to place Nicaragua on her feet politically and financially would have been useless, and the interest of the New York bankers...would be seriously imperiled.[153]

To protect American property, the U.S. kept the marines in Nicaragua until 1933 (although the force was reduced to a 100 in 1913).[154]

In 1913, new elections were held under U.S. supervision. The liberals refused to participate and Diaz was reelected. Under Diaz, the Chamorro–Bryan Treaty gave the U.S. exclusive rights to build

---

152 Cox, Isaac Joslin, 711.

153 Walker, Thomas W., *Nicaragua, The Land of Sandino*, 19.

154 "Nicaragua – United States Intervention, 1909-33," Library of Congress, http://countrystudies.us/nicaragua/10.tm.

an inter-oceanic canal across Nicaragua, a renewable ninety-nine-year lease to the Great and Little Corn Islands in the Caribbean, and a renewable ninety-nine-year option to establish a naval base in the Gulf of Fonseca. This blocked the Germans and Japanese, in exchange for which Nicaragua was supposed to receive $3 million dollars. But U.S. officials who handled Nicaragua's finances channeled much of the money into payments for foreign creditors.[155]

Nicaragua's inability to service debt repayment led it back to the New York bankers. The bankers, at first, tried to assume direct collection of the entire country's revenue via the central bank. When this failed, they amassed treasury notes totaling $1,000,000 and bought the controlling interest in Nicaragua's National Railway. Nicaragua used the funds to pay its current debt and increase the stock of the National Bank.[156]

Because the liberals boycotted the 1916 election, conservative Emiliano Chamorro was then elected to replace Diaz. The 1920 election was no different, even though the liberals participated. Backed by the U.S. (in what was viewed by the liberals as a fraudulent election), Emiliano Chamorro's uncle, Diego Manuel Chamorro, became his next successor.

By then, the country's financial position improved. It reduced its debt of over $32,000,000 to less than one fourth that amount because the country's economic activity had doubled with each decade.[157] It now owned the National Bank outright, and had repurchased the Pacific Railroad stock. Harbors and sanitary measures had both been improved, and plans were underway for road-building.

In 1924, Chamorro was replaced by Carlos Solorzano. Solorzano requested that U.S. forces remain to help Nicaragua build a national military. This marked the creation of the National Guard, after which U.S. troops left Nicaragua in 1925. Solorzono was then forced from power by former president General Emiliano Chamorro.

From fear that the liberal-conservative conflict would install another liberal, the U.S. Marines were returned to Nicaragua in 1926. However, American fears were realized when Chamorro resigned in favor of another former president, Adolfo Diaz, and former liberal Vice President Sacasa claimed the right of successor.

---

155 Walker, Thomas W., *Nicaragua, The Land of Sandino*, 20.
156 Cox, Isaac Joslin, 720.
157 Ibid., 737.

The outcome of Sacasa's efforts was a U.S.-mediated agreement, which allowed Diaz to remain in office until the end of his elective term. Under the Pact of Espino Negro, U.S. forces supervised the 1928 elections. Both the government and the liberals were obliged to disarm. Sacasa refused to sign the agreement and went into exile once more. The U.S. took over the military and strengthened the National Guard. Then the U.S. oversaw the peaceful election of liberal Jose Maria Moncada, with whom the conservatives made peace.

By now, the U.S. could live with a liberal in office because the regime was controlled from a number of points: "the American embassy, the Marines, the Guardia Nacional (which included U.S. Army officers), the High Commissioner of Customs, the Director of the Railway, and the National Bank. Under the circumstances, it no longer mattered whether the chief executive was a liberal or conservative."[158]

Sandino and Somoza

Augusto Cesar Sandino led a rebel liberal group which also refused to sign the Pact of Espino Negro. A highly nationalist figure, Sandino attracted like-minded members of the urban middle class and the revolutionary rural poor. Sandino was not a communist (he ousted Agustin Farabundo Marti, the martyr of the 1932 uprising in El Salvador, precisely because he was a communist), but he was a guerrilla fighter, whose overarching goal was to evict the United States. He fought a hit-and-run campaign against the U.S. Marines that finally convinced President Roosevelt to withdraw U.S. troops.

This occurred after a free and fair election in which a more acceptable liberal candidate, Juan B. Sacasa, became president in 1933. It also marked a change of leadership in the Guardia Nacional, for which U.S. Minister Matthew Hanna chose Anastasio Somoza Garcia, Sacasa's liberal nephew.[159] Under the U.S. development model, the Guardia Nacional was meant to serve as a constabulary (combining the roles of an army and a police force), but not as a force independent of the army.

Somoza suspected that Sandino led many more guerillas than claimed. When Sandino signed a peace pact under President Sacasa, he demanded the Guardia's disarmament, making it hard to reach

---

158 Walker, Thomas W., *Nicaragua, The Land of Sandino*, 21.

159 Anderson, Thomas P., *Politics in Central America: Guatemala, El Salvador, Honduras, and Nicaragua*, Revised Ed. (New York: Praeger, 1988) 175.

an accord. When they did, Somoza had Sandino arrested, driven to the airfield and shot. Somoza at first denied involvement, then admitted to the crime, and began to exert control over the Sacasa administration.

To prevent Somoza from becoming president, Sacasa's support-ers planned to attack him in his fortress of La Loma, but were per-suaded to refrain by Arthur Bliss Lane, the current U.S. minister. By then, Somoza controlled the Guardia and was also backed by a paramilitary force, publicly known as Blue Shirts.[160] Using intimi-dation, Somoza became the liberal candidate for the 1936 election. He was then duly elected, after which he combined the Guardia leadership with the office of the presidency as the best possible means to maintain his hold on power.

Somoza called an Assembly in 1939 to rewrite the constitution and limit the term of the president to six-years, with no reelection possible except in the case of Somoza. Somoza was then elected to serve for an eight-year term from 1939–1947.

This was acceptable to President Roosevelt. He assigned a North American major to establish a Nicaraguan Academia Militar for officers of the Guardia, who spent their senior year at the School of the Americas (the U.S. military training center in Panama).[161] Eventually, Somoza's National Guard controlled most government-owned enterprises, including the national radio and telegraph net-works, the postal and immigration services, health services, the in-ternal revenue service, and the national railroads.[162] Somoza turned the Guardia against the people by encouraging corruption and ex-ploitation. According to Thomas W. Walker:

> ...gambling, prostitution, smuggling and other forms of vice were run directly by the guardsmen. In addition, citizens soon learned that in order to engage in any of a variety of activities— legal or not—it was necessary to pay bribes or kickbacks to guard officers or soldiers. In effect, rather than being a profes-sional national police and military force, the guard was a sort of Mafia in uniform, which served simultaneously as the personal bodyguard of the Somoza family.[163]

Meanwhile, Somoza controlled the political machinery through the Liberal Nationalist Party, or the Partido Liberal Nacionalista

---

160 Ibid.
161 Ibid.
162 "Nicaragua – The Somoza Era, 1936-74," Library of Congress, http:// countrystudies.us/nicaragua/11.htm.
163 Walker, Thomas W., *Nicaragua, the Land of Sandino*, 27.

(PLN). He controlled the legislature and the judicial system while using the National Guard to repress political opposition, giving him absolute power.

Unsurprisingly, Somoza amassed a fortune in World War II through agricultural exports and acquisition of industrial enterprises. He owned many German properties which the government confiscated and sold to him for a fraction of their worth, as well as textile companies, sugar mills, rum distilleries, the merchant marine lines, the national Nicaraguan Airlines, and La Salud dairy (the country's only pasteurized milk facility). Somoza made more money through economic concessions to national and foreign companies, bribes, and illegal exports, until his fortune at the end of the 1940s was US $60 million dollars.[164]

As a U.S.-supporter, Somoza received military and economic aid, especially during World War II, when the Nicaraguan economy was important to the wartime plan. But, in 1945, President Roosevelt died and the new president, Harry Truman, wanted Somoza to step down. This was also true within Nicaragua, where Somoza was being opposed by new political parties, such as the Independent Liberal Party (Partido Liberal Independiente – PLI), labor, and business groups. Somoza then left office but retained his hold on power.

---

164 "Nicaragua – The Somoza Era, 1936-74."

Chapter Eleven: Nicaragua — The Somoza Dynasty

In 1947, Somoza convinced the PLI to nominate Leonardo Arguello for president. When Arguello was sworn in, Somoza remained the chief director of the National Guard and expected Arguello's obedience. In the words of Thomas P. Anderson:

> Arguello...had the quaint notion that he was really president...
> [H]e demanded that Somoza resign as jefe [leader] and go into
> exile. In a twinkling, he was overthrown in May 1947 and a So-
> moza relative, Benjamin Lacayo Sacasa installed in his place.[165]

The Truman administration denied Sacasa recognition, so Somoza named an Assembly to rewrite the constitution. The Assembly appointed Somoza's uncle, Victor Roman Reyes, as president
and the new constitution contained anti-communist language to
placate the United States. The U.S., however, maintained non-rec-
ognition. Diplomatic relations were broken until 1948.

Despite U.S. interference, Nicaragua remained underdeveloped.
Its infrastructure consisted of rudimentary installations, with less
than 700 kilometers of all-weather roads and only 400 kilometers of
usable railroad tracks. Shipping was confined to the port of Corinto
(which badly needed repair), and more than three quarters of the
labor force was still devoted to agriculture. Because the majority
of the populace was illiterate and untrained, it offered little hope

---

165 Anderson, Thomas P., *Politics in Central America: Guatemala, El Salvador,
Honduras, and Nicaragua,* 175.

to the nascent industrial sector, and the range of national exports remained limited to coffee, gold, rice, sesame, and bananas.[166]

Controlling the Opposition

Under Somoza's regime, public discontent led to union organization with demands for price controls and government relief. The unions desired a national labor code, affordable public health care, a minimum wage and the right to strike.

In 1945, Somoza responded to these demands with new labor laws. He allowed union organization, but authorized groups of employers to "defend their economic rights." In 1948, any union worker could be fired after thirty day's notice. The same precondition allowed employee lock-outs. Strikes related to "public service and businesses of collective interest" became criminal, while employer crackdowns were legalized. Although labor won wage gains within certain sectors, Somoza's legal "concessions" reduced union participation to under 2,000 people.[167]

Meanwhile, conservatives attacked Somoza on presidential succession. Because the constitution prohibited two consecutive terms, conservatives forced Somoza to engage in power-sharing. Emiliano Chamorro (Somoza's presidential choice) was allowed to serve for another six-years in exchange for opposition membership in his Cabinet, the legislature and the judiciary. Called the Pacto de los Generales, the agreement facilitated conservative control of the ministries of finance and education, and direct municipal elections. A free and fair election occurred in 1950.[168]

Somoza's Foreign Policy

Somoza's anti-communist policy impacted other Central American countries. Most affected was Guatemala, which favored land reform (and directly threatened the interests of the U.S.-owned United Fruit Company), under President Jacobo Arbenz. Accused of communism, Arbenz was forced to resign under a CIA-sponsored assault of psychological and political warfare, while Somoza and other leaders hosted Guatemalan exiles who trained to invade Guatemala.[169]

---

166 Gambone, Michael D., *Eisenhower, Somoza, and the Cold War in Nicaragua, 1953-1961* (Westport, CT: Greenwood, 1997) 33.

167 Ibid.

168 Ibid., 52.

169 "Guatemala '54," http://www.gwu.edu/nsarchiv/NSAEBGB/NSAEBB4/.

Somoza told U.S. State Department officials, "Just give me the arms and I'll clean up Guatemala for you in no time."[170] He accordingly designed a plan (which Washington declined) to invade Guatemala with the help of Venezuela, Colombia and the Dominican Republic. Somoza reactivated ODECA (the Organization of Central American States), which was initially conceived as an economic and political union, but now came to embody an anti-communist organization.

As part of the Caribbean Area Reserve, Nicaragua was intended to lead Central and South America in defense of the Panama canal. Troops from Nicaragua, Brazil, Honduras, Guatemala, Cuba and Colombia were to be deployed in concert under a foreign attack. The plan's dual purpose was for Nicaragua to stabilize Central America. Few countries in the 1950s had forces to match the Guardia Nacional, let alone Somoza's degree of control. As ever, Somoza endeared himself to the Guard by giving it the power to pillage, an observation Americans repeatedly noted.

Foreign Aid and Development

In 1950, the outbreak of the Korean War produced a boom in Nicaraguan exports that led to a trade surplus. This, combined with lower external debt and fiscally conservative policies, earned Nicaragua a high credit rating, which attracted IBRD lending. A Nicaraguan advisory commission recommended a five-year development plan, encompassing transportation, communications, agriculture, industry, education, health and energy. In addition, the World Bank issued 1,427 loans (valued at sixty-nine million cordobas) to private manufacturing, agricultural and industrial interests.[171]

Under the Eisenhower administration, Somoza was treated kindly. Together with Nicaragua, Eisenhower introduced the Cooperative Agricultural Program, the Cooperative Educational Program, the Cooperative Business Administration Program, the Cooperative Vocational and Rural Education Program, and the Cooperative Health Program—a series of initiatives that cost the United States $8.9 million in nonmilitary aid between 1953 and 1957.[172] In 1954, Nicaragua's first universal income tax broadened its revenue base and reduced export-dependency. According to Michael D. Gambone, all of this served the Somoza family:

170 Gambone, Michael D., 89.
171 Ibid., 52.
172 Ibid., 22.

Though tax policy, labor policy, transportation policy, and a host of other official activities, Somoza could control and manipulate the Nicaraguan economy in a manner that bore little resemblance to market forces or private interests outside the family. As the Somoza family's fortunes rose in the early part of the decade, so too did the possibility of an elite backlash.[173]

In 1952, Somoza defused this threat by creating the Banco Nicaraguense (BANIC) and Banco de America (BANAMERICA). This allowed people outside the Somoza family to access commercial credit, as well as funds from the World Bank, INFONAC, the National Bank, and the Central Bank. By this means, Somoza encouraged diversification, while allowing agricultural and industrial elites to share the growth and prosperity of the early 1950s.

During this time, Nicaragua received major foreign investment, not only from the United States but also from Britain, France, Germany, Israel, Cuba and El Salvador. Foreign direct investment attracted some of the biggest names in industry, like Quaker Oats, General Mills, Pepsi-Cola and Fox Head Breweries. New markets for Nicaraguan exports developed in Germany Japan, Holland, Italy, and other Central American countries.

The Succession of Luis Somoza

By mid-decade, exports dropped, and economic stagnation threatened more decay. Military clashes with Costa Rica (in 1955) and Honduras (in 1957) interrupted inter-regional trade. Then, on September 21, 1956, Somoza was shot by Nicaraguan poet Rigoberto Lopez Perez. Somoza was rushed to the Panama Canal Zone and treated by Eisenhower's own doctors, but he died eight days later.[174]

Somoza left behind a fortune of U.S. $100–$150 million, comprised of bank holdings, properties and industries. He also prearranged the peaceful presidential succession of his son Luis Somoza Debayle.

Unlike his brother Anastasio, who attended West Point and received control of the Guardia Nacional, Luis was taught economics and engineering at the University of California, Louisiana State University and the University of Maryland. When Luis became president, Anastasio imprisoned his political opponents,[175] some of

---

173 Ibid., 60.

174 Anastasio Somoza killer file, http:///.moreorless.au.com/killers/somoza. html.

175 Walker, Thomas W., *Nicaragua, The Land of Sandino*, 29.

whom were tortured. The government imposed press censorship and suspended many civil liberties.[176]

In the 1957 elections, the Conservative Party refused to participate, so the brothers created a puppet opposition party, the National Conservative Party (Partido Conservador Nacional - PCN), to maintain the pretense of democracy. Luis won the 1957 election with almost no resistance. Then he re-imposed restrictions on presidential terms and favored liberalization to encourage the opposition.

In 1961, Luis allowed the Cuban exile brigade to use coastal Caribbean military bases for the Bay of Pigs invasion.[177] This endeared him to the United States, as much as his technocratic background and more conciliatory style of ruling.

The Economic Climate

During the mid- to late 1950s, Nicaraguan exports declined in value and volume. Cotton, which comprised the bulk of exports in 1955 dropped from $31 million to $21.8 million in 1957. The value of coffee plummeted from $27.9 million in 1955 to $13.9 million in 1959. A reduction of primary exports produced a $15 million balance-of-payments deficit in 1956. There was also a drop in investment, making the country's annual per capita GDP decrease from U.S. $222 to $200.[178]

In response, Luis initiated social welfare programs. He invested in public housing, education, social security and agrarian reform. The Social Security Law of 1957 made the government responsible for basic health care and housing in the capital of Managua. Two years later, the Law of Family Protection made special grants available to low-income families with large numbers of children. The government offered public food assistance and opened the National Granary to distribute grain to the poor.[179]

These policies meshed well with the U.S. Alliance for Progress, which was launched in reaction to Fidel Castro's successful revolution in Cuba. Designed to promote social and economic development in Latin America, the Alliance favored superficial reform through moderate political means. Thomas W. Walker explains:

---

176 "Nicaragua – The Somoza Era, 1936-74."
177 Ibid.
178 Gambone, Michael D., 95.
179 Ibid., 168.

[W]hile creating jobs for an expanded bureaucracy and providing opportunities for further enrichment of the privileged, [Alliance for Progress developmentalism] had little positive impact on the lives of the impoverished majority of Nicaraguans, and "democracy" was a façade. Elections were rigged and the National Guard, as always, provided a firm guarantee that there could be no real reform in the political system.[180]

Opposition and Accommodation

In 1959, the first attempt to overthrow the Somaza regime was led by Pedro Joaquin Chamorro (publisher and editor of *La Prensa*), who was beaten and forced into exile.[181] Then, in 1962, a group named after nationalist guerilla Augusto Cesar Sandino began to press for change. The Sandinista Front of National Liberation (Frente Sandinista de Liberacion Nacional - FSLN), became a thorn in Somoza's side and would remain so until it toppled his regime.

In 1963, Luis maintained a low profile and selected Rene Schick Gutierrez as his presidential choice. Gutierrez supported Luis and was replaced by the equally malleable Lorenzo Guerrero Gutierrez in 1966. Because Luis did not want his brother Anastasio to run for president, he ensured that it was prohibited by Nicaragua's constitution. In 1966, this was revised, and the Liberal National Party nominated Anastasio for president.

In the 1967 elections (which were widely viewed as fraudulent), Anastasio was opposed by the Union Nacional Opositora (a combined party of Independent Liberals and Christian Democrats), backing Dr. Fernando Aguero for president. Pedro Joaquin Chamorro staged a massive protest involving between 40,000 and 60,000 people.[182] Forty demonstrators were shot by the Guardia, and Chamorro was imprisoned once more.

Anastasio rejected compromise, nor did he need it to expand his political base. He ruled through force and intimidation. And, much like his father, Anastasio encouraged corruption and exploitation by the Guardia Nacional. He even gave the Guard political power. His cousin, Noel Pallais Debayle, headed the National Development Bank. His brother-in-law, Guillermo Sevilla Sacasa, served as Nicaragua's ambassador to the United States. Anastasio's uncle, Manuel Debayle, headed the national electric company. His wife Hope

---

180 Walker, Thomas W., *Nicaragua, The Land of Sandino*, 29.

181 Anderson, Thomas P., *Politics in Central America: Guatemala, El Salvador, Honduras, and Nicaragua*, 176.

182 Ibid., 177.

headed Social Security, and his cousin, Luis Pallais, ran the liberal newspaper *Novedades*, which backed Anastasio's regime.[183] When Anastasio's presidential term was due to end in 1971, he arbitrarily extended it until 1972. This strengthened his opposition, causing Anastasio to form a pact with conservative leader Fernando Aguero (brokered by U.S. Ambassador Turner Shelton) whereby power would pass to a triumvirate, comprised of two liberals and Aguero. Though this took place in 1972, Anastasio retained control of the National Guard as the power behind the scenes. He therefore had no problem getting reelected in 1974.

Increased resistance to Anastasio's corrupt regime stemmed from the Christmas earthquake of 1972, which killed over 10,000 people and leveled 600 square blocks in Managua. Responding to the crisis, foreign governments including the United States sent aid to rebuild the city. But Anastasio (who already possessed a fortune of over $300 million) stole much of the aid, took kickbacks on government contracts, and allowed the National Guard to loot the city.[184] Nor did he rebuild Managua. Funds from the Agency for International Development (AID) went into building luxury homes for members of the National Guard.

The people did not forget. When Anastasio announced his bid for reelection in 1974, he was resisted by his own party. It also inspired business groups, the traditional elite and unions to form a new political party, organized by Pedro Joaquin Chamorro and former Minister of Education Ramiro Sacasa. The Democratic Liberation Union (Democratica de Liberacion – Udel) was created to promote political pluralism, but, in this, it failed when Anastasio was reelected in 1974.

The FSLN

Since the early 1960s the FSLN tried terrorism and guerrilla tactics to bring down the Somoza dynasty. Founded by Carlos Fonseca Amador, Silvio Mayorga and Tomas Borge Martinez, the movement stemmed from student activism but grew to became much more. With its Marxist-Leninist mindset, the party advocated social and economic reform to benefit the poor, hoping to end the system under which the poorest half of the nation received 15 percent of the income, the poorest fifth received 3 percent, and the richest 5 per-

183 Ibid., 178.
184 "Nicaragua – The Somoza Era, 1936-74."

cent enjoyed 30 percent, as well as privileged access to health care and elite education.[185]

Nicaragua was a country where one baby in eight died before age one, two out of three children were undernourished, and two out of three farmers were landless or had plots too small for sub-sistence. In Somoza's "investor's dream," six out of ten deaths were caused by preventable and curable diseases, and over half the popu-lation was illiterate.[186]

In contrast, the Somoza family fortune skyrocketed to $500 mil-lion. The Somozas owned half the country's agriculture and vast amounts of industry, including the agricultural firm Agrotecnica S.A., a Nicaraguan cigar-making firm, the television network Tele-vision de Nicaragua, S.A., the Mamenic steamship lines, the Banco de Centro America, a half interest in the Intercontinental Hotel and stock in the Lanica Airline.[187]

In 1969, many FSLN leaders, including Julio Cesar Buitrago, were killed in a shootout with the Guardia in Managua. The same year, Carlos Fonseca Amador was arrested on charges of bank rob-bery. His release came in 1970, after the FSLN hijacked a Costa Ri-can airliner and demanded Fonseca's freedom.

In 1974, the FSLN held an elite group of Managuans hostage until Anastasio agreed to their ransom, an FSLN national radio broadcast, and the release of fourteen FSLN members. Immediately after, Anastasio declared martial law and sent the Guardia into the countryside with permission to conduct pillage, arbitrary impris-onment, rape, torture, and the summary execution of hundreds of helpless peasants.[188]

Anastasio developed a death squad—the Anti-Communist league of Nicaragua—and received help from the United States and CONDECA (the Central American Defense Council) to commence counterinsurgency. Under a state of siege, many FSLN leaders, in-cluding Fonseca, were killed, while others were forced into exile.

---

185 Sklar, Holly, *Washington's War on Nicaragua* (Boston: South End Press, 1988) 10.

186 Ibid., 10.

187 Anderson, Thomas P., *Politics in Central America: Guatemala, El Salvador, Honduras, and Nicaragua*, 178.

188 Walker, Thomas W., *Nicaragua, The Land of Sandino*, 32.

The Beginning of the End

U.S. policy changed when President Jimmy Carter replaced Gerald Ford. Carter promoted human rights and dealt with Anastasio's regime through a combination of non-military and humanitarian aid. Once Anastasio realized that the FSLN was too scattered and beaten to do further damage, he lifted the state of siege and restored freedom of the press.

The United States wanted Anastasio to step down in 1981. It pictured a new government led by business elites with strong ties to Washington, but what it wanted was Somocismo, *sans* the Somozas, instead of real change.

Meanwhile, the FSLN refused to die. It launched new attacks aimed at National Guard posts in 1977, with the support of businessmen, clergy and professionals who called for a new government that would include the FSLN and became known as "The Twelve."

Due to Somoza's terror, support for the FSLN was growing. On January 10, 1978, the murder of *La Prensa* editor and publisher Pedro Joaquin Chamorro mobilized the populace. Crowds took to the streets, burning Somoza's buildings and chanting anti-Somoza slogans. As the government tried to cover up Chamorro's murder, the chambers of commerce and industry called for a nationwide strike that lasted for two weeks and shut down the country.

There were rural and urban uprisings, which the National Guard put down with tanks, armored cars, 50-caliber machine guns, helicopter gun ships, and two light planes that strafed entire neighborhoods. When it was leaked, in August, that Anastasio received a letter from President Carter applauding his human rights record, this proved too much for the Nicaraguan people. The FSLN seized the National Legislative Palace and held 1,500 people hostage[189] to win a list of "stinging" demands, including "U.S. $500,000 ransom, airtime on radio and space in the press, government capitulation to the demands of striking workers, and safe passage out of the country for fifty-nine political prisoners and the guerrillas."[190]

Panama and Venezuela vied for the "honor" of hosting the exiles, while the Nicaraguan people were encouraged to fight without them. The Broad Opposition Front demanded Anastasio's resignation and called for another nationwide strike that paralyzed the country, this time for a month. There were more urban uprisings,

---

189 "Nicaragua – End of the Anastasio Somoza Debayle Era," Library of congress, http://countrystudies.us/nicaragua/13.htm.

190 Walker, Thomas W., *Nicaragua, The Land of Sandino*, 37.

which the government put down with bombing, strafing, summary executions and the murder of noncombatants, including young males and children.

According to Holly Sklar:

> [T]he Guard laid siege to the rebellious cities, cutting off food and utilities, and bombing and strafing by air. Guardsmen then carried out "Operation Clean-Up." The Inter-American Commission on Human Rights reported that "many persons were executed in a summary and collective fashion for the mere reason of living in the neighborhoods where there had been activity by the FSLN; young people and defenseless children were killed." It was "a crime to be a male between the ages of 12 and 30," said one refugee. In Matagalpa, reported Amnesty International, guardsmen castrated the owner of the Hotel Soza before machine-gunning him and his whole family. "In some areas," said Amnesty, 'all males over fourteen years old were reportedly shot dead."[191]

Somoza Must Go

The Carter administration began weighing its options. Although it wanted to maintain the ruling system complete with "Somocismo," it realized that Anastasio had to go. Anastasio tried to arrange succession with the few politicians still willing to listen and the Carter administration suggested a peace-keeping force be supplied by the OAS (Organization of American States) to "reassure the National Guard" and keep the Sandinistas from gaining power.

Meetings were held between William Jorden and the FAO (Frente Amplio de Oposicion), which was a coalition of 16 organizations including 3 labor unions, 4 factions of the Conservative Party, 2 socialist parties, the Independent Liberal Party, Los Doce (The Twelve), and a party called the MDN (Movimiento Democratico Nicaraguense). Jorden tried to broker a compromise between the FAO and Anastasio, but the FAO insisted Somoza must go and that the Guardia be disbanded, along with the Somoza-controlled Congress.[192]

The FSLN frantically increased its membership, recruiting students and rural activists. It also resolved disagreements between its three factions. The Guerra Prolongada Popular (GPP) favored a drawn-out war of attrition, whereas the Proletarian tendency favored a long campaign of recruitment. The Insurrectionist tendency

---

191 Sklar, Holly, 17.
192 Anderson, Thomas P., 182.

was linked to business groups in Managua[193] and sought the broadest base, but insisted on proper Marxism.

It was because of this that Robelo Callejas, the FAO spokesperson, distrusted the Sandinistas. Washington supported the FAO and this caused a more radical party to form: the Movimiento Pueblo Unido – MPU. The MPU joined Los Doce to form the Frente Patriotico Nacional (FPN), which aligned with the FSLN.

FSLN leadership was shared by its three factions, with Tomas Borge, Henry Ruiz and Bayardo Arce Castano representing the GPP. Carlos Nunez, Luis Carrion Cruz and Jaime Wheelock Roman led the Proletarian tendency. Daniel and Humberto Ortega Savedra and Victor Manual Tirado Lopez headed the Terceristas.

Washington tried to encourage plebiscitary democracy (the goal of the FAO) by arranging for a $65.7 million dollar loan from the IMF. When Anastasio balked, the Carter administration cut off bilateral aid, but half of the IMF loan was delivered to Somoza in June.

The Sandinistas attacked Managua then retreated to Masaya to facilitate Somoza's departure via the Las Mercedes Airport. The following were chosen to comprise the government in exile: Alfonso Robelo and Violeta Barrios de Chamorro (the widow of Pedro Joaquin Chamorro)—both of whom were non-Marxists—plus Sergio Ramirez, Daniel Ortega Saavedra, and Moises Hassan, who were each Sandinistas.[194] The junta called for a mixed economy, political pluralism and a nonaligned foreign policy.

The United States tried to preserve the National Guard and insert its own candidates into the mix, suggesting Adolfo Calero, General Julio Gutierrez of the Guardia, Emilo Alvarez (a conservative), Ernesto Fernandez (a liberal friend of Somoza), Mariano Fiallos (another liberal) and conservative Jaime Chamorro of *La Prensa*. The junta objected that this would preserve Somocismo. Too, they already compromised by including an MDN candidate and prominent conservatives in Alfonso Robelo and Violeta Barrios de Chamorro.[195]

In the junta's "Plan to Achieve Peace," submitted to Washington on July 11:

> Somoza was to resign to congress which in turn would cede power to the junta. The junta would dissolve the Somocista

193 Ibid., 181.

194 "Nicaragua – The Sandinista Revolution," Library of Congress, http:// countrystudies.us/nicaragua/14.htm.

195 Anderson, Thomas P, 186.

congress and carry out a cease-fire; guardsmen who immediately ceased fighting would be eligible to join a new Nicaraguan army (with a Sandinista core). Guardsmen and others guilty of serious crimes would be tried.[196]

On July 16, 1979, Anastasio agreed to surrender the government to Francisco Urcuyo, the president of the lower house, who would then handle the transfer of power to the Sandinista junta, with Anastasio exiled to Florida. The junta entered Leon on July 19th to take the oath of office. From there it went on to Managua, where it was received by a triumphant people. The Somoza dynasty, which endured for four decades, was finally defeated.

Unbeknownst to the junta and its supporters, an American named "Bill," wearing Red Cross insignia, had just landed in Managua to extract Colonel Justiniano Perez. Over the next few months, "Bill" would extract other Guardia members from exile in Guatemala and El Salvador, until they numbered 130—enough to resurrect the old Guardia and depose the Sandinistas.[197]

---

196 Sklar, Holly, 24.
197 Ibid., 34.

Chapter Twelve: Nicaragua — Opposition to the Sandinistas

As part of post-World War II planning to deter anti-communist states from joining the liberal camp, U.S. interference helped Nicaraguan conservatives develop external markets and promote foreign investment. Under the liberal Somozas, Washington shifted alliances, but "liberal" never referred to left-leaning reformers. It defined crop-growers, merchants and exporters who prospered from free trade, contrasting with Spanish-born conservatives who lost protectionism.

During the difficult postwar years, Luis Somoza Debayle adopted palliative measures to provide access to health care and alleviate widespread hunger, but these were discontinued under Anastasio. During Anastasio's reign, the Guardia was abusive and the Somoza fortune grew.

Anastasio's corruption, continual abuse of power and the plight of poor peasants who were kept landless and illiterate created the FSLN. Much of Nicaragua supported the FSLN, despite government-sponsored violence to discourage support for the rebels. Defenseless, innocent peasants were raped, tortured, arrested and summarily executed, eliciting the opposite of the Guardia's intent. Support for the FSLN multiplied and, with the murder of Pedro Joaquin Chamorro, even the elite and business sectors called for a new government to include the FSLN. The junta that was formed adopted a mixed economy with prominent socialist policies aimed at being fair.

Insofar as the phases of colonization are coercion, persuasion, bargaining and indoctrination, the U.S. used a combination of measures to control Nicaragua. Above all, U.S. clientelism catered to the wealthy and empowered the Somozas. But lacking indoctrination, the Sandinista victory and U.S. inability to control the revolution forced Washington to drop all pretense of negotiation. The U.S. reverted to coercion from fear that Sandinista socialism would radicalize Central America and "export revolution."

The Result of the War for Liberation

The harm to Nicaragua that resulted from revolution was by no means small-scale:

> The Sandinistas had won, but the cost had been tremendous. No exact casualty statistics were kept by either side, but estimates of the dead ranged from 40,000 to 50,000. Even accepting the lowest figure, this represented a higher casualty rate than that in the U.S. Civil War. Another 100,000 had been wounded, and lay, often without proper medical attention, in makeshift hospitals about the country; 40,000 children had been orphaned, and 8,000 tons of emergency food relief were needed every day to prevent famine. The economic costs were equally staggering, the best estimate of war damage being $1.3 billion, with the national debt, which the Sandinistas promised to repay, standing at $1.6 billion.[198]

As noted by Holly Sklar:

> The ruins of the war rested on a foundation of poverty. The UN Economic Commission for Latin America (ECLA) estimated that 62.5 percent of the pre-revolutionary Nicaraguan population lived in a state of critical poverty. Two out of three Nicaraguans did not have enough income to cover their most basic needs. More than one out of three Nicaraguans lived in 'extreme poverty.' They 'did not even have sufficient income to cover the value of the minimum shopping basket of food considered necessary in order to meet their biological nutritional needs.' Infant mortality was 121 per 1,000 live births. Less than 20 percent of pregnant women and children under five received any health care. In rural areas where nearly half the population lived, 93 percent of the homes had no safe drinking water. Less than one in ten rural children were able to finish primary school. More

---

198 Anderson, Thomas P., *Politics in Central America: Guatemala, El Salvador, Honduras, and Nicaragua*, 189.

than half the Nicaraguan population is under sixteen years old. The revolution promised a better future.[199]

The new ruling junta exerted immediate control over health, housing, education and private property appropriation. Under MINSA (the Ministry of Health), it made healthcare universal. It also increased health facilities to reach urban areas and train qualified personnel. There was a noticeable shift from curative to preventive care, and the government opened childcare facilities. It also built a countrywide health network to address physical and mental disabilities, drug and alcohol abuse, physical abuse and abandonment.

The Ministry of Social Welfare merged with the Nicaraguan Social Security Institute to form the Nicaraguan Institute of Social Security and Social Welfare (INSSBI). In 1982, this extended benefits to nearly twice the amount of workers. More than half the payments were for deaths and injuries caused by Somoza's "counterrevolutionary aggression."[200] The junta promoted labor-intensive reconstruction and increased the minimum wage.

MINVAH (the Ministry of Housing and Human Settlements) organized the repair and rebuilding of earthquake-damaged Managua. It built 1,146 new houses and repaired 4,676 others.[201] MINVAH also empowered urban homeowners to gain title to their land, introduced rent control and restructured mortgages. By 1982, the number of houses under construction grew to 5,762, with a focus on the poor.

In 1980, Nicaragua earned UNESCO's prize for advancements in education, by reducing the illiteracy rate from over 50 percent to 13 percent. It also promoted literacy in Miskito, English, and Sumu, as well as Spanish. By 1983, the junta established 17,377 education collectives (CEPs), spread throughout the country. Education was expanded from preschool to graduate studies, and school enrollment more than doubled between 1979 and 1984.[202]

To implement land reform, the junta confiscated 20 percent of the nation's farmland, including 1,200 estates owned by the Somozas and their supporters. It also seized control of five sugar mills, three slaughterhouses, the whole tobacco industry, dairy plants,

199 Sklar, Holly, 36.
200 Walker, Thomas W., ed., *Revolution & Counterrevolution in Nicaragua* (Boulder, CO: Westview Press, 1991) 193.
201 Ibid., 192.
202 Sklar, Holly, 43.

rice mills, cotton gins, coffee processing facilities and other agro-industrial facilities.[203] Foreign-owned mines were nationalized and the junta restored the national banks, which Somoza and his supporters had looted and de-capitalized. Like mining, the banking and the insurance industries were eventually nationalized.

Between 1978 and 1980, public sector output via monopolized agro-exports grew from 15 percent of GDP to 36 percent. However, the government used price surpluses resulting from export growth to create a price buffer for the products of private landowners during years of dearth. Loans were made available to private industry and agriculture, and these sectors were supported by the Superior Council of Private Enterprise (COSEP). Finally, the Ley de Amparo (law of protection) "gave Nicaraguan citizens the right to seek redress for, and question the legality of, the everyday activities of government."[204]

The Early Government Structure

The Fundamental Statute of the Republic of Nicaragua abolished the constitution, presidency, Congress, and the courts, so the nine-person directorate ruled by decree under emergency powers.[205] Prominent business elites who endorsed the revolution were included in the early government, and the COSEP (their official organization) was awarded five seats of the original thirty-three in the Consejo de Estado (Council of State).[206]

There were also popular organizations for government participation, including Sandinist Defense Committees (CDSs), the Sandinist Youth, the Sandinist Workers' Central (CST), the Luisa Amanda Espinos Association of Nicaraguan Women (AMNLAE), and the Rural Workers' Association (ATC). The Sandinist Popular Army maintained control of defense. Along with the Sandinist Police, members of the Sandinist Popular Army were trained by per-

---

203 Spalding, Rose J., *Capitalists and Revolution in Nicaragua: Opposition and Accommodation* (Chapel Hill: University of North Carolina Press, 1994) 65.

204 Walker, Thomas W., *Nicaragua, The Land of Sandino*, 61.

205 "Nicaragua – THE SANDINISTA YEARS, 1979-90," Library of Congress, http://countrystudies.us/nicaragua/15htm.

206 Spalding, Rose J., 67.

sonnel from Cuba, Eastern Europe and the Soviet Union.[207] The government's third line of defense was the Sandinist Popular Militia.[208] According to Thomas W. Walker:

> Nearly two-thirds of the adult population belonged to one or more of the mass organizations, and many others participated occasionally through special mobilizations. Participation was not limited merely to providing physical labor for government projects. The mass organizations were involved more and more in planning, organizing, administering, and evaluating a wide range of public programs.[209]

Under increased resistance from national business leaders over the social agenda, the government coalition began to unravel. The Sandinistas tried to increase the Council of State by fourteen more members, with twelve to be chosen by the FSLN.[210] Then Violeta Barrios de Chamorro and Alfonso Robelo resigned from the junta.

Seven months later, UPANIC president Jorge Salazar was killed by Sandinista state security for engaging in a counterrevolutionary conspiracy.[211] Salazar became a martyr for the business community, but the public-private sector partnership did not completely collapse. It took external interference and the depiction of Daniel Ortega as the "Nicaraguan Castro" (by the Reagan administration) to mobilize the private sector against the Sandinista state.

Foreign Aid in the Early Years

Throughout 1980, war-torn Nicaragua needed $800 million in outside assistance, and $200 to $250 million annually thereafter. The U.S. initially provided $8 million in disaster aid and approved another $39 million for various specific projects. After that, Carter requested $75 million in Congressional appropriations, of which $5 million was intended to be grant.

People who pointed to Soviet assistance as evidence of "communist" Nicaragua, ignored the junta's request for U.S. military aid. Fighting with 3,000 Guardia members who regrouped in Honduras, the Sandinistas were hard-pressed to defend their revolution. But President Carter's request for $5.5 million in military aid to complement the $75 million nonmilitary appropriation was dropped dur-

---

207 "Nicaragua – THE SANDINISTA YEARS, 1979-90."

208 Walker, Thomas W., *Nicaragua, The Land of Sandino*, 40.

209 Walker, Thomas W., ed., *Revolution & Counterrevolution in Nicaragua*, 190.

210 "Nicaragua – THE SANDINISTA YEARS, 1979-90."

211 Spalding, Rose J., 67.

ing committee.[212] Nicaraguan officers were offered military training at the U.S. Army's School of the Americas in Panama, but this organization had trained more than 4,693 members of Somoza's National Guard, such that it wasn't surprising when the Sandinistas declined.[213]

Even nonmilitary aid became controversial. Before releasing funds, the U.S. Congress required certification that the Government of Nicaragua was not cooperating with or harboring any international terrorist organization or aiding, abetting or supporting acts of violence or terrorism in other countries. Congress pledged to terminate aid in the event of "gross violations of internationally recognized human rights," "violations of the right to organize and operate labor unions free from political oppression," or "systematic violations of free speech and press,"[214] and if Soviet, Cuban or other foreign forces were stationed in Nicaragua.

By 1984, Mexico provided Nicaragua with over $500 million in credits. France, West Germany, Spain, Holland, Italy, Sweden and Canada also provided aid. The World Bank and UN agencies made loans to Nicaragua during the early years, whereas the Soviet Union and its allies (with the exception of Cuba) were slower in responding. Although the USSR and its satellites did offer aid, this was to fill the needs-gap during the 1980s, as countries led by the United States began to withdraw aid and block multilateral funds. At the request of the United States, the IDB (Inter-American development Bank) made no loans to Nicaragua after 1981.[215]

Nicaragua had become a Cuban conduit for arming revolutionaries in El Salvador. Too, the Nicaraguan army and police force were trained by the USSR and its allies. Nicaragua received Soviet-bloc military supplies worth $5 million in 1979. This rose to between $6 and $7 million in 1980 and, by 1981, Soviet-bloc arms shipments rose to 900 tons at a cost of $39 to $45 million.[216] The U.S. blocked the Sandinistas from buying arms through France.

---

212 Lamperti, John, *What Are We Afraid Of?: An Assessment of the "Communist Threat" in Central America: a Narmic-American Friends Service Committee Study* (Cambridge, MA: South End Press, 1988) 44.

213 Ibid., 44.

214 Sklar, Holly, 42.

215 Lamperti, John, 27.

216 Sklar, Holly, 112.

The El Salvador Situation

The Carter administration put a hold on the remainder of the $75 million Nicaraguan appropriation and stopped allowing arms traffic to the El Salvadoran rebels.[217] In early 1971, Nicaragua got the message.

However, its support for El Salvador had nothing to do with Marxism and much to do with state terror. As Cynthia J. Arnson notes:

> [U.S. ambassador to El Salvador Robert] White's analysis of the source of the violence in El Salvador was reinforced by three congressmen, Representatives Bob Edgar (D-Pa.), Barbara Mikulski (D-Md.), and Gerry Studds (D-Mass.), who had visited Central America in January 1981. They stated that 'by far the greatest responsibility for violence and terrorism rests with those forces now receiving U.S. guns, helicopters, grenades, and ammunition.' Government troops, they concluded, had been 'waging a systematic campaign of harassment, torture and murder against large segments of the Salvadoran population.' Later that day, William Doherty, executive director of the American Institute for Free Labor Development, stated that 'right wing security forces' had carried out 80 percent of the murders of peasants involved in El Salvador's agrarian reform program. What appeared to be near unanimity about the problem of political violence in El Salvador stood in sharp contrast to [U.S.] administration portrayals. [218]

In Nicaragua and El Salvador, both populations were fighting U.S.-sponsored death squads. Their lives were intolerable and miserably disadvantaged.

But, for the Reagan administration, this was preferred policy. Unlike Nicaragua's so-called "totalitarian dictatorship," other Latin American countries did not "cruelly repress" their people. The fact that Latin American death squads committed every human rights violation listed as a trigger for U.S. aid termination was overlooked because these states were staunch U.S. allies and a necessary bulwark against communist encroachment.

Heeding U.S. warnings, Nicaragua ceased aid to the El Salvadoran rebels and expelled 2,200 Cuban advisors.[219] But according to

---

217 Lamperti, John, 29.

218 Arnson, Cynthia J., *Crossroads: Congress, the President, and Central America*, 2nd ed. (University Park, PA: Pennsylvania State University Press, 1993) 59.

219 "Nicaragua HISTORY, http:www.nationsencyclopedia.com/Americas/ Nicaragua-HISTORY.html.

Wayne Smith, head of the U.S. Interests Section in Cuba, the Reagan administration "had no wish to work with the Sandinistas."[220]

The "Totalitarian Dungeon"

Reagan attacked the Sandinistas over non-democratic ascension and support for the public sector. They were also accused of cruelty for resettling the Miskito Indians. In the latter case, Americas Watch wrote:

> In Nicaragua there is no systematic practice of forced disappearances, extrajudicial killings or torture—as has been the case with the "friendly" armed forces of El Salvador...Nor had the government practiced elimination of cultural or ethnic groups, as the [Reagan] Administration frequently claims; indeed in this respect, as in most others, Nicaragua's record is by no means so bad as that of Guatemala, whose government the Administration consistently defends. And yet it is Nicaragua, and not Guatemala or El Salvador, which Mr. Reagan calls a 'totalitarian dungeon.'[221]

Socialism—barely tolerated in distant allies, like former Yugoslavia—was impermissible in Latin America. In line with the domino theory, the U.S. prevented revolution from spreading to El Salvador and instigated counterrevolution within Nicaragua.

Scorning the positive aspects of Sandinista reform, Reagan's political platform included the following language:

> "We deplore the Marxist Sandinista takeover of Nicaragua and the attempts to destabilize El Salvador, Guatemala, and Honduras...We oppose the Carter Administration aid program for the government of Nicaragua. However, we will support the efforts of the Nicaraguan people to establish a free and independent government...We will return to the fundamental principle of treating a friend as a friend and self-proclaimed enemies as enemies, without apology."[222]

In October, 1980, Cleto DiGiovanni—a high-level clandestine CIA operative until late 1978—advocated economic warfare. Reagan canceled loans and PL480 food credits, using his influence to block international loans. His administration provided foreign aid to Nicaraguan private business interests and other influence groups that opposed the Sandinistas. These were the COSEP and its member organizations: the Social Action Committee of the Moravian Church on the Atlantic Coast, the Archdiocese of Managua, and

---

220 Arnson, Cynthia J., 72.
221 Lamperti, John, 31.
222 Sklar, Holly, 62.

the American Institute for Free Labor Development (AIFLD). The last had longstanding ties to the CIA. When a grant of $5.1 million was appropriated for 1982, the Sandinistas rejected it as private sector aid, noting that "the agreements have political motivations designed to promote resistance and destabilize the revolutionary government."[223]

The Coming of the Contras

The administration toyed with the idea of direct intervention, but chose to rely instead on former Guardia members in exile, who were known within Nicaragua as the *contrarevolucionarios* (counter-revolutionaries), thus the name "contra." On November 23, 1981, Reagan signed National Security Decision Directive 17 (NSDD-17), authorizing the CIA to "work with foreign governments as appropriate" to conduct political and "paramilitary" operations "against [the] Cuban presence and Cuban-Sandinista support infrastructure in Nicaragua and elsewhere in Central America."[224] The CIA was allocated $19.95 million to build a 500-man force. This was to complement the 1,000-man force being built by Argentina, for which Washington paid $50 million.

The Sandinistas appealed to U.S. neutrality legislation, which prohibited U.S. territory from being used for hostilities against countries with which the U.S. was at peace.[225] Reagan denied connection with the contra training camps and claimed the neutrality laws did not apply in any case. The Sandinistas commenced a crackdown within Nicaragua, arresting private-sector leaders who published a critical communiqué in October, 1981.

By 1982, the CIA was able to work with two factions. The first, headed by Eden Pastora (known as Comandante Zero), was the result of a Sandinista leadership split, which inspired the creation of the Sandinista Revolutionary Front (FRS). The second included former members of Somoza's National Guard, which Pastora would not work with due to Somocismo "taint." The CIA preferred the Somocismos, renamed the Fuerza Democratica Nicaraguense (Nicaraguan Democratic Force – FDN) and headed by Enrique Bermúdez, a

---

223 Ibid., 66.
224 Ibid., 98.
225 Arnson, Cynthia J., 78.

former colonel in the National Guard and Somoza's military attaché in Washington.[226]

Contra spokesperson Edgar Chamorro explained:

> 1982 was a year of transition for the FDN...From a collection of small, disorganized and ineffectual bands of ex-National Guardsmen, the FDN grew into a well-organized, well-armed, well-equipped and well-trained fighting force of approximately 4,000 men capable of inflicting great harm on Nicaragua. This was due entirely to the CIA which organized, armed, equipped, trained and supplied us.[227]

The FDN recruited Nicaraguan foot soldiers via bribes, family ties and terror. According to Chamorro:

> FDN units would arrive at an undefended village, assemble all the residents in the town square and then proceed to kill—in full view of the others—all persons suspected of working for the Nicaraguan Government or the FSLN, including police, local militia members, party members, health workers, teachers, and farmers from government-sponsored cooperatives. In this atmosphere, it was not difficult to persuade those able-bodied men left alive to return with the FDN units to their base camps in Honduras and enlist in the force.[228]

The CIA told the contras that damage to farms or crops would be politically counterproductive. This changed in 1984, when Sandinista social programs became the primary target. Aligned with religious leaders, the contras spread the belief that the Sandinistas would eliminate private property and persecute religious faith.

Low Intensity Conflict

Between 1983 and 1987 Reagan's policy was as follows:

> While expressing verbal support for a negotiated settlement of differences, the Reagan administration seemed to be following the recommendations of the Rand Corporation's 1984 report: rejection of accommodation as untenable, emphasis on 'diplomatic efforts to isolate the regime, raise the regime's costs, reduce the support it receives from Latin America and Europe,' and a strengthening of 'the rebel forces to concentrate their attacks on economic targets.' This was part of a conscious shift to a new type of military strategy, 'low-intensity" conflict'...The goal was...to squeeze the economy by forcing a massive diversion of resources into defense. The strategy aimed to exacerbate social

---

226 Draper, Theodore, *A Very Thin Line The Iran-Contra Affairs* (New York: Hill and Wang, 1991) 16.

227 Sklar, Holly, 117.

228 Ibid.

problems and tensions, eroding popular support for the revolution by making it ineffective in people's lives and to produce a heavy psychological impact on the civilian population.[229]

In this, Reagan was successful. When Nicaraguan brought its case to the World Court in 1984 (after the U.S. mined its harbors), direct and indirect damage was more than $1.6 billion (equivalent to four years of Nicaraguan export earnings). Defense expenditures rose to 37 percent of the national budget in 1983 and more than half the national budget in 1985.[230]

The World Court issued a preliminary restraining order against the U.S, ruling 15 to 0 that the U.S. refrain from blockading or mining the Nicaraguan ports. Then, ruling 14 to 1 (with the U.S. judge dissenting) the Court found that Nicaragua's political independence and sovereignty "should be fully respected and should not be jeopardized by any military or paramilitary activities."[231] But the U.S. preempted Nicaragua before the suit was filed by announcing it would ignore Court rulings for a period of two years (in violation of the World Court treaty).

The U.S. did not lack allies. On October 1, 1983, CONDECA, the Central American Defense Council, (once been headed by Somoza), was reactivated by El Salvador, Honduras, Guatemala and Panama.

> CONDECA military leaders met secretly to discuss the legality of a joint military action for the 'pacification of Nicaragua.' They agreed that the contras 'can establish a government somewhere in [Nicaraguan] territory, and, once recognized internationally, can ask for aid from CONDECA.'[232]

This plan never came to fruition because, in 1984, the Sandinistas held their first national elections.

The 1984 Elections

Ignoring the opposition, the Sandinista leadership chose November 4, 1984 as the date of presidential and legislative elections and set 6 years as the term of elective service. Overseen by the Supreme Electoral Council, the elections were open to anyone age sixteen or older.

Participants included: the FSLN and its presidential candidate, Daniel Ortega; The Democratic Coordinator (Coordinadora Dem-

---

229 Walker, Thomas W., *Revolution and Counterrevolution in Nicaragua*, 196.
230 Ibid., 197.
231 Sklar, Holly, 169.
232 Ibid, 162.

ocratica – CD); a coalition of labor unions, business groups and four centrist parties; the PLI; the PPSC; the Democratic Conservative Party (Partido Conservador Democratica – PCD); the communists; the socialists; and the Marxist-Leninist Popular Action Movement.[233] The CD refused to register, claiming the process was rigged, and urged Nicaraguans to boycott as the means to discredit the outcome.

Fully 75 percent of the electorate voted. The FSLN won 67 percent of the votes, the presidency and sixty-one of the ninety-six seats in the new National Assembly. Twenty-nine of the remaining seats were garnered by the three conservative parties, and three seats went to independent leftist groups.[234] The opposition accused the government of manipulating the outcome through control of state and party organs, and by lowering the voting age. Reagan declared Ortega a "dictator," and the elections were dismissed as a "Soviet-style sham."[235]

Opposition and Resolution

Support for the Contras was not overwhelming in Congress. In fact, Washington alternated between funding and de-funding, concerned for the potential for a Vietnam-style conflict or a Sandinista overthrow, which, in the words of one speaker was, "none of our goddamn business." Congress passed two Boland Amendment prohibiting direct support for a Sandinista overthrow and suspended aid to the Contras in 1986. This created the impetus for the Iran–Contra scandal, in which revenue from Iranian weapons purchases was illegally used to fund the Contras. Before this, aid from Taiwan and Korea allowed the Reagan administration to circumvent the Boland Amendments.

President Daniel Ortega then sued for peace with his neighbors. Under the Esquipulas II agreement, the presidents of Guatemala, Honduras, El Salvador, Nicaragua and Costa Rica called for "amnesty for persons charged with political crimes, a negotiated cease-fire, national reconciliation for those countries with insurgencies (Guatemala, El Salvador and Nicaragua), an end to all external aid to insurgencies (U.S. support to the Contras and Soviet and Cuban support to guerrillas in Guatemala and El Salvador), and democrat-

---

233 "Nicaragua – Institutionalization of the Revolution," Library of Congress, http://countrystudies.us/nicaragua/17.htm.

234 Ibid.

235 Lamperti, John, 29.

ic reforms leading to free elections in Nicaragua."[236] After stalling and manipulating the Contadora process (earlier regional peace efforts), the U.S. finally urged the Contras to enter negotiations.

At the Central American summit of January 15, 1988, President Daniel Ortega agreed to hold talks with the Contras, which he did in March. The result was a cease-fire agreement, a commitment to lift the state of siege, and consent to new elections.

By now, Nicaragua was in ruins:

> In human and economic terms, the price of U.S. intervention was appalling. Between 1980 and 1989, the total death toll—Nicaraguan military, contra, and civilian—was officially put at 30,865. Tens of thousands more were wounded, orphaned, or left homeless. As of 1987, property destruction from CIA/contra attacks totaled $221.6 million; production losses, $984.5 million. Nicaraguan economists estimated monetary losses due to the trade embargo at $254 million and the loss of development potential from the war at $2.5 billion. Even as the Nicaraguan government requested $12.8 billion dollars in damages, it noted that the human suffering could never be quantified, let alone repaid: "No such reparation can revive the human lives lost, or repair the physical and psychological injuries suffered by a population that has endured an unrelenting campaign of armed attacks and economic strangulation...The full impact of such a policy on a small, impoverished nation is simply incalculable."[237]

Even worse, the Ortega government was faced with painful reforms.

---

236 "Nicaragua – The Regional Peace Effort," Library of Congress, http://countrystudies.us/nicaragua.htm.

237 Sklar, Holly, 344.

CHAPTER THIRTEEN: NICARAGUA — IMPLEMENTING NEOLIBERALISM

The devastation wrought by war was staggering. But, in 1988, the government of Nicaragua also had to contend with Hurricane Joan, which left 432 people dead and 230,000 homeless, with damage estimated at U.S. $1 billion.[238] Hyperinflation (caused by too much money chasing after too few goods) had risen to 30,000 percent, and foreign aid was half of what it had been in 1984. The government took extreme measures to bring the economy under control, including currency devaluations, severe reductions in government subsidies and employment, and an increased reliance on liberal free-market measures.[239] Government ministries were merged and given smaller, restrictive budgets at a time when social needs were greater than ever before. Enrollment in Social Security rose from 122,597 to 286,495 between 1979 and 1989, while people receiving pensions rose from 7,918 to 67,352.[240] MINVAH was phased out completely, leaving home repair and reconstruction largely to the private sector.

Between 1984 and 1986, the government ceased favoring the public sector through agrarian reform. State property holdings fell

---

238 "Nicaragua – The Regional Peace Effort."
239 Walker, Thomas W., *Revolution and Counterrevolution in Nicaragua*, 201.
240 Ibid., 202.

from 1.3 million manzanas[241] to 948,000 manzanas by the late 1980s, and uses of private property included collective, semicollective and individual modes of production. By freeing internal markets, the government encouraged the opening of peasant stores, which provided crucial goods to people in rural areas. Efforts were made to substitute the production and sale of cheap exports for traditional peasant staples, in hopes of garnering foreign exchange to cover fiscal expenditures, address payments on foreign debt and balance-of-payment problems.

But 1988 and 1989 were years of deep recession. According to Walker, three major problems were: "unprecedented peacetime levels of negative real growth, hyperinflation and severe external imbalance."[242] The first was due to wartime destruction, the second involved low production and, in the third case, imports outstripped exports by nearly $600 million. Rampant inflation required currency devaluations and the nation's external debt rose from $1.6 billion in 1979 to $6 billion by 1986.

From 1981, austerity and efficiency became economic imperatives. Nonmilitary spending was cut from 23.5 percent of GDP in 1984 to 16.5 percent in 1987. To combat hyperinflation, the government strove to increase exports, contain domestic demand, and cut the fiscal deficit from 24 percent to 10 percent of GDP. Ortega was forced to relax price controls and dismantle the National System of Wages and Labor.[243] "Shock treatment" also required a new cordoba, valued 1,000 times greater, which contracted the money supply by an estimated 10 percent concurrent with an official devaluation of 10 new cordobas to the dollar, followed by a maxi-devaluation of 80 new cordobas to the dollar. The merging of public sector ministries eliminated 8,000 jobs.

In the short run, these measures dampened inflation, but prices were driven up by 600 percent due to local shortages of goods. Unions saw no choice but to protest when the average wage declined to 7 percent of minimum consumption. But the government wasn't done.

It resorted to further devaluations, the nearly complete elimination of price controls and subsidies, credit rationing in favor of private producers, and credit indexation to establish real interest rates. This:

---

241 One manzana is the equivalent of 1.6 acres.
242 Ibid., 248.
243 Ibid., 263.

...essentially opened the economy fully to the operation of market forces, but without popular mobilization in support of the measures and without a clear indication of the long-run gains to be won from such IMF-style austerity. Carlos Vilas suggested it was the worst of both worlds, undergoing the austerity of an IMF package without the benefits of receiving the external financial assistance.[244]

Ortega was under extreme pressure to hold new elections, which he scheduled for the fall of 1990, hoping the U.S. would halt non-military aid to the contras but resume bilateral and multilateral aid to Nicaragua.

The UNO Victory

Between 1984 and 1988, the NED (American National Endowment for Democracy) channeled $1.9 million in aid to non-Sandinista political parties, private sector and religious groups, trade unions and the media. In mid-1989, the amount increased to $3.5 million, as appropriated by Congress.[245]

Opponents of the Sandinistas created the National Opposition Union (Union Nacional Opositora – UNO) from twelve conservative and liberal parties, plus two communist factions. In mid-1989, they fielded Violeta Barrios de Chamorro (publisher of *La Prensa* and former member of the ruling junta), as their presidential candidate for the 1990 elections.

The FSLN framed the UNO as supporters of Somocismo and U.S. imperialism, in hopes that Nicaraguan nationalism would carry it through the polls. The UNO, on the other hand, promised peace and prosperity while claiming the Sandinistas had destroyed the Nicaraguan economy. In the end, Violeta de Chamorro won 55 percent of the popular vote against FSLN Daniel Ortega's 41 percent.

The FSLN cooperated to make Chamorro's succession peaceful, but abuses did occur. According to the U.S. Library of Congress:

> Sandinista bureaucrats systematically ransacked government offices and gave government assets to loyal government supporters, destroyed records; consolidated many of the government agencies...and passed legislature to protect their interests once they were ousted from government.[246]

244 Ibid, 264.

245 Arnson, Cynthia J., 235.

246 "Nicaragua – The UNO Electoral Victory," Library of Congress, http://countrystudies.us/nicaragua/19.htm.

Before leaving office, the FSLN granted "full and unconditional amnesty" to those who had committed crimes "against the public order and the internal or external security of the state." This covered their own crimes as well as the opposition's and was justified as the means to block political reprisals. Also passed were labor acts to limit rights of dismissal. Danilo Aguirre said, "To leave [the workers] without a new labor code would not only be an irresponsible act, but for a revolutionary, treason against the working class, and the FSLN can't do that."[247] Lastly, FSLN property laws gave all owners, including organizations, full title to their land, whether confiscated or not. For President Chamorro, all three measures would prove controversial.

The Policies of Chamorro

Neoliberal transitions stemming from top-down dissemination typically begin with multilateral institutions. Encouraged by the U.S., this is how they work:

> The IMF and the World Bank facilitate the movement toward economic reform both by disseminating the classical liberal ideology and by providing partial financing of the structural adjustment process. The U.S. government directly supports this transition through USAID programs and the zealous promotion of free trade...But the U.S. government and international financial institutions cannot simply dictate policy reform. A crucial mechanism through which external actors wield influence is the training of a domestic technocratic elite that links local and international economic actors. This insular elite...mediates the transfer of the economic ideology and associated policy prescriptions as it oversees the local initiation and implementation of the policy reform.[248]

Multilateral and bilateral funds accompany U.S. strong-arming to "ease the pain of transition." Spalding then explains why authoritarian rulers are most successful with reforms:

> To succeed in this effort, the economic team needs firm support from the president and a political system weighted heavily toward executive control. If the executive branch is too weak, the dispersal of power through a series of institutions that compete for control can give opponents of the neoliberal project an instrument through which to block the reform. When the legislature serves as an effective check on presidential dominance, powerful groups may succeed in diverting the economic

247 Close, David, *Nicaragua: The Chamorro Years* (Boulder, CO: Lynne Reinner, 1999) 48.

248 Spalding, Rose J., 158.

program by riddling it with exemptions and loopholes, if not derailing the project altogether. Centralization of political authority in the hands of the executive, on the other hand, allows a president committed to the new agenda to pursue it with fewer impediments. The ability of the president to rule in effect by decree, in spite of any formal divisions of power or constitutional constraints, fosters the implementation of economic restructuring. Neoliberal reform is also promoted when executive power extends deep into the bureaucracy, which otherwise could undermine the effort.[249]

The hardships imposed by neoliberal reforms require mass organizations and anti-statist ideology to be successfully overcome, which means labor must be weakened and opposition silenced. Here's why:

> Various groups in civil society, including both popular sectors and privileged elites, will have reason to object to the new economic model. The immediate, and often longer-term, impact of the neoliberal project is the withdrawal of economic supports that have buffered important segments of the popular classes. Subsidies on basic goods and services are terminated, causing price hikes; wage indexation is eliminated, allowing real wages to tumble; agrarian reform land may be returned to former owners or made available for sale, fostering reconcentration of the land; public sector employment is cut, leading to a ripple of job loss in adjacent sectors; and import competition increases, resulting in a loss of industrial jobs. There is a strong tendency for popular groups to resist paying the high social costs of the transition to free market capitalism.[250]

Nicaragua's neoliberal supporters included the Bush administration, its technocratic advisors, and multilateral institutions. To the advantage of reform, the country's political power also remained concentrated within the presidency, a concentration that was militantly opposed under Sandinista rule).

In 1990, Chamorro received foreign loans and donations totaling U.S. $456 million, $1.3 billion in 1991, and another $800 million for 1992. By then, Nicaragua had received U.S. $450 million through the World Bank, IMF and IDB.[251]

Nicaragua was devastated when Chamorro came to power. With a per capita GDP of U.S. $500, it was one of the poorest nations in the entire Western Hemisphere, and more than half the la-

---

249 Ibid., 158.
250 Ibid.
251 Ibid., 161.

bor force was either unemployed or underemployed.[252] Chamorro's opposition stemmed from labor, big business, the contras and confiscados (people whose land was seized).

Resistance to job loss, repeated devaluations and industrial privatization provoked strikes in May and July of 1990, in March, April and May of 1991, in November of 1992, in June and September of 1993, and in August and November of 1995.[253] Promised blocks of privatized shares were delayed in delivery, and wages didn't compensate for the inflation of import prices under devaluations. Unemployment of 60 percent rose to 89 percent across rural areas.[254]

Health programs, previously free, began imposing user fees. And formerly subsidized services, such as water, light, electricity, public transportation and telephones now charged market rates.

To deal with the confiscados, Chamorro processed 5,384 claims for the return of over 15,000 expropriated urban and rural properties, and issued 1,000 certificates of devolution to ex-Somozas before suspending the process amid accusations of mismanagement and corruption.[255]

The contras (now called the recontras) refused to disarm and reintegrate unless FSLN-member Humberto Ortega was dismissed as army chief. By keeping Ortega, however, Chamorro won the power to downsize defense. So she created a contra resettlement zone of 25,000 hectares, with a promise to build schools, hospitals and infrastructure.[256]

As recontra uprisings continued, demobilized Sandinistas (calling themselves recompas) took up arms again. They fought from 1991 until 1992, when common grievances against the government led them to join forces, calling their new group revueltos.[257]

The End of the Chamorro Regime

Repression was not an option because the military Sandinistas sympathized with the people, so Violeta held Nicaragua together through collective bargaining tactics and by reducing the fiscal deficit to 8% of GDP.

---

252 "Nicaragua Introduction," http://workmall.com/wfb2001/nicaragua/nicaragua_history_introduction.html.

253 Close, David, 77.

254 Ibid., 99.

255 Spalding, Rose, 165.

256 Close, David, 95.

257 "Nicaragua Introduction."

She was criticized increasingly for cooperation with the FSLN, until the UNO coalition divided into two factions. The faction of Alfredo Cesar Aguirre demanded a complete break from military Sandinistas. The other preferred cooperation with the FSLN, under Antonio Lacayo Oyanguren. Members of the U.S. Senate backed Aguirre's faction and threatened to freeze aid if the FSLN remained.

In 1992, Aguirre attacked Humberto Ortega, the commander of the national army, and high-ranking police officials, even as he accused Lacayo of fraud and embezzling government funds. In what many viewed as a coup, Aguirre declared himself president of the National Assembly.

The U.S. then froze $116 million in aid, pending restructuring of the police.

Chamorro sacked top leaders of the Sandinista police and, using executive powers, authorized the military to seize the congressional building and remove Aguirre as president. She appointed a provisional administration to serve until new elections, but, in the process, lost the support of her entire political base.[258]

In 1996, Arnoldo Aleman, former mayor of Managua and leader of the Liberal Constitutionalist Party (PLC), defeated FSLN leader Daniel Ortega at the polls.

The Aleman–Bolanos Reforms

President Aleman and Vice President Enrique Bolanos Geyer were inaugurated on January 10, 1997. Although their election was marred by allegations of corruption, Aleman had strong support from right-wing groups in and outside Nicaragua, which helped him to further economic progress. The country suffered Hurricane Mitch in 1998, but Aleman and his presidential successor Bolanos still managed to achieve the following reforms:

1. The army was cut by three-fourths.

2. 351 government-owned businesses were privatized, as 30 percent of GDP.

3. Voluntary retirement was introduced for public employees.

4. Defense outlays fell from 14 percent of GDP to less than 3 percent.

5. Between 1990 and 1999, public sector employment was reduced from 285,000 employees to 80,000.

---

258 Ibid.

6. In 1995, regulatory institutions were created for telecommunications and energy.

7. In 1997, water and sewerage were regulated.

8. Public service rates were revised, with gradual adjustments to recover long-run marginal costs.

9. In 1998, the National Assembly approved laws to privatize the government telephone company (ENITEL) and liberalize exploration and sale of hydrocarbons.

10. In 1997, the law of the government-owned electricity company (ENEL) was modified to permit private sector participation.

11. In 1991, the first private bank (after the reestablishment of democracy), began to operate. The Superintendency of Banks was also reestablished and reform of the Central Bank restored its autonomy. Ceilings on interest rates were abolished, reserve requirements restored, and laws mandating Central Bank financing of the fiscal deficit and state banks abolished.

12. Government-owned export trading monopolies were abolished to encourage private exports, under a realistic exchange rate and lower import tariffs. The highest nominal import tariff rate was reduced from 60 percent to 10 percent in 1999. The extensive price controls of the 1980s were abolished.[259]

13. From 1994–1999, real GDP grew at an annual average rate of 4.8 percent. Foreign investment came back, with private capital inflows almost doubling from $97 million in 1996 to $184 million in 1998. FI peaked at $300 million in 1999 and dropped to $265 million in 2000. Inflows fell to $132 million in 2001, and then to $95 million in 2002.[260]

Even so, the United Nations Development Program (UNDP) reported that as of June, 1994:

> 74.8 percent of Nicaraguan families lived in poverty, with 43.6 percent in extreme poverty or indigence. Total unemployment (official unemployment plus underemployment) reached 60 percent of the economically active population, affecting principally youth and women.[261]

---

259 "A Strengthened Poverty Reduction Strategy," Government of Nicaragua, August 2000, 14-15.

260 "Nicaragua FOREIGN INVESTMENT," http;//www.nationsencyclo-pedia.com/Americas/Nicaagua-FOREIGN INVESTMENT.html.

261 Ibid.

Once-cured diseases returned with a vengeance, and suicides set a record in 1997.

Self-Reproducing Debt and North–South Conflict

Economic growth did not reach the population because loans from multilateral institutions were used to retire old debt. According to a paper entitled "The IMF and Financial Sector Reform in Nicaragua":

> [M]uch of the foreign aid upon which Nicaragua remained highly dependent—between 1991 and 1995, foreign assistance represented an annual average of 29.9 percent of GDP—"leaked" abroad as interest payments and amortization of foreign debt. During the first half of the decade, an annual average of 12 percent of GDP flowed back out of the country. Despite these payments, by the end of 1995 the country carried the highest level of foreign debt as a percentage of GDP in the world, so that, for every dollar produced, five dollars were owed in foreign debt.[262]

In sum, there was little or no debt reduction. Xabier Gorostiaga, S.J. (an economist and rector of the Central American University in Managua) claimed Latin America's foreign debt was $250 billion in 1980. Latin American countries paid off $285 billion within the prior decade, but the debt still increased to $450 billion. In Gorostiaga's words, "the debt reproduces itself and forces us to increase our exports without getting the benefit of that increase."[263]

Gorostiaga decries Nicaragua's "champagne-cup democracy," where 20 percent of the nation controls 83 percent of its product, while the middle classes are shrinking and 60 percent of the people survive on six percent of GNP. To him, the chances of real democracy coming to Nicaragua are slim, if they even exist. If achieved, the South's first demand would be to democratize the World Bank, IMF and United Nations. "For the North," Gorostiaga says, "his would be an unacceptable demand...I don't have a crystal ball, but I think a serious North–South confrontation before the end of the century is very probable...That is why the North is in a very serious crisis. It is being challenged by the cultures and civilizations of the South, by the majority of the world's population."[264]

262 "The IMF and Financial Sector Reform in Nicaragua," http://www.developmentgap.org/imfnicaragua.html.

263 "Struggling for Survival in the Global Marketplace," EPICA, http://www.epica.org/Library/globalization/marketplace.htm.

264 "Struggling for Survival in the Global Marketplace," EPICA, http://www.epica.org/Library/globalization/marketplace.htm.

Gorostiaga's fear is not unique. The IMF, World Bank and other multilateral institutions have been beset with complaints and grievances since the onset of the Structural Adjustment Program. Public unrest over reform has unseated two different governments (Indonesia and Argentina). This, combined with the threat of insurgency, produced a new "human face" for Structural Adjustment Programs. Multilateral institutions began to insist on Strategic Poverty Reduction Papers for continuance of loans, and also introduced 100 percent debt relief under the HIPC initiative (for Highly Indebted Poor Countries) in 2005.

Aleman Charged With Corruption

In August 2002, Aleman was charged with participation in a $100 million fraud during his presidential term. Broadcast live on national television, evidence revealed that Aleman's close family and friends were also involved in the scheme. This came after President Enrique Bolanos swore to fight corruption at all levels in January 1992.[265]

In the decision of Judge Juana Mendez, the following were implicated in Aleman's money laundering:

- Amelia Aleman – former president Aleman's sister
- Alvaro Aleman – former president Aleman's brother
- Mayra Estrada de Aleman – Alvaro Aleman's wife
- Arnoldo Aleman Estrada – Mayra and Alvaro Aleman's son
- Alfredo Fernandez – former president Aleman's secretary
- Byron Jerez Solis – former Chief of Department of Taxes
- Ethel Gonzalez de Jerez – Byron Jerez' wife
- Valeria Jerez Gonzalez – Byron Jerez' daughter
- Esteban Duque Estrada – former Minister of Finance
- Jorge Solis Farias – former president of ENITEL[266]

Over 80,000 people signed a petition to strip Aleman of immunity. In retaliation, Aleman forced the parliament to block an IMF-mandated program for fiscal reform.

Since Nicaragua could not receive further IMF funds until the program was implemented, Bolanos stood to lose his fight in the interest of economic stability. Nor did the IMF soften its stance to

---

265 Korsgaard, Christian, "Ex-president Aleman charged with corruption," *MS Central America,* http://www.ms.dk/sw4260.asp.

266 Korsgaard, Christian, "Nicaragua facing political chaos," *MS Central America,* http://www.ms.dk/sw4246.asp.

encourage anti-corruption. To the Nicaraguan people, the IMF was co-responsible for the Aleman scandal. It made more stringent demands of Bolanos than it had of Aleman, demanding government cuts and increased revenue even during recession. Ana Quiros from the independent NGO Coordinadora Civil gave this analysis of the IMF's position:

> [T]he IMF was during the reign of Aleman so afraid of a return to power of the leftist Sandinistas that irregularities and corruption were permitted. It is a repetition of the US philosophy during the Somoza dynasty in our country, when Franklin D. Roosevelt said that "yes, he's a son of a bitch, but he's our son of a bitch". The IMF deliberately pretended not to see what was happening.[267]

A Strengthened Poverty Reduction Strategy

Despite the introduction of Strategic Poverty Reduction Strategies, the plight of the poor did not improve. In 1999, Nicaragua showed six percent economic growth, but 44 percent of the populace lived on less than a dollar a day. Too, this economic growth was predicated on the loss of 100,000 jobs, wage freezes and the loss of health care services.[268]

Nicaragua released its "Strengthened Poverty Reduction Strategy" in August of 2000, placing the blame for the poor on "a mismanaged effort to create a command economy, inconsistent fiscal and monetary policies, and a civil war"—all events of the 1980s, for which it blamed the Sandinistas (who did more for the poor than any other regime) more than a decade after they fell. According to the SPRS, Nicaraguans in the 1990s had the same per capita income they had earned in the 1950s.[269] By 1998:

> ...almost 48 percent of Nicaragua's citizens remained in poverty, 17.3 percent in extreme poverty...Over a fifth of the poor remain unemployed, almost twice the national average. Underemployment is even worse—a third of the poor are underemployed; one out of two poor females is underemployed...Their access to safe water, to electricity, sanitation, and even roads is usually half or less the access levels of the non-poor....almost 30 percent of the poor are illiterate; they average just over 3 years of schooling, more than 50 percent below the national average...over 30 per-

267 Korsgaard, Christian, "International community is co-responsible," *MS Central America*, http://www.ms.dk/sw4255.asp.

268 "Nicaragua – Economic Growth Amid Poverty and Corruption," LatAm, http://ips.org/geneva/solidarity/nic0906a.html.

269 "A Strengthened Poverty Reduction Strategy."

cent of poor children, and 40 percent of extremely poor children are malnourished.[270]

In response, the SPRS was based upon four pillars:

1. A continued modernization of the state to increase both its focus and efficiency in providing services to the poor

- which will require a real GDP growth rate of 5.5 percent over the next 5 years, entailing further moves toward a private sector-driven market economy.
- This includes plans for privatization of electricity, telephone, water, and port services, and specific actions to encourage agricultural expansion, including rural infrastructure.

2. A complementary promotion of greater equity by increasing the access of the poor to the benefits of growth, with special emphasis on rural communities, women, indigenous groups, and residents of the Atlantic Coast

- This includes improvement in the coverage, quality, and integration of public education, health, nutrition, and population services, mostly in rural areas.
- Also, more and better-staffed rural health posts and centers will improve the health of the poor.

3. More transparency and accountability through participatory processes that include targeted communities, beneficiaries, and local leaders

- This will require strengthening public institutions and developing a greater understanding of the poor's vulnerabilities.
- There will also be a transfer of responsibility to some local governments.

4. A broader participation of all members of Nicaraguan society in the SPRS.

- This will include, among others, laws to improve access to government information, laws to extend modern governmental procurement practices throughout the public sector, laws to standardize the national and local civil service, and laws to modernize the penal code.
- The government will also train judges, regulators, and other public servants, restructuring obsolete procedures and institutions.[271]

---

270 Ibid., v.
271 Ibid., vi.

The government projected that implementation would cost U.S. $1.1 billion in capital spending during 2001–2003,[272] which would have to be funded by donors. Too, it could not be undertaken without HIPC debt relief of an annual U.S. $100 million after 2001.

For its progress to be measured, the government set targets:

Target 1:	Reduce extreme poverty by 25 percent by the year 2005.
Target 2:	Increase the net primary school enrollment rate from 75 percent to 85 percent by the year 2005.
Target 3:	Reduce the maternal mortality rate from 148 to 129 per 100,000 live births by the year 2005.
Target 4:	Reduce the infant mortality rate from 40 to 32 per 1,000 live births and mortality of children under five years of age from 50 to 37 per 1,000 live births by the year 2005.
Target 5:	Increase access to reproductive services to individuals of appropriate age.
Target 6:	Implementation of a strategy for sustainable ecological development by the year 2005.
Target 7:	Reduce chronic malnutrition in children under 5 to 17 percent by 2002 from 19.9 percent, to 13 percent by 2005 and to 7 percent by 2015.
Target 8:	Between 1999 and 2000, increase the national coverage of access to water to 75.5 percent from 66.5 percent and the national access to sanitation to 50.2 percent from 36 percent. Increase access to safe water and sanitation in rural, dispersed areas to 54 percent from 39 percent by 2005 and access to sewerage in urban areas to 47.3 percent from 33.6 percent.
Target 9:	Reduce the illiteracy rate to 17 percent by 2002 from 19 percent in 1998, and to 10 percent in 2015.*

* Ibid., 21-24.

Measured by these standards, there was no significant change by October of 2002. Instead, the Nicaraguan Institute of Statistics and Censuses revealed that 60 percent of Nicaraguans (just over three million) could not cover their basic requirements, and of these, one million suffered extreme distress.[273]

---

272 One eighth of then-current GDP.

273 "Three Million Nicaraguans Below the Poverty Line," Nicaragua Network Hotline, 21 October 2002, http://www.hartford-hwp.com/

In November of 2002, the IMF required the government to implement school autonomy legislation to reduce national funding. Parents would have to pay for textbooks, supplies, uniforms, and user fees or keep their children out of school. This, despite the fact that, at the time, U.S. law required the U.S. IMF executive director to vote against any loans that introduced user fees for education or health.[274]

Punishing Nicaragua?

By September 2003, U.S. aid dropped to an annual average of $38 million, fueling the impression that Nicaragua was still being punished "for having attempted to obtain its independence and exercise its right to self-determination." In the words of Toni Solo, "The U.S. subsidizes its own industries at record levels, but is rigidly free-market with Nicaragua." It destroyed the network of cooperative farms through "lack of access to credit, spiraling costs, and stagnant or falling prices." In the aftermath, "hundreds of destitute families camped out for months on the roads leading to the coffee growing areas, pleading for work. Television showed pictures of children in Matagalpa, the coffee capital, with levels of starvation usually associated with Africa."[275]

Nicaragua's health care system is impoverished and, due to privatization, the cost of utilities skyrocketed, forcing many Nicaraguan families even deeper into debt. After a slight increase in 1997, wages were frozen. Now most people subsist on U.S. $2.00 per day.

To help their families, 40 percent of school-age children do not attend classes, and 65 percent never finish secondary education. In the maquilas of the Las Mercedes Free Trade Zone, Nicaraguan women work in foreign-owned garment factories for *49 cents an hour*.[276]

Toni Solo concludes:

arhcives/47/437.html.

274 "IMF Loan Conditions for Nicaragua Require Privatization Measures That Would Enrich Corporations at the Expense of the People," *Public Citizen*, 4 December 2002, http://www.hartford-hwp.com/archives/47/413.html.

275 Solo, Toni, "Neoliberal Nicaragua is a Neo-Banana Republic," *Z Magazine*, http://www.thirdworldtraveler.com/Central_America/Neo_LIberal_Nicaragua.html.

276 "Country vignettes: Nicaragua," Solidarity Network, http://www.maquilasolidarity.org/resources/maquilas/nicargua.htm.

[M]ost people in Nicaragua are worse off than they were 20 years ago. The Clinton and Bush Jr. regimes intervened decisively to ensure the elections of Arnoldo Aleman and Enrique Bolanos; one a crook, the other a stooge. Under the aegis of the U.S. and the World Bank, these proxies, and Violeta Chamorro before them, put in place the disastrous policies that have reduced most Nicaraguans to ever-deepening penury. The hopes of the poor majority for a decent life have disappeared. The sign at the end of the neoliberal route for Nicaragua reads loud and clear: "Dead end. Made in the U.S.A."[277]

The World Bank and the IMF

In March of 2003, the World Bank announced it would supply Nicaragua with project and investment loans of between $120 and $160 million, including a $15 million Programmatic Structural Adjustment Credit (PSAC). This was to help the country with its Poverty Reduction Strategy, which was submitted to the World Bank and International Monetary Fund in September of 2001, because poverty still affected 45.8 percent of the people, with the situation made worse by Hurricane Mitch (1998), the crisis in international coffee prices, and drought and migration in recent years. The World Bank prioritized the following:

1. Promoting faster growth by raising productivity and improving competitiveness in the private sector;

2. Upgrading the country's productive infrastructure, especially in rural areas;

3. Expanding human capital through investments in basic health and primary education;

4. Building expertise and efficiency in the public sector, and fighting corruption; and

5. Developing a social protection program for the poor and most vulnerable.[278]

The World Bank promoted cooperation with the IFC (International Finance Corporation), which claimed that impediments to private investment were weaknesses in the financial sector, property rights, and corporate and legal governance.

In the same month, the IMF threatened to cut off funding, based on a budget revision submitted to the national legislature by Presi-

---

277 Ibid.

278 "Nicaragua – Country Assistance Strategy," World Bank, http://web.worldbank.org/WBSITE/EXTERNAL/COUNTRIES/LACEXT/NICARAGUA.

dent Bolanos. The appropriations at issue were a small wage raise for public and civil servants and money for the Institute for Rural Development, the Emergency Social Investment Fund, and the Nicaraguan Institute for Municipal Development. The legislature also eliminated an interest payment of $24.5 million that was due on the internal debt of $1.69 billion. The last was controversial because most of Nicaragua's internal debt was owed to private banks (President Bolanos' biggest supporters). These banks charged 20 percent interest while defaulting on tax payments of $200 million.[279]

As one reporter noted:

> [T]he reaction from much of civil society and within the assembly to the threats from the IMF was quick and furious. Alejandro Bendana, director of the Center for International Studies quipped, "We have never elected the IMF to be our government." Likewise, an FSLN deputy, Roberto Gonzalez, complained, "We are not the deputies of the IMF, or of the WB [World Bank]; we serve the people, and that is why, with this budget, we are trying to create initiatives that improve the conditions of the people."

The Nicaraguan Center for Human Rights (CENIDH) released this statement:

> Since 1990, a succession of Nicaraguan governments has made agreements with the IMF on the backs of the Nicaraguan people. None of these has led to any improvement; rather the overall quality of life for the majority has been constantly deteriorating. The Nicaraguan people are the victims of a new dictatorship, that of the IMF, which imposes fundamentalist economic models through authoritarian and anti-democratic means. These models serve only to deepen our dependence and under-development.[280]

Although Bolanos and the legislature compromised, the IMF took a rigid stand on water privatization, which was under a moratorium due to public resistance. Unless Nicaragua privatized, it would, again, be in noncompliance with the IMF program.

On December 21, 2005, the IMF issued a press release concerning 100 percent debt relief for 19 countries under the Multilateral Debt Relief Initiative (MDRI). In addition to Nicaragua, the countries chosen for debt relief included Benin, Bolivia, Burkina Faso, Cambodia, Ethiopia, Ghana, Guyana, Honduras, Madagascar, Mali,

---

279 "Nicaragua: IMF Threatens Nicaragua with aid cut-off," *Central America/Mexico Report*, March 2003, http://www.rtfcam.org/report/ volume_23/No_1/article_2htm.
280 Ibid.

Mozambique, Niger, Rwanda, Senegal, Tajikistan, Tanzania, Uganda and Zambia.[281]

Nearly half the countries chosen for debt relief were formerly socialist. Just as many were authoritarian. In the former, the program may discourage reversion. In the latter, pro-Western states have been attacked by groups like Jubilee South and the Latin American Solidarity Coalition for incurring external debt by extra-legal means. Therefore, the IMF responded to two sets of criticisms, attempting to change its image.

Debt relief offers hopeful prospects and we should definitely applaud that. But if we put it in perspective, Nicaragua sought war reparations after U.S. support of the contras in the amount of $18 billion, long before it was offered relief in the amount of $6.7 billion.

---

281 "IMF to Extend 100 Percent Debt Relief for 19 Countries Under the Multilateral Debt Relief Initiative," IMF, http://imf.org/external/np/sec/pr/2005/pr05286.htm.

CHAPTER FOURTEEN: EL SALVADOR — THE MILITARY AND THE OLIGARCHY

In 1524, a Spanish expedition led by Pedro de Alvarado reached El Salvador. It was met with resistance by the Pipil (descendants of the nomadic Nahua, who were conquered by the Mayans). Defeated in 1524, the Spaniards returned in 1525 and 1528 to finally subdue the Pipil. They were seeking mineral wealth, which they did not find. Instead, their source of wealth became *encomienda* tribute, a system under which the natives, who lived on communal lands, supplied the Spaniards with goods and services. This process grew so abusive that the clergy replaced *encomienda* tribute with the *repartimiento* system.

For slave wages, the natives worked plantations for the export of cacao and indigo. Meanwhile, Crown grants of land transformed the Spaniards and *criollos* into a traditional oligarchy. The capital city of San Salvador became the second city of the Captaincy (or Kingdom) of Guatemala.

The natives were denied literacy and even subsistence farming. They perished on a large scale due to European diseases. The surviving mix of Mestizos suffered greatly from deprivation.

Independence

El Salvadoran independence was achieved through a collective movement of Guatemala, Honduras, Nicaragua and Costa Rica, which broke free of the Spanish Crown on September 15, 1821. Like Nicaragua, El Salvador was briefly conquered by Mexico's emperor Agustin de Iturbide, after which it joined the United Provinces of Central America on July 1, 1823.

The federation was first ruled by liberals who favored foreign investment, a laissez-faire economy and non-privileged Church. However, their social, political and economic reforms were reversed in 1826 by conservatives seeking protectionism and the supremacy of the Church. In 1829, Francisco Morazan restored liberal control.

Despite strong support for war against conservative Guatemala, Morazon was defeated in March 1840 and El Salvador withdrew from the Federation in January of 1841. It then maintained independence, although attempts were made to form the Greater Republic of Central America (Republica Mayor Centroamerica) from 1895 to 1898.

The Coffee Republic

Between 1871 and 1927, liberals dominated El Salvador and made coffee their primary export. Land concentration became greater than ever, until one hundred families owned the bulk of the land. A mere 14 families controlled the country's wealth.

To support the coffee growers, the government constructed roads, railroads and port facilities. It also abolished communal lands and passed anti-vagrancy laws to ensure that sufficient labor was available to farms.[282] In 1833, an indigenous uprising led by Anastasio Aquino was put down by troops hired by the landowners.

Instead of taxing exports, the government taxed the consumption of imports by those who were well-off. Because this taxation was offset by spending on infrastructure and the creation of a National Guard (Guardia Nacional – GN) to keep the workers under control, the wealthy did not contest it. From 1921 on, the Guardia Nacional provided security to coffee growers. Each farm had a Guardia unit, and farm-owners paid regional commanders to guarantee the loyalty of their troops.

In these years, President Santiago Gonzalez (1871) was an unsuccessful autocrat. What followed was a flurry of takeovers, noted only to demonstrate frequency.

---

282 "Chapter 1A. Historical Setting," *Countries of the World*, January 1, 1991, http://www.highbeam.com/library/doc3.asp?DOCID=1P1:28384241&num=15&ctrlInfo.

Guatemala overthrew El Salvador's Andres Valle in 1876. In 1885, President Rafael Zaldivar was ousted by force. His opponent, Francisco Menendez, was overthrown and executed by General Carlos Erzeta in 1890. Erzeta was ousted by Rafael Gutierrez in 1894. Gutierrez was replaced by General Tomas Regalado in the bloodless coup of 1898. Regalado peacefully transferred power to Pedro Jose Escalon in 1903. Escalon was followed by Fernando Figueroa in 1907. President Manuel Enrique Araujo was assassinated in 1913. President Carlos Melendez was succeeded by his brother Jorge, who then chose his brother-in-law Alfonso Quinonez Molina to rule.[283] Carlos, Jorge, and Alfonso institutionalized the supremacy of the landed oligarchy. Each them belonged to the powerful Coffee Growers Association (Asociacion Cafetalera).

Quinonez created Liga Roja (a network of armed vigilante groups), which he paid to fix votes, disperse demonstrations and report on subversive developments. In 1922, the Liga Roja and the National Guard killed many, including female market sellers who protested price changes determined by the exchange rate.[284]

Labor and Politics

After the formation of the Central American Congress of Workers in 1911, organizational proliferation culminated in the Great Confederation of Workers of El Salvador (COES), to which 200 union delegates contributed. More radical union organizers from Guatemala and Mexico promoted political groups, like the El Salvadorean Communist Party (Partido Comunista de El Salvador – PCS), the Anti-Imperialist League and the Red Aid International (Socorro Rojo Internacional – SRI).

One of the communists, Augustin Farabundo Marti (el Negro), was expelled from El Salvador for radical activism. He returned in 1925 to join the Regional Federation of Salvadorean Workers, and was promptly re-expelled. When Marti returned a second time, President Pio Romero Bosque had him jailed. Marti went on a hunger strike, until support from the General Association of Salvadorean University Students (AGEUS) convinced the President to release him. Marti then traveled to Nicaragua, where he joined Augusto Cesar Sandino to fight a guerrilla war against U.S. forces.

---

283 Ibid.

284 Dunkerley, James, *The Long War: Dictatorship and Revolution in El Salvador* (London: Junction Books, 1982) 20.

Unable to convert Sandino to communism, Marti returned again to El Salvador.

President Romero Bosque (Don Pio) tolerated unions until campesino organization (involving over 80,000 people) compromised the oligarchy. He then banned demonstrations, rallies and leftist literature and, in protest, the peasants signed a petition. Don Pio had most of them jailed, and the Campaign for the Liberation of Political Prisoners was formed. However, more repression followed. Over 1,200 were jailed between November 1930 and February 1931.[285] One of them was Marti, who was then re-expelled.

For the first time in El Salvador, Don Pio extended the political system in 1919.[286] Leftist parties were not allowed to run, but the military and oligarchy accepted a semi-reformist president, renowned for paying his workers double the going rate. President Arturo Araujo's speech to the second congress of the COES, made him a friend of peasants and workers.

Between 1928 and 1931, coffee export prices fell by 54 percent, and agricultural wages were cut.[287] Food production, which coffee had always crowded out, declined even more, and the depth of deprivation became inhumane.

Because of his popularity and extravagant campaign promises, the oligarchy refused to participate in Araujo's government. Araujo then betrayed the peasants and workers, which led to social unrest. Repression failed and necessitated concessions. Araujo scheduled municipal elections for December, 1931 and allowed participation by the leftist PCS. This proved too much for the oligarchy, and also aroused the military. The result was a coup d'état by junior military officers, who placed Araujo's vice president, General Maximiliano Hernandez Martinez, in the presidency.

Martinez and la Matanza

The elections went forward and the PCS participated, but Martinez refused to certify the outcome for the PCS. Denied a path to power, the PCS planned a revolt. Its leaders were arrested and the

---

285 Montgomery, Tommie Sue, *Revolution in El Salvador: From Civil Strife to Civil Peace*, 2nd ed. (Boulder, CO: Westview Press, 1995) 35.

286 Baloyra, Enrique A., *El Salvador in Transition* (Chapel Hill, NC: University of North Carolina Press, 1982) 8.

287 "El Salvador: Chapter 1B. Economic Crisis and Repression," *Countries of the World*, January 1, 1991, http://www.highbeam.com/library/doc3.asp? DOCID=1P1:28384242&num=40&ctrlInfo.

uprising that followed induced *la matanza* (an official massacre), leaving 10,000 to 30,000 dead. The government regained control in towns where insurgents held power (only 10 percent of which rebelled).[288] Marti and two students were subsequently tried and killed.

News of the uprising brought three U.S. warships and two Canadian vessels into El Salvador's waters. A U.S. Marine platoon was offered to quell the disturbance. But President Martinez, whom the U.S. did not recognize because his position stemmed from a coup, replied that there was no need, so the offer was withdrawn.[289]

The shock of *la matanza* reverberated throughout El Salvador. To the oligarchy, violence against communism was appropriate — never mind that the insurgency stemmed from hunger rather than politics. Campesino unions were outlawed, as were all political parties. Under President Martinez, 1932 marked the beginning of military rule.

Faced with financial difficulties, Martinez issued a debt moratorium (that affected a US $21 million loan), imposed protective tariffs, devalued the colon, and established the Banco Hipotecario and the Cajas de Credito Rural to provide credit to the oligarchy.[290] In moves opposed by the oligarchy, Martinez continued Araujo's policy of limited land reform and raised export taxes. Martinez tried to extend his rule by legislative fiat, and sparked a failed coup, as well as a general strike, which forced him to resign in May of 1944. In October, his successor, General Andres Ignacio Menendez, was overthrown by the military, but not before Menendez reinstated freedom of the press, abolished Martinez' secret police, and allowed other political parties to participate in his cabinet.

In 1945, Colonel Osmin Aguirre y Salinas manipulated elections in favor of General Salvador Castaneda Castro.[291] Castaneda allowed political organization and made limited reforms meant to appease the left. He issued a general political amnesty and undertook a reorganization of the government and the army. When reform proved ineffective, it caused another general strike that led to a state of siege until Castaneda was overthrown by another coup.

---

288 Stanley, William Deane, *The Protection Racket State: Elite Politics, Military Extortion, and Civil War in El Salvador* (Philadelphia: Temple University Press, 1996) 41.

289 Dunkerley, James, 29.

290 Baloyra, Enrique A., 11-12.

291 Anderson, Thomas P., *The War of the Dispossessed: Honduras and El Salvador, 1969* (Lincoln, NE: University of Nebraska Press, 1981) 26.

From 1931, politics in El Salvador followed the model provided by Tommie Sue Montgomery in her book *Revolution in El Salvador*:

- Consolidation of power by the new regime
- Growing intolerance of dissent and increasing repression
- Reaction from two quarters: the public and a progressive faction within the army officer corps, culminating ultimately in a
- Coup d'état, led, by progressive officers, that when successful led to
- Promulgation of various reforms
- Reemergence within the army of the most conservative faction, and
- Consolidation of that power once more.[292]

The coup leaders appointed three mid-level officers and two civilians to five-member junta called the Revolutionary Council. The Council was dominated by Major Oscar Osorio, who resigned in March, 1950 to run as the presidential candidate of the Revolutionary Party of Democratic Unification (Partido Revolucionario de Unificacion Democratica – PRUD). Osorio defeated Colonel Jose Asencio Menendez of the Renovating Action Party (Partido Accion Renovadora – PAR) and tried to establish the PRUD as the country's sole political force.

Limited Reform

In 1950, Osorio invested in social security, housing, health care and sanitation. He also initiated public works and tried to encourage industry, increase production and diversify agriculture. Cotton production rose from 9,800 harvested hectares in 1942 to 19,030 hectares in 1951. By 1965, 122,300 hectares were cultivated. This helped El Salvador break away from mono-crop agriculture, but, in the process, squatters and subsistence farmers were pushed off of the land.

Impoverishment also deepened under import substitution. Coffee profits invested in manufacturing created jobs for the people. But for every job gained, 100 jobs were lost. Nor could manufacturing prosper in a nonviable domestic market. The majority of the populace could not afford the output. Real land reform could have produced a class of small operators, but the oligarchy opposed this for fear it would threaten their interests.

---

292 Montgomery, Tommie Sue, 38.

In 1950, Osorio reformulated the constitution in line with state intervention to:

> ...assure all the inhabitants of the country an existence worthy of a human being, to guarantee the social function of property, and to regulate relations between labor and capital through limits on the working day, the right of association, collective contracts, and a formal minimum wage.[293]

Again, land reform was blocked.

To succeed him, Osorio chose Lieutenant Colonel Jose Maria Lemus, and visible army troops encouraged his election. President Lemus tried to emulate Osorio, but a drop in export prices limited government revenues and stalled further reform.

Repressing the Communists

Revolution in Cuba inspired El Salvador's peasants and workers to seek Lemus' overthrow after 1959. Students called for a true democratic transition, and the reply was more repression. Under banned free speech and expression, the dissidents were detained.

Fear within the military that Lemus was losing control led to a bloodless coup. On October 26, 1960 a second military–civilian junta included Fabio Castillo (a university professor and known Cuban sympathizer). The perceived threat of communism prompted the oligarchy and junior officers of the military to overthrow the new junta. From then on, El Salvador was controlled by anti-communist, anti-Castro politics, and Lieutenant Colonel Julio Adalberto Rivera was the only junta member to participate after its overthrow.

As a new force in El Salvador, the Christian Social Democrats (PDC) appealed to middle- and upper-class activists who sought economic growth and political stability. Jose Napoleon Duarte Fuentes (one of the PDCs founders), emphasized reform, application of moral principles to political and economic life, and the rejection of Marxism.[294]

To legitimize its government, the junta included the PDC. Those who wished to collaborate formed a splinter party, known as the PCN (National Conciliation Party). Running for the PCN, Lieutenant Colonel Julio Adalberto Rivera became president in 1961. His

---

293 Dunkerly, James, 35.

294 "El Salvador THE CHRISTIAN DEMOCRATS: A CENTRIST ALTERNATIVE?" Library of Congress, http://workmall.com/wfb2001/ el_salvador/el_salvador_history_the_christian_democrats.

only opponent was a donkey, sarcastically supplied by AGEUS (the student organization).

In 1963, the U.S. helped El Salvador create two organizations to combat communism. These were ORDEN (Organizacion Democratica Nacional), which was developed by the State Department, CIA and the Green Berets, and ANSESAL (the Salvadorean National Security Agency). Headed by General Jose Alberto Medrano, their complex, multi-tiered paramilitary and intelligence networks extended from the executive office to remote villages. ORDEN operated in rural areas to indoctrinate the peasants on the benefits of democracy. Communists were reported to ANSESAL, and ANSESAL worked with the president. Assassination was the remedy. Communists were killed by ORDEN, or by the army or National Guard. Sometimes the death squad Mano Blanca (White Hand) was responsible for the murders.[295]

Medrano's top protégés were Nicolds Carranza, Domingo Monterrosa, and Roberto D'Aubuisson, the last of whom would become widely known.

ORDEN claimed as "few" as 50,000 members and as many as 150,000. But not all members were loyal to the cause. Some peasants joined for protection from ORDEN patrols. Only 5 to 10 percent acted as ORDEN's eyes and ears.[296]

Political Pluralism and Economic Growth

In 1964, new rules called for proportional representation in the Legislative Assembly. This allowed the PDC to win fourteen seats in the Assembly and thirty-seven mayoralties. Duarte became mayor of San Salvador, and was then reelected in 1966 and 1968.

In 1967, the PCN, PDC, and PAR comprised the leading parties. The PAR was accused of communism and denied media access. The PDC was treated similarly. The PAR did better than the PDC, but the PCN's Colonel Fidel Sanchez Hernandez became president.

El Salvador's abandonment of import substitution meant the PCN was aided by manufactured exports and economic growth. The American Alliance for Progress helped create a boom in housing, school construction, health facilities, and water and sewage projects. The army engaged in construction, and El Salvador began receiving foreign investment. FI rose from $43 million in 1959 to $114.6 million in 1969.

---

295 Montgomery, Tommie Sue, 56.
296 Ibid.

A new minimum wage for agricultural workers produced thousands of unemployed, as well as starving, landless people The number of subsistence farmers shrank from 55,769 in 1961 to 17,019 in 1971. The number of landless campesinos increased from 30,451 in 1961 to 166,922 by 1975.[297] Labor became dependent on limited, seasonal work.[298]

The Soccer War

Landless peasants moved into neighboring Honduras as squatters on the land. Their presence was resented by Hondurans, as was El Salvador's better performance in the Central American Common Market (CACM). El Salvador's export growth was felt keenly in Honduras and, in the economic downturn, the squatters were a scapegoat for Honduran president Oswaldo Lopez Arellano. Arellano expelled the squatters, sometimes using the Honduran military. Unwanted in El Salvador, the squatters produced a strain on social services and undermined stability.

Harassment at a soccer match between Honduras and El Salvador exacerbated tension. El Salvador briefly invaded Honduras and killed 2,000 people, leaving tremendous damage. Honduras closed its market to the other country's exports, and El Salvador lost the economic "safety-valve" that had helped control its landless peasants.

Parties that had supported the war were left divided. The PDC left the National Unity Front and made agrarian reform a major issue for 1972.

In January 1970, the convocation of the National Agrarian Reform Congress classified concentrated landholdings as "unproductive," contrary to public interest, and "subject to government taking." PDC support for land expropriation placed it in conflict with the military and oligarchy. It then lost three seats in the Legislative Assembly and seventy municipalities.[299] Undaunted, the PDC sponsored Duarte for president in 1972.

---

297 Montgomery, Tommie Sue, 58.

298 Anderson, Thomas P., *The War of the Dispossessed: Honduras and El Salvador, 1969*, 31.

299 "El Salvador: Chapter 1C. The 1969 War with Honduras," *Countries of the World*, January 11, 1991, http://www.highbeam.com/library/doc3asp?DOCID=1P1:2834243&num=31&ctrlInfo.

The Molina Victory

The pro-communist victory of Salvador Allende Gossens in Chile served to encourage communism all over Latin America. The PCS infiltrated the National Democratic Union (Union Democratica Nacional – UDN) and made it a communist front. The PDC joined a coalition called the United National Opposition (Union Nacional Opositora – UNO), unaware that some of its members were more radical than they appeared. Against these two groups, the PCN ran Colonel Arturo Armando Molina on its presidential ticket.

The UNO became a victim of harassment, kidnappings and assault, which it blamed on the Guardia Nacional. The PCN attempted to disqualify UNO candidates in the mayoral elections for San Salvador, San Miguel, Usulutan, Sonsonate, La Union and San Vicente. The UNO's Duarte may have beaten Molina in the presidential race, even though ballots were "doctored" by the military. When the votes were "recounted," Molina was declared the winner.[300] The country was incensed over blatant fraud.

On March 25, 1972, Colonel Benjamin Mejia launched an unsuccessful coup. Most of the military defended Molina. Duarte's radio address garnered no support for the rebels. Instead, Duarte was detained, beaten and exiled, while Molina relied on ORDEN to quell trouble in rural areas.

Kidnappings, ransoms and terrorism became everyday occurrences. Those claiming responsibility were the People's Revolutionary Army (Ejercito Revolucionario del Pueblo – ERP) and the Farabundo Marti Popular Liberation Forces (Fuerzas Populares de Liberacion Farabundo Marti – FPL), both of which grew out of the PCS. These parties created mass organizations to exploit radical Roman Catholics. The largest organization was the 60,000-member Revolutionary Popular Bloc (Bloque Popular Revolucionario – BPR). Together, they conducted public demonstrations, strikes, building seizures and propaganda campaigns. They also set the stage for repression on a inconceivable scale.

Death squads had existed since the establishment of ORDEN. In 1975, the Anti-Communist Armed Forces of Liberation by Wars of Elimination (Fuerzas Armadas de Liberacion Anti-comunista de Guerras de Eliminacion – FALANGE) and the White Warriors Union (Union de Guerreros Blancos – UBG) went public.

Following demonstrations in July 1975 and February 1977, the government issued the Law for the Defense and Guarantee of Public

---

300 Stanley, William Deane, 89.

Order, which eliminated civilian protection from the military. The military already fired on protestors, but now there was a "tenfold increase in political assassinations, a tripling in the prosecution of 'subversives' and a doubling in the number of 'disappeared.'"[301]

Fraud and Violence

The UNO participated in the elections of 1974, but discovered they were rigged and declined to run candidates in 1976. It revived hopes for the presidency in 1977 and ran Colonel Ernesto Clara-mount Roseville against General Carlos Humberto Romero Mena of the PCN. Mena won again through fraud.

Dropping all pretense of government-sponsored reform, Romero increased violence and the insurgents reacted in kind. Bombings, kidnappings and assassinations were stepped up by the rebels to inspire insurrection.

Under Romero, persecution of Christians became routine because of humanitarian criticism underlying political agitation. The slogan of the UGB was "Be Patriotic—Kill a Priest." The UGB's War Bulletin No. 6 accused 46 Jesuits of "terrorism" and gave them a limited time to leave the country, after which their execution would be "immediate and systematic."[302] The new Archbishop of San Salvador, Oscar Arnulfo Romero, had boycotted the President's inauguration, and U.S.-Salvadorean relations during the term of President Carter (who championed human rights), sank to an all-time low.

Alarmed by these events, many groups combined to form the Popular Forum (Foro Popular), which called for an "end to repression, the establishment of political pluralism, short-term and long-term economic reforms (including agrarian reform) and the incorporation of the mass organizations into the government."[303] Formed just after the downfall of Nicaragua's Somoza, the new Popular Forum sparked military fears that a broad coalition could now overthrow Romero.

The result was another coup, led by Colonel Adolfo Arnoldo Majano Ramos. Majano's military junta thought reform was essential to stability. It supported land reform and officially disbanded ANESAL (which had directed ORDEN).

---

301 "El Salvador: Chapter 1C. The 1969 War with Honduras."
302 Dunkerley, James, 107.
303 "El Salvador: Chapter 1C. The 1969 War with Honduras."

Supported by the military and oligarchy, ANESAL became the National Intelligence Agency – ANI).[304] Major Roberto D'Aubuisson Arrieta—a member of the executive security agency—was bankrolled by the oligarchy for organizing death squads.

In January, 1980, the junta reorganized, but anti-leftist violence escalated. In the second junta, Majano remained a military representative. The non-military members were two Christian Democrats. In a pact of January 9th, the military promised the Christian Democrats it would support the nationalization of external trade, carry out land reform, nationalize the banking system, and include popular organizations in politics to be protected from violence. Phase three of the plan (which wasn't implemented past phase one) involved expropriating properties larger than 1,250 acres and granting them to the workforce as cooperatives.[305]

Death squads and insurgents kept the country under siege. The insurgents regrouped to form the Revolutionary Coordinator of the Masses (Coordinadora Revolucionaria de las Masas – CRM) and called for more demonstrations and strikes, as well as the junta's overthrow.

This led to a third junta, in which Duarte participated, having returned from exile.

Major "Blowtorch"

Roberto D'Aubuisson, leader of ANESAL, retired from the military after the coup against Romero. He moved to Guatemala but returned in 1980. His nickname, Mayor Soplete (Major Blowtorch), was inspired by television broadcasts in which he accused priests, civilian leaders and others of "terrorist conspiracy." The people whom D'Aubuisson denounced were murdered almost at once.

D'Aubuisson's death squads were receiving financial support from El Salvador's exiles in Miami. A 1981 embassy cable stated that:

> [Six Salvadorean millionaires in self-imposed exile] have directed and financed right-wing death squads for nearly a year, that they are trying to destroy the moderate reformist government by terrorizing its officials as well as the businessmen who cooperate with its reform program [and] that a wave of recent kidnappings is very likely their work...they organize, fund and direct death squads through their agent Roberto D'Aubuisson.[306]

---

304 Montgomery, Tommie Sue, 76.
305 Stanley, William Deane, 194.
306 Montgomery, Tommie Sue, 76.

One of D'Aubuisson's suspected victims was Archbishop Romero, who tried to mediate between conservatives and reformists. He was shot through the heart while celebrating mass on March 24, 1980.

As for the United States, Tommie Sue Montgomery supplies the following:

> [C]ivilian and military officials of the U.S. government supplied electronic, photographic, and personal surveillance of individuals who were later assassinated by death squads; kept key security officials on the Central Intelligence Agency (CIA) payroll; furnished intelligence files that D'Aubuisson used for his television programs; instructed Salvadorean intelligence operatives in the use of investigative techniques, combat weapons, explosives, and interrogation methods that included "instruction in methods of physical and psychological torture"...[307]

The United States violated its own laws, which prohibited providing material or financial support for foreign police, prisons or other law enforcement bodies.

Majano's followers uncovered a coup plot in which D'Aubuisson was involved. D'Aubuisson was arrested then released without trial, while attempted assassinations forced Majano into exile.

Washington's plans were for Duarte to take power and stage new elections in 1982. But first it had to contend with a reconstituted guerrilla movement called the Farabundo Marti National Liberation Front (Frente Farabundo Martipara la Liberacion Nacional – FMLN), which became the umbrella organization for leftist opposition, much like the Nicaraguan FSLN.

---

307 Ibid., 135.

CHAPTER FIFTEEN: EL SALVADOR — THE WAR AND ITS AFTERMATH

On January 10, 1981, FMLN guerrillas launched what they called the "final offensive" in their first public broadcast.

By then, the U.S. had reorganized and retrained the military for Vietnam-style pacification. Having released the "White Paper," the U.S. asserted:

> [T]he insurgency in El Salvador had been progressively transformed into another case of indirect aggression against a small Third World country by communist powers acting through Cuba; and that Cuba, the Soviet Union and other communist states...are carrying out what is clearly shown to be a well-coordinated, covert effort to bring about the overthrow of El Salvador's established government and to impose in its place a Communist regime with no popular support.[308]

Washington's allegations were partly false. The El Salvadorean guerrillas received a cool reception in Moscow, and Nicaragua had ceased to supply them with arms.

The defeat of the rebels "final offensive," led to a second attempt in July of 1981. The insurgents took prisoners of war (for whom it asked the Red Cross to assume responsibility) and conducted major economic sabotage. The Army struck back, but its victims

---

308 Dunkerley, James, 178.

were helpless civilians. An attack in El Mozote left 482 dead, 280 of whom were under age fourteen.[309]

Nicaragua circumvented El Salvador's government in attempts to mediate between the insurgents and the U.S. because, as Guillermo Ungo put it, "there's no point in talking to the clowns if you can talk to the owner of the circus."[310] Washington rebuffed Nicaragua from no desire to compromise while the FMLN remained on a war footing.

Before President Carter left office, he reversed his policy of denying El Salvador military aid on humanitarian grounds. A total of $10 million was appropriated for "non-lethal" military aid, and this was hugely augmented under President Reagan.

Trying to Undercut the Left

Washington supported the Salvadorean military, but also the ruling junta, headed by Duarte. It attempted to undercut the complaints of the left through three phases of land reform (which, as mentioned before, never passed phase one). Where land was expropriated, peasants were shot for forming cooperatives and landowners reclaimed their property through deals with the military.

Washington demanded new legislative and mayoral elections in 1982, followed by a presidential election in 1983. But this took place under siege; no necessary freedoms were in place. To quote Tommie Sue Montgomery:

> [T]he media were under government control; the popular organizations had been decimated and disbanded by late 1980; state-sponsored terror was the norm, with over 30,000 civilians killed and 600,000 refugees since the October coup; leaders of legal parties on the left of the political spectrum were threatened with death if they returned...voting was required by law, but in El Salvador Defense Minister Garcia advised citizens that failing to vote was treasonable. Furthermore, voters were told their cedulas (identity cards) would be stamped, and the voting system was such that it was possible to determine who had voted for whom.[311]

D'Aubuisson ran for office as the head of a new party, the Alianza Republicana Nacionalista (Nationalist Republican Alliance – ARENA). Backed by right-wing groups in and outside of El Salvador (with the help of U.S. Senator Jesse Helms), D'Aubuisson's

---

309 Montgomery, Tommie Sue, 152.

310 Dunkerley, James, 179.

311 Montgomery, Tommie Sue, 156.

platform was a mix of the 1980 U.S. Republican creed and neo-Nazi principles.

Three other parties ran against ARENA: the PCN (Party of National Conciliation), the Christian Democrats (PDC), and the Democratic Action Party (AD). Ballots were thought to be rigged, since the final tally of votes was 1,551,687 and only 1.2 million citizens were eligible to vote. But the Christian Democrats gained 35.5 percent of the vote (twenty-four seats), ARENA garnered 25.8 percent (nineteen seats), and the PCN won 16.8 percent (fourteen seats).[312] Although the parties agreed not to contest the outcome, D'Aubuisson tried to oust the PDC and name himself provisional president. In response, the U.S. sent a Congressional delegation to inform D'Aubuisson he would not be an acceptable candidate.[313] Instead, the U.S. backed Alvaro Magana, head of the Banco Hipotecario and banker for the military.

D'Aubuisson, became head of the Constituent Assembly, where he named ARENA members to sabotage agrarian reform. He also placed Hector Antonio Regalado (a well-known organizer of death squads, similar to D'Aubuisson) in charge of Assembly security.

The Christian Democrats Take Control

Due to inter-party bickering and D'Aubuisson's control of the Legislative Assembly, presidential elections did not take place in 1983. First, a new constitution had to be written, which the parties could not agree on. The war continued apace, and El Salvador seethed with terror and violence.

In 1984, the U.S. routed $1.4 million to the Christian Democrats and the UPD (Popular Democratic Unity party). Jose Napoleon Duarte became president in a runoff with D'Aubuisson. Then, in 1985, the PDC won 33 seats in the Legislative Assembly and 153 of 262 mayoralties, under a pact with the UPD to place "rural and urban labor representatives in charge of labor relations and agrarian reform, respect human rights and begin a dialogue with the FMLN."[314]

The ARENA-controlled Assembly attacked Duarte's budget and accepted only a skeleton of what the country required. Agrarian reform was gutted to the tune of $9.16 million, leaving a symbol-

---

312 "El Salvador: Chapter 1D. The Civil Conflict Begins," *Countries of the World*, January 11, 1991, http://www.highbeam.com/library/doc3.asp?DOCID=1P1:28384244&num=61&ctrlInfo.

313 Stanley, William Deane, 196.

314 Montgomery, Tommie Sue, 179.

ic appropriation of $4 dollars. Duarte increased export revenues to subsidize basic consumer goods. He also maintained protective tariffs favored by industrialists. The distribution of credit was skewed toward political interests.

By now, U.S. aid of $1 million per day kept El Salvador afloat. Under wartime devastation, per capita GDP fell by 23 percent between 1979 and 1982. Export earnings declined by 35 percent. Unemployment reached 27 percent. IMF assistance required voluntary adjustment to create:

> ...unification of the exchange rate, exchange and import restrictions, a more aggressive export promotion program, new fiscal revenue-generating mechanisms, agrarian reforms, a macroeconomic and external debt management committee, and strict monetary policies to curb the country's accelerating inflation rate.[315]

In order to curb inflation, the government employed monetary targets, price controls, wage controls, and exchange rate freezes. But when price controls were relaxed in 1985, inflation skyrocketed to 22 and then 32 percent. The government intervened in employer–labor wage negotiations, while slow monetary growth resulted in lower real wages. The Central Reserve Bank controlled foreign exchange to discourage capital flight and rationed credit in favor of exports via interest rates. The National Industrial Development Bank provided credit to industry.

Despite taxes on sales, exports, property, income, capital gains and profits, new foreign loans paid for most development initiatives. Foreign debt rose from US $88 million in 1970 to US $1.5 billion by 1986. Between 1980 and 1986, U.S. aid rose to $2.5 billion in military and economic aid.[316]

In the process, spending for government-owned banks, the National Water and Sewerage Administration (ANDA), the National Telecommunications Administration (Antel), and the National Electric Company (CEL) rose to US $135 million by 1985. Health care allocations decreased from 10 percent of the budget in 1978 to 7.5 percent in 1986. Social security and welfare spending increased from US $11 million in 1976 to US $31 million in 1985.[317]

315 "El Salvador: Chapter 3B. Monetary and Credit Policies," *Countries of the World,* January 11, 1991, http://www.highbeam.com/library/doc3asp?DOCID=1P1:28384250&num=82&ctrlInfo.

316 Ibid.
317 Ibid.

A Chance for Peace

Duarte met with the FMLN to negotiate terms for a cease-fire at the United Nations General Assembly. For the day of October 15, 1984, a cease-fire was declared. People lined the streets, waving flags and white paper doves. They shouted, "We want peace!"

The day's meeting went smoothly and both sides issued press communiqués. The next meeting was set for one month later but Duarte did not attend. At a meeting of November 30th, he accused the FMLN of a hard-line attitude and efforts to ruin the peace.

On February 21st, 60,000 public and private workers, teachers and cooperatives hit the streets to demand new negotiations and the withdrawal of failed economic reform (which had devalued the colon, imposed price increases and banned luxury imports).

Between March and November 1985, sixty-three strikes took place, fifty-three of which were attended by 46 organizations and 60,000 workers. The government response was to reinstate repression rather than move toward peace. Then 100 unions, representing 350,000 people, formed the National Unity of Salvadorean Workers (UNTS). The UNTS protested economic austerity and the U.S.–IMF role. Its demand for further peace talks led to the U.S.-sponsored creation of the UNOC (National Union of Workers and Peasants), which was pro-government and opposed the UNTS.

In 1987, the Esquipulas agreement (forged by Central American leaders, including Costa Rican president Oscar Arias, who received the Nobel Peace Prize), put pressure on Duarte to reopen negotiations. The FMLN declared a five-day truce during talks in mid-September. They met on October 4th, and then again in late October. However, nothing changed.

On January 23, 1989, the FMLN asked for a six-month delay in the presidential election, military non-interference, participation of the Democratic Convergence (formed from the left-wing parties of the MPSC, MNR, and PSD) on the Central Elections Council, and a provision for absentee voting. In return, the FMLN would participate in, and abide by, the election. Duarte rejected the plan, but the parties met again on February 20th.

The FMLN offered to demilitarize, become part of national politics, and integrate with the army in exchange for military reform.[318]

---

318 Montgomery, Tommie Sue, 215.

Cristiani and the FMLN

ARENA derailed the agreement in expectation of winning the presidency. The FMLN fought the army across the country as Alfredo Cristiani, ARENA's presidential contender won. Cristiani was more conciliatory than D'Aubuisson. He offered new talks, and meetings were held in August 1989. More talks followed in September and October. Cristiani demanded a cease-fire, but couldn't guarantee the insurgents' safety. Between them, they established the National Commission for the Consolidation of Peace (COPAZ), to implement guarantees for "life, liberty, and freedom of organization and assembly; reform of the electoral system; and improvement of the justice system."[319] The FMLN offered peace, but the bombing of El Salvador's largest and most militant trade union federation (FENASTRAS) convinced them the government wasn't prepared.

The FMLN launched its largest offensive ever on the capital of San Salvador. Negotiations were renewed. The UN Secretary General served as a mediator, and an agreement was reached in Switzerland, followed by talks in June, July and August. At the last meeting, the FMLN proposed to eliminate the military, as had been done in Costa Rica. It asked for a new civilian police and a special tribunal to prosecute human rights abuses.

In September, UN negotiator Alvaro de Soto stepped in. He conducted separate talks and proposed the abolition of two out of three security forces plus the military intelligence apparatus, and the establishment of a three-person commission to investigate human rights abuses. Though the proposal was not accepted, the parties moved closer together.

The Bush administration unsuccessfully lobbied Congress to continue military aid. Congress decreased it by a fifty percent and conditioned further release on the continuance of peace talks and investigation into the murder of six Jesuit priests. Then renewed guerrilla warfare brought the deaths of two U.S. servicemen, and President Bush restored military aid. UN negotiator de Soto was accused of being too soft.

Days before new elections and a predicted ARENA majority, Nicaraguan president Violeta Chamorro unveiled an FMLN proposal to re-involve the UN. July of 1991 marked the beginning of ONUSAL, the UN Observer Mission to El Salvador. When talks resumed in September at New York, the government was pressured by the "Group of Friends" (Spain, Mexico, Venezuela and

---

319 Ibid., 216.

Columbia), along with the United States. The FMLN dropped its demand for inclusion in the Army and settled for incorporation in a National Civilian Police (PNC) and a role in the Peace Commission (COPAZ). On January 16, 1992, a final accord was reached. The parties agreed to reduce the military, purify the officer corps, eliminate the security forces (to be replaced by the PNC), and implement economic, social, electoral and judicial reforms.

Between June 30th and December 17th, 12,362 guerrillas demobilized. The government reduced the Army by half and abolished its intelligence apparatus, rapid-reaction battalions, National Guard and Treasury Police.

In the Aftermath

Joseph S. Tulchin and Gary Bland describe El Salvador after the war:

> More than 75,000 lives have been lost; hundreds of thousands have been injured and maimed; 0.5 million people have been displaced from their homes in El Salvador; and about 1 million people have been forced to flee the country and live as refugees. For those remaining in El Salvador, damage from the war has resulted in a substantially lower quality of life. The cost of the war to the economy between 1981 and 1990 has been estimated to be more than $2 billion.[320]

By 1993, IMF Adjustment produced unified exchange rates, reduced and unified tariffs, simplified taxation (including a value-added tax), several privatized banks, agricultural reform, and a Social Investment Fund to "cushion the potentially negative impact of adjustment on the poor."[321] The results were 1.6 percent growth of GDP between 1989 and 1990, and a GDP increase of 3.8 percent between 1990 and 1992.

Between 1989 and 1994, imports increased over exports, and the country's trade deficit grew from US $524 million to US $1.125 billion. This was paid for with foreign remittances of US $1 billion. El Salvador received aid grants of US $284 million, of which two were from the World Bank for structural adjustment, leading analysts to

---

320 Tulchin, Joseph S. and Gary Bland, *Is There a Transition to Democracy in El Salvador?* (Boulder, CO: L. Reinner Publishers, 1992), 106.

321 Rubio, Roberto, and Karen Hansen-Kuhn, Fondacion Nacional para el Desarrollo and The Development Gap, November 6, 1995, http://www.hartford-hwp.com/archives/47/069.html.

believe that growth was not fuelled by exports (then US $817 million). Instead, the apparent cause was remittances, aid and loans.[322]

Stratification continued, with the country's richest 20 percent increasing its share of income from 43 percent in 1989 to 54.2 percent in 1991. The income share of the poorest 20 percent dropped from 5.6 to 3.4 percent.[323] The people who benefited from growth were those who possessed resources. Landless peasants, small-scale farmers, industrial and service sector workers, public employees, and small-scale business people were left out of the loop.

To cushion the impact on these groups, the Salvadoran Social Investment Fund (FISS) provided $3.5 million[324] to promote domestic production, infrastructural improvements, and occupational training. This was supposed to help low-income groups pay for education, health and nutrition.

In September 1996, the legislature legalized the 49 percent sale of the telephone company ANTEL. Seven electricity distributors were to be sold in 1997, and the telecommunications system was to be privatized in two years.[325]

In 1999, IMF recommendations included a new tax code and broadened value-added tax (VAT). The government was expected to dampen wage demands to promote private savings and strengthen the banking sector. Investments in human capital and infrastructure were also to be made.[326]

In 2003, the IMF urged El Salvador to broaden the tax base further, increase the VAT, and maintain "prudence" on wages.[327] By 2005, it summarized the changes.[328]

322 Eriksson, John, Alcira Kreimer, and Margaret Arnold, *Post-Conflict Reconstruction: Country Case Evaluation* (Washington, DC: World Bank, 2000) 43.

323 Rubio, Roberto and Karen Hansen-Kuhn.

324 Tulchin, Joseph S., and Gary Bland, 113.

325 "IMF Approves Stand-By Credit for El Salvador, International Monetary Fund, Press Release Number 97/11, March 3, 1997, http://www.imf.org/external/np/sec/pr/1997/pr9711.htm.

326 "IMF Concludes Article IV Consultation with El Salvador," International Monetary Fund, Public Information Notice (PIN) no. 99/104, November 15, 1999, http://www.imf.org/external/np/sec/pn/1999/pn99104.htm.

327 "IMF Concludes Article IV Consultation with El Salvador," International Monetary Fund, Public Information Notice (PIN) No. 03/149, December 22, 2003, http://www.imf.org/external/np/sec/pn/2003/pn03149.htm.

328 "El Salvador: 2004 Article VI Consultation—Staff Report; Staff Statement; Public Information Notice on the Executive Board

Value added-tax (VAT) adopted	1992
VAT raised from 10 to 13 percent	1995
VAT base broadened	2001–03
Modernization of state and payroll cuts	1995 &2001
Ethics code for civil servants introduced and civil service law reformed	2001–02
Nominal salaries for most civil servants maintained broadly stable	2000–04
Laws for privatization of telecommunication and electricity company	1996
Sale of four regional electricity distribution companies (75 percent) and three thermal generating plants	1998–99
Break-up and partial sale of the state telecoms monopoly (ANTEL)	1998
Approval for reforming the public social security and pension system	1996
Transition from pay-as-you-go pension system to fully-funded private accounts initiated	1998
Provision for early retirement plan	2004
Replacing of short-term public debt for longer-term bonds intensified	2002
Central bank recapitalized	1993
De facto exchange rate peg adopted	1994
Approval of central bank autonomy law	1996
Introduction of U.S. dollar as legal tender initiated	2001
Preferential access to U.S. textile market under Caribbean Basin Initiative	Early 1990s
Trade liberalization, further reducing tariffs and non-tariff barriers	1992–95
External tariffs from Central American Common Market (CACM) adopted	1996

Discussion; and Statement by the Executive Director for El Salvador," International Monetary Fund, Country Report NO. 05/271, August 2005.

Free-trade agreements with Chile, Dominican Republic, Mexico, and Panama	1998–2001
Liberal regime for FDI introduced	1999–2000
Central American Free-Trade Agreement with the United States ratified	2004
Privatization of Banks (nationalized in 1980)	1992–94
Public bank (two-tier) created to assume development lending from central bank	1994
Banking law to strengthen the supervisory powers of regulators and tighten prudential regulations	1999
Reforms to banking law to strengthen protection of depositors, improve supervisory powers to take preventive and corrective measures against banks, and introduce consolidated supervision	2002
Liquidity buffers strengthened further and prudential regulations moved closer to international standards	2003–04
Labor code reformed to ease rules on fringe benefits and hiring/firing of workers	1994
Minimum wage code maintained stable	1998– 2002–04

El Salvador's currency was switched to the U.S. dollar to strengthen the private sector. In practice, it increased the prices of goods.

The poor (representing 43 percent of the nation, with 19 percent living in extreme degradation), were especially hurt by the change. Many survived via foreign remittances, which climbed to US $2.5 billion in 2004, and reduced the impact of poverty by 7 to 8 percent.[329]

In 2004, President Antonio Saca hoped to stimulate growth by attracting more foreign investment. His "Opportunities" program cost the government US $440 million and included a health fund, the "2021 Plan for Education," the "Get Connected" program (to provide 90,000 computers to educational centers), a small credit program, and the Solidarity Network. The last program offered a subsidy of US $15.00 per month to families in absolute poverty, provided their children went to school and received medical check-ups. However, $15.00 a month translated to fifty cents per day—

---

329 "El Salvador: Political Will Needed," *Social Watch El Salvador*, August 19, 2005.

well below the poverty standard of US $2.00 per day and closer to absolute poverty, measured at US $1.00 per day.[330]

In 2004, growth was 1.5 percent. Low levels of poor-quality investment failed to produce jobs and income. Meanwhile, external debt grew to US $8.273 billion by June 2005, with a fiscal deficit of US .327 billion during the same year.[331]

The IMF recommended raising the fiscal surplus to 1 percent of GDP by 2006. This required further reform of taxes, government spending, and the nation's pension system. Trade reform had to be "deepened" and infrastructural constraints addressed. More flexibility on wages was a given expectation.

At the time, the minimum *daily* wage was: US $4.80 for commercial, industrial, construction and service employees; US $2.47 for agricultural workers; and US $3.57 for seasonal agricultural workers. The law required a full-time, minimum-wage employee to be paid for an 8-hour day of rest in addition to the 44-hour workweek, and a bonus of one month's average wage, plus two vacation weeks a year.[332] But, at 60 to 30 cents per hour, this was a bargain in any case. Now fringe benefits hit the chopping block, even as wages declined.

The FMLN "Threat"

The IMF claimed that the country's sluggish growth was due to election uncertainties in 2004, when it looked, for the first time, as if the FMLN might win. According to Rose Likens, U.S. ambassador to the region, "The FMLN generated worry." She said, "Salvadorans have the right to decide what they want, but we also have to react on the basis of what happens in March of 2004." Likens stressed that an FMLN victory, would require U.S. relations to be further "analyzed," from concern for "democratic values" and the future of U.S. investments.[333]

Her comments rallied the right, and publicity was issued to deal with the FMLN threat: an FMLN victory would mean thousands

---

330 Ibid.

331 CIA – The World Factbook – El Salvador, http://www.cia.gov/cia/ publications/factbook/print/es.html.

332 "El Salvador," U.S. Department of State, http://www.state.gov/g/drl/ rls/hrrpt/2002/18331.htm.

333 "El Salvador: U.S. Seen Interfering in Electoral Process," *NotiCen: Central American & Caribbean Affairs*, http://www.highbeam.com/library/doc3. asp?DOCID=1G1:103133896&num=42&ctrlInfo.

of penniless Salvadoreans returning to the country en mass, with-drawal of foreign investment, and a threat to CAFTA (the Central American Free Trade Agreement).

In 2006, ARENA took no chances on the presidential election. The FMLN claimed that ARENA-organized thugs harassed and physically assaulted FMLN supporters, during its campaign. In one incident a pregnant woman was hospitalized. In another, a mob of "ARENA members attacked activists with rocks, machetes and sticks" while the activists posted signs on the outskirts of town."[334] The National Police released the suspects, alleging that FMLN vic-tims were "unable to identify" their attackers.

The Human Rights Situation

In 2002, there were no reports of political killings or people "disappeared," but according to the U.S. State Department the Na-tional Police resorted to abusive use of force, shootings, kidnapping for ransom and improper treatment during detainment. People were arbitrarily arrested and detained, and 706 of 3,303 complaints were for violation of personal integrity by government authorities. The last applied to torture, inhuman or degrading treatment, and disproportionate use of force. However, the PCN took corrective action in response to filed complaints. It dismissed 372 employees and sanctioned 520 others. Five former officers were sentenced to prison terms for participation in kidnapping. The Attorney General and the Supreme Court dismissed unqualified judges and prosecut-ed four others.

The government established a Truth Commission for war time abuses. Entitled "From Madness to Hope: The Twelve-Year War in El Salvador," the report tracked the implementation of death squads and chronicled government slaughters, such as the massa-cre at El Mozote. It also dealt with the "disappeared" and found D'Aubuisson involved in the murder of Archbishop Romero.

The purpose of a Truth Commission is to hold criminals ac-countable and facilitate national healing. However, the Commis-sion had no power, beyond recommendation. Linking the death squads and military massacres to a corrupt and discredited legal system, the Commission requested judicial reform. It also recom-

---

334 "Armed ARENA Groups Attack FMLN, Seriously Injuring Activists," Committee in Solidarity with the People of El Salvador, January 16, 2006, http://www.cispes.org/english/Communiques_-_Action_Alerts/index.html.

mended removal of police and military criminals and a system of penalties in the event they were to be tried.

Noam Chomsky provides a rendition of a particularly gruesome event:

> The results of Salvadoran military training are graphically described in the Jesuit journal *America* by Daniel Santiago, a Catholic priest working in El Salvador. He tells of a woman who returned home one day to find her three children, her mother and her sister sitting around a table, each with its own decapitated head placed carefully on the table in front of the body, the hands arranged on top "as if each body was stroking its own head." The assassins, from the Salvadoran National Guard, had found it hard to keep the head of an 18-month-old baby in place, so they nailed the hands onto it. A large plastic bowl filled with blood was tastefully displayed in the center of the table.[335]

No one in El Salvador wants to return to the state of violence and widespread insecurity that marked the years of the war.

---

335 Chomsky, Noam, "The Crucifixion of El Salvador," http://www.third-worldtraveler.com/Chomsky/ChomOdon_ElSalvador.html.

CHAPTER SIXTEEN: HONDURAS — LAND OF INSTABILITY

Although Christopher Columbus discovered Honduras in 1502, it was 1523 before Gil Gonzalez Davila led an expedition into the Golfo de Fonseca, and not until 1524 that the conquest began. Then Gonzalez Davila vied with Cristobal de Olid for possession of Honduras. Olid, who acted for Hernan Cortes, developed his own ambitions. He fought Gonzalez Davila and Francisco de Las Casas. Cortes sent Las Casas to reclaim the territory from Olid. Olid captured Davila and Las Casas, but his captives converted his own followers and had Olid beheaded. Cortes then came to assert authority over Honduras. He returned to Mexico in 1526.

Diego Lopez de Salcedo became the first royal governor of Honduras, but ended up imprisoned for ambitions toward Nicaragua. His abrasive ruling style provoked native revolts, which he put down with massacres. Thousands died in the Olancho and Comayagua valleys.[336] Like all Central American countries, Honduras suffered indigenous depopulation due to disease, mistreatment, and the exportation of slaves to the Caribbean islands. The country bordered on collapse by 1534.

In 1536, Pedro de Alvarado discovered gold. Native exploitation became greater and crueler. Led by a native named Lempira, the natives revolted in 1537. Lempira was then murdered during nego-

---

336 Stokes, William S., *Honduras: an Area Study in Government* (Westport, CT: Greenwood Press, 1974) 17.

tiations. Native resistance was broken, though sporadic uprisings continued through 1539. Between 1539 and 1541, the indigenous population fell from 15,000 to 8,000.[337] The natives were replaced with African slaves, and the colonists owned 2,000 by 1545.

After Spanish Rule

Under Spanish rule, Honduras belonged to the *audiencia* of Guatemala. Its main population centers were the rival cities of Comayagua and Tegucigalpa. When Honduras declared independence in 1821, Tegucigalpa supported a Central American state, whereas Comayagua favored the Mexican empire of General Augustin de Iturbide. Comayagua prevailed until March of 1823, when Iturbide was overthrown.

Honduras joined the United Provinces of Central America and produced its most prominent liberal leader, Francisco Morazan. The federation collapsed after a conservative uprising in Guatemala, after which the Central American Congress removed Morazan from office on May 30, 1838.

The next leader, Francisco Zelaya Ayes, was succeeded by General Francisco Ferrera, Honduras's first elected president. Ferrera's two-year term was followed by five years of alternation between president and minister of war. In 1847, Ferrera allowed Juan Lindo Zelaya (a fellow conservative) to take over. Zelaya transferred power to the liberals, led by Trinidad Cabanas, in 1852.

In 1855, Guatemala invaded Honduras to install conservative president Santos Guardiola. The next target was Nicaragua, where the Central American republics ousted William Walker.

In 1862, Guardiola's honor guard assassinated him. Leadership changed hands twenty times in the following decade. Conservative General Jose Maria Medina served eleven times, only to be ousted by Guatemala in 1876. From then until 1882, liberal president Marco Aurelio Soto was backed by Guatemalan general Justo Rufino Barrios. When Soto fell from grace, Barrios backed General Luis Borgran, until 1891. Through a manipulated election in 1893, General Poinciana Leiva took over as an authoritarian ruler.[338]

---

337 "Honduras: The Era of the Conquistadores," Library of Congress, http://workmall.com/wfb2001/honduras/honduras_history_the_era_ of_the_conquistadores.html.

338 "Honduras: The Development of an Independent Nation," Library of Congress, http://workmall.com/wfb2001/honduras/honduras_history_ the_development_of_an_independent_nation.html.

In 1894, Domingo Vasquez was replaced by Policarpo Bonilla, the leader of the Liberal Party of Honduras (Partido Liberal de Honduras – PLH), backed by Nicaragua's Jose Santos Zelaya. Bonilla implemented a new constitution in 1895, and ensured that his successor was General Terencio Sierra. Sierra was overthrown by General Manuel Bonilla in 1903.[339]

Bonilla started the National Party of Honduras (Partido Nacional de Honduras – PNH) to give the conservatives cohesion. He also favored the Standard Fruit Company, which was allowed to build roads and lay rail, and improve inland water facilities to expand external trade. Investors in Honduras were largely exempt from taxes, including the Honduras Rosario Mining Company (NYHRMC), which exported US $700,000 in bullion to the United States each year.

In February 1907, exiled Honduran liberals overthrew Bonilla with the support of Nicaragua's president Zelaya. Their provisional ruling junta gave way to General Miguel Davila, after U.S. intervention.

The Boundary Disputes

Britain and Honduras disputed sovereignty over the Islas de la Bahias. Honduras also claimed the boundary of the Coco River, whereas Nicaragua claimed all land westward to the Patuca. Two separate boundary agreements were proposed in 1870 and 1889, but neither was ratified in Honduras.

Negotiators from both sides agreed to accept King Alfonso XIII of Spain as the Central American mediator. By December 1906, the east bank of the Coco River stretching to Nicaragua and including Puerto Cabo became the Honduran boundary. However, Nicaragua underwent revolution in 1912, and a new, hostile government claimed the Patuca line.[340]

From 1969, Honduras and El Salvador also disputed borders. The Honduran municipality of Santiago de Jocoara (now Santa Elena) contested El Salvador's claims to Nino de Dios de Arambala and Asuncion de Nuestra Senora de Perquin. Between 1869 and 1941,

339 Munro, Dana G., *The Five Republics of Central America: Their Political and Economic Development and Their Relation with the United States*, ed. David Kinley (New York: Oxford University Press, 1918) 123.

340 Anderson, Thomas P., *The War of the Dispossessed: Honduras and El Salvador, 1969*, 41.

they attempted fifteen separate agreements. However, the border dispute persisted to contribute to the Soccer War.

Stabilizing Honduras

Because Central American states interfered frequently in Honduras, the U.S. proposed the Central American Peace Conference of 1907. The parties ignored a Honduran proposal to reestablish the Central American federation, but agreed to a Permanent Central American Court of Justice for resolving their disputes. Each state pledged not to support former leaders in exile and to make legal extradition possible. Finally, they agreed to withhold recognition of governments seized by power or revolutionary means.

The treaty's first test stemmed from Honduras. Opponents of President Davila invaded in 1908, allegedly supported by Guatemala and El Salvador. Davila, in turn, resisted with the help of Nicaragua. The case was submitted to the Court, where complaints from both sides were dismissed. However, the revolt collapsed from within, allowing Davila reprieve.

Honduran external debt of US $120 million convinced the Taft administration that instability would persist if this matter wasn't addressed. New York reduced the debt in exchange for Honduran bonds. The U.S. took control of Honduran customs while the bankers controlled its railroad.

The Honduran National Congress withheld ratification, and opposition led to revolt in 1911. Rather than turn to the Court, the U.S. selected Tomas Dawson to mediate a provisional president. Dawson appointed Francisco Bertrand, who promised early elections. Manuel Bonilla replaced him in 1912, but died a year later, restoring Bertrand to the presidency. Bertrand won another election and served until 1920.[341]

Between 1911 and 1920, the U.S. kept the peace. It sent warships to discourage revolutions and opposed manipulation by the country's banana companies. By 1917, the Cuyamel Fruit Company began extending rail lines into Guatemala with support from Honduras. This brought Guatemalan troops to the border on behalf of the United Fruit Company. U.S. mediators intervened, but the issue defied solution until 1930.

---

341 "Honduras: Chapter 1B. The Development of an Independent Nation," *Countries of the World*, January 11, 1991, http://www.highbeam.com/library/doc3.asp?DOCID=1P1:28384576&num=20&ctrlInfo.

The Banana Companies

Unlike Central American oligarchies, which controlled land and labor to monopolize produce and exports, native Honduran producers lacked the size and capital to become an elite group. Instead, foreign-backed production was controlled by the Vacarro brothers between 1899 and 1910. Their interests were incorporated with the Standard Fruit Company and the Cuyamel Fruit Company. The latter belonged to Samuel Zemurray. In 1910, the United Fruit Company came to Honduras, built the Tela Railroad Company, and extended its reach to areas controlled by Cuyamel and Standard Fruit.

Honduras endowed the companies with huge land grants, hoping a national railroad would be built to link major cities and access the Caribbean. Instead, the banana companies focused on fertile areas, and left the country underdeveloped, ignoring the government's wishes. The government hired private contractors, but only achieved a rail line of fifty-seven kilometers.[342]

Boom towns grew from the banana companies in port cities and San Pedro Sula. They introduced sanitation and rudimentary health care, but also engaged in banking. Established by the Vacarro brothers, the Banco Atlantida became the most powerful bank in Honduras and extended loans to the government when the New York bankers wouldn't.

Banana production increased from 6 million bunches in 1910 to 29 million in 1930. By 1919, a million acres of coastal land was held by five owners. Seventy-five percent belonged to United Fruit, Cuyamel and the Vacarros.[343] Honduras became a mono-crop country (often called a banana republic), with the majority of exports controlled by foreign interests.

In 1917, the banana workers struck against the Cuyamel Fruit Company, and could only be controlled by the Honduran military. Workers rebelled against Standard Fruit in 1918 and, in 1920, a general strike ensued. The U.S. sent a warship and Honduras arrested the strike leaders. To appease the workers, Standard Fruit increased the daily wage to $1.75.

---

342 Euraque, Daraio A., *Reinterpreting the Banana Republic: Region and State in Honduras, 1870-1972* (Chapel Hill, NC: University of North Carolina Press, 1996) 4.

343 Schulz, Donald E., and Deborah Sundloff Schulz, *The United States, Honduras, and the Crisis in Central America* (Boulder, CO: Westview Press, 1994) 9.

Problems of Succession

Bertrand meant to prevent elections in 1919, but General Rafael Lopez Gutierrez recruited local liberals, Guatemala and Nicaragua in an attempt to overthrow him. El Salvador denied Bertrand assistance, and he was forced to step down under U.S. insistence. The U.S. installed Francisco Bogran until October of 1920, when Gutierrez replaced him through an unfair election.

There were 17 uprisings between 1920 and 1923. The U.S. held another conference of the Central American republics on the U.S.S. Tacoma. The presidents pledged, once again, to prevent their respective countries from being used for insurrections. The meeting was followed by a conference in Washington, which produced the General Treaty of Peace and Amity of 1923. The governments pledged to limit their armies and deny recognition to any government achieved through revolution.

In 1923, no candidate in Honduras gained a majority vote. The National Congress was left to choose from General Tiburcio Carias Andino, former president Policarpo Bonilla, and Dr. Juan Angel Arias) and failed to reach a decision. Gutierrez announced he'd remain in power until new elections took place.

Arias challenged Gutierrez, with the support of United Fruit. Armed conflict between government troops and the rebels led to looting and arson, causing US $2 million in damage. When Guiterrez died soon after, his cabinet ruled the country. Carias was blocked by the United States, which held new mediation on board a U.S. cruiser. General Vicente Tosta became interim president, and agreed to appoint a cabinet involving all the parties. A U.S. arms embargo and denial of international loans kept Tosta from reneging. New elections brought PNH candidate Miguel Paz Barahona to power.

Following Barahona, Mejia Colindres won decisively against General Tiburcio Carias. Colindres took office with great expectations, only to have them shattered during the Great Depression. Banana exports declined after 1930. Thousands of workers were laid off and wages plummeted. Government repression quelled the labor strikes, but it had to borrow US $250,000 from the fruit companies in order to pay the army.[344]

---

344 "Honduras: The Restoration of Order, 1925-31," Library of Congress, http://workmall.com/wfb2001/honduras/honduras_history_ the_restoration_of_order_1925-31html.

Stability at a Price

Because the constitution prohibited reelection, the Congress granted General Carias another six years in office from 1936. Ultimately, he served until 1949. The 1930s and 1940s were the years of Jorge Ubico in Guatemala, Maximiliano Hernandez Martinez in El Salvador, Anastasio Somoza in Nicaragua, and Tiburcio Carias in Honduras.[345] Carias, in similar authoritarian style, allowed no more congressional elections. He appointed ministers to positions based on personal loyalty, stifled the press and popular organizations, and filled the jails with dissidents.

Under Carias, the United Fruit Company flourished. It bought out the stock of the Cuyamel Fruit Company and expanded like an "octopus" (the Hondurans called it el pulpo) to cover fertile land in Honduras. Journalists who criticized the company and its operations in Honduras were either bribed or "disappeared" into Carias' jails. United Fruit employees became the minister of war, the president of Congress and the head of the Supreme Court.

Carias' cronies ran gambling and prostitution rings, as well as liquor monopolies. They imposed tribute on businessmen and intimidated citizens through networks of local informers, imprisoning or assassinating political opponents."[346]

The United States valued stability during World War II, but support for Carias disappeared as the war came to an end. Citizens of Honduras began to call for change, until the fruit companies viewed him as a threat to political consensus and an obstacle to modernization. Carias allowed free elections in 1948.

Galvez and the Guatemala Invasion

In 1949, conservative president Manuel Galvez proved more lenient. He permitted freedom of the press and the right to organization. His laws established an eight-hour workday, paid holidays for workers, limited employer responsibility for work-related injuries, and regulations for the employment of women and children.[347]

Galvez expanded roads and exports, and also paid the nation's external debt within the strict guidelines set by British creditors.

345 Schulz, Donald E., and Deborah Sundloff Schulz, 16.
346 Ibid., 17.
347 "Honduras: STRONGMAN RULE, 1932-63, Library of Congress, http://workmall.com/wfb2001/honduras/honduras_history_strongman_rule_1932_63.html.

He established the Banco Central de Honduras and the Banco Nacional de Fomento to offer credit to agriculturalists and reformed education. Before then, literacy extended to only 35 percent of the populace.[348]

The actions and propaganda of Jacobo Arbenz Guzman, Guatemala's left-leaning ruler, created tensions in and outside Honduras. Arbenz's agrarian reform threatened the interests of the United Fruit Company, and earned U.S. enmity. The Galvez administration harbored Guatemalan exiles who continued to oppose Arbenz but Galvez withheld support until a series of strikes in 1954.

Workers' grievances included wages, working conditions, medical benefits, overtime pay, and the right to collective bargaining.[349] By May 21, the movement spread to include other industries, with a total of 35,000 on strike. Galvez met with the Central Strike Committee then arrested several leaders, claiming that they were communists linked to Guatemala. The leaders were replaced with pliant workers, who agreed to limited wage increases and recognition of their unions by the fruit companies.[350]

Honduras received U.S. arms shipments and became the staging ground for an assault against Arbenz. Arbenz fled soon after the fighting, and was replaced by Castillo Armas.

Diaz is Overthrown

The 1954 elections produced the same confusion as the 1924 elections. None of the candidates (former president Carias, Abraham Williams Calderon and Ramon Villega Morales) obtained a majority vote. In this case, the National Congress was boycotted to instigate national crisis.

During Galvez's absence, Vice President Julio Lozano Diaz declared himself interim president. He promised to appoint cabinet members from all major parties and replaced the suspended Con-

---

348 Anderson, Thomas P., *The War of the Dispossessed: Honduras and El Salvador, 1969,* 50.

349 "Honduras: Aborted Reform, 1954-63," Library of Congress, http://workmall.com/wfb2001/honduras/honduras_history_aborted_reform_1954_63.html.

350 Brett, Donna W., "Chapter 6 Facing the Challenge: the Catholic Church and Social Change in Honduras," *Central America: Historical Perspectives on the Contemporary Crises,* ed. Ralph Lee Woodward (New York: Greenwood Press, 1988) 109.

gress with a new Council of State. A constituent assembly was formed to write a new constitution.

Diaz raised taxes and contracted international loans to pay for development plans. He produced the first labor code, which legalized strikes and organization, offered minimum wage provisions, and regulated hours and working conditions. This won the support of labor, but Diaz reduced the Council of State to a consultative body and tried to subordinate other parties to his National Unity Party (Partido de Unidad Nacional – PUN). In July of 1956, Diaz arrested and exiled Villeda Morales and other PLH leaders. In August, he crushed an uprising with 400 troops.[351]

When Diaz rigged the assembly elections to favor PUN candidates, the army and air force revolted. Led by Major Roberto Galvez, they established a short-term junta. Elections for the assembly and presidency were held in October and November of 1957. Ramon Villeda Morales became president on January 1, 1958.

The Military Intervenes Again

Villeda attempted to modernize Honduras through IMF and World Bank loans. He built roads, schools and hospitals, funded health care and fought illiteracy. At the time, he described Honduras as "a country of the 70s—70 percent illiteracy, 70 percent illegitimacy, 70 percent rural population, and 70 percent avoidable deaths."[352] Villeda launched a major program for agrarian reform. He also created the National Agrarian Institute to address uncultivated land belonging to the fruit companies, which fulfilled no social function.[353]

Since 1930, the population doubled, and grew at an annual rate of 2.8 percent. This strained the country's resources, and land seizures by campesinos were fought by large land owners. In the late 1950s, 50 percent of rural people were landless or land-poor. The presence of Salvadorean squatters and the growth of large estates for cattle, cotton and coffee had transformed rural farming into subsistence efforts. The land was overworked and over exploited. Increasing militancy and organization by peasants had culminated in violence against land owners.

---

351 "Honduras: Aborted Reform, 1954-63."

352 Schulz, Donald E., and Deborah Sundloff Schulz, 27.

353 Brockett, Charles D., *Land, Power, and Poverty: Agrarian Transformation and Political Conflict in Central America* (Boulder, CO: Westview Press, 1998) 186.

Under the government's land reform, 75,000 acres of national and communal lands were distributed to peasants.[354] The National Association of Honduran Peasants (Asociacion Nacional de Campesinos de Honduras – ANACH) was created by the government to counteract radicalization.

ANACH competed with the Francisco Morazan Movement (MFM) and the Revolutionary Party (PR), both organizations of Castroite inspiration that developed guerrilla cells. Their cells were destroyed and some of their members killed. Others were exiled or imprisoned.[355] Also organized were the Roman Catholic Comite Coordinador de Organizaciones Democraticas de Honduras (CORDEH), the Christian Democratic Party (PDC); and a student organization, the Frente Revolucionario Estudiantil Social Cristiano (FRESC).[356]

Since the government repressed opposition, Honduras received an inflow of US $200 million in foreign investment between 1961 and 1965. That figure doubled between 1963 and 1967. Thirty-five of the sixty-three biggest firms evolved between 1960 and 1968, and the five largest firms were 100 percent controlled by U.S. multinationals.[357]

Villeda's reforms were consistent with the Kennedy administration's Alliance for Progress program, and Honduras received ample funding. Opposition to reform stemmed from the National Federation of Agriculturists and Stockraisers of Honduras, which represented the large landowners. Military support waned after the creation of the Civil Guard (Guardia Civil) as an independent police in 1957.

In 1963, it appeared that Modesto Rodas Alvarado would win the presidential election, and his left-leaning PLH politics made the military nervous.[358] On October 3, 1963, the military seized power. Colonel Lopez Arellano declared himself president, Villeda and Alvarado were exiled, and the U.S. broke off diplomatic relations.

At first, Lopez nullified reform by de-funding the National Agrarian Institute. He became close to the PNH and established a

---

354 Schulz, Donald E., and Deborah Sundloff Schulz, 29.

355 Aguilar, Ernesto Paz, "9 the Origin and Development of Political Parties in Honduras," *Political Parties and Democracy in Central America*, ed. Louis W. Goodman, William M. LeoGrande, and Johanna Mendelson Forman (Boulder, CO: Westview Press, 1992) 164.

356 Brett, Donna W., 112.

357 Schulz, Donald E., and Deborah Sundloff Schulz, 33.

358 Brockett, Charles D., 186.

loose organization called the Mancho Brava. The latter consisted of shock troops, authorized to "attack and kill" the regime's enemies.

Lopez distrusted the Alliance for Progress, and the funds he accepted were channeled to his supporters. [359] The economy took a downturn for lack of public investment under widespread corruption and graft. The use of the Central American Common Market (CACM) as a vent for Honduran exports was preferred to internal markets because better jobs and wages to give people the means of purchase would eventually inspire political demands.

In the legislative elections of 1965, Lopez ensured that Mancho Brava thugs and members of the army were present at the polling stations. His party gained 35 of the 64 seats. Then the Assembly claimed the right to appoint the president, giving Lopez another term.

The Soccer War

The scapegoats of the regime were Salvadorean squatters who migrated to Honduras seeking land and work. The government decided to expropriate squatters' lands for agrarian reform, and this pleased Honduran peasants, as only the foreigners suffered. The Honduran Secret Police (Departimiento de Investigaciones Nacionales – DIN), the Mancho Brava, Honduran army and vigilantes forcibly expelled the Salvadoreans, employing rape, torture and murder. By July 1969, 20,000 Salvadoreans fled back to El Salvador.

Preexisting tensions were caused by El Salvadorean troops entering Honduras in pursuit of alleged criminals. Now participation in the World Cup games incited retaliatory harassment and El Salvador invaded.

Some 130,000 Salvadoreans were expelled from Honduras, causing both countries severe economic damage. Two thousand Hondurans were killed as the Salvadorean air force struck and the army captured Nueva Ocotepeque. In return, the Honduran air force attacked Salvadorean oil storage facilities. In a fight that lasted one hundred hours, the two countries' relations were irreparably damaged. They both lost the benefits of the Central American Common Market, and diplomatic relations would not be restored until 1980.

---

359 Anderson, Thomas P., *Politics in Central America: Guatemala, El Salvador, Honduras, and Nicaragua*, 131.

Power Behind the Scenes

After the Soccer War, no amount of nationalism could keep Lopez in office. The economy was in shambles and agrarian reform had stumbled. The PNH and the PLN divided the Assembly seats between them then held a presidential election. Ramon Ernesto Cruz narrowly won, but Lopez Arellano remained in power behind the scenes as chief of the armed forces.

Lopez disrupted the Cruz regime by dismissing Rigoberto Sandoval, who oversaw the pace of agrarian reform. Then Lopez seized power during a feud between the PNH and the PLN.

During Lopez's second term, he pushed land reform. New decrees allowed the government to force landholders to rent underutilized properties, and led to the establishment of 500 peasant settlements. Then lands totaling 600,000 hectares were distributed to 120,000 families over the next five years.[360]

Lopez called a meeting of Latin American countries that included Colombia, Ecuador, Costa Rica, Nicaragua, Honduras, Guatemala and Panama. The issue of a proposed impost on fruit exports, translated to fifty-cent charge per crate of bananas. Initiated on April 25, 1974, the impost was protested by the U.S. ambassador and the company United Brands. Eli Black, the chairman of United Brands, bribed Lopez and economics minister Abraham Bennaton Ramos to cancel the export impost on August 24, 1974.[361] The scandal, known as Bananagate, reverberated through Honduras and led to Lopez's ouster via military coup. On March 31, 1975, General Juan Alberto Melgar Castro took power.

---

360 Anderson, Thomas P., *The War of the Dispossessed: Honduras and El Salvador, 1969,* 158.

361 Schulz, Donald E., and Deborah Sundloff Schulz, 43.

CHAPTER SEVENTEEN: HONDURAS — THE IMPACT OF THE CONTRAS

As violence escalated in Nicaragua during the late 1970s, Honduras found itself in an uncomfortable position. It did not want to support the unpopular Somoza regime but found itself likewise confounded with regard the FSLN, the Marxist Sandinista movement. When it captured German Pomares, a leader of the FSLN in March 1978, it refused to extradite him to Nicaragua and instead flew him to Panama. The government collaborated in attacks on Sandinista base camps to a certain extent, but sold arms to the Sandinistas at the same time that it sold intelligence to Somoza.[362] And during the course of the war, Honduras found itself host to an increasing number of Nicaraguan refugees.

In the meantime, the regime of Melgar Castro was facing its own challenge. Charged with corruption and protecting narcotics traffic in which members of the military were alleged to have participated, the regime came under increasing right-wing criticism. Student movements read this criticism as the prelude to another coup, and took to the streets to defend Melgar, which, in turn, signaled to the military that Melgar had lost control of public order. They therefore wasted no time in replacing him with a three-member junta, of which General Policarpo Paz Garcia was the leader.

---

362 Ibid., 55.

Paz was faced with defiance from the peasants, who returned to land seizures as the means to force the government to reengage in agrarian reform. Labor also gave him problems, as the cost of living had risen by 25 percent annually between 1975 and 1979. Textile workers struck violently in San Pedro Sula in March of 1979, and a massive strike of 14,000 sugarcane workers occurred later in October during the middle of harvest. Likewise, 6000 workers struck against United Brands, in a struggle that dragged on into 1980. In the end, large gains were made by labor, including a 66 percent wage hike over three years.[363]

The New Significance of Honduras

When the Sandinistas won their war in Nicaragua, the Carter administration was faced with a fait accompli. It therefore became increasingly important to avoid a domino effect in the rest of Central America, with the threat to El Salvador from the FMLN looming large in the minds of Americans. The Carter administration praised the Paz government for making "progress toward democracy," and it was clear that Honduras would become the "new Nicaragua" or bulwark against communism within the Central American sphere.

U.S. aid to Honduras rose to US $53.1 million in 1980, and military assistance increased from US $2.3 million to US $3.9 million.[364] The U.S. Congress agreed to loan the country 10 Huey helicopters so that they could patrol the Salvadorean border, and Green Berets were sent to patrol the area in the company of Honduran soldiers.

This was the time when an alleged massacre occurred on the Sampul River in El Salvador, involving Salvadorean and Honduran forces which were said to have participated in a joint counterinsurgency operation. Some six hundred were said to have been killed as the Honduran troops forced peasants fleeing El Salvador back over the border where they were gunned down by Salvadorean troops. A Roman Catholic group, headed by Bishop Carranza, recorded the scene as follows:

> The previous day, trucks and other vehicles filled with soldiers from the Honduran army arrived in Guarita...They continued... to the Sumpul River, the frontier between Honduras and El Salvador. They cordoned off the left bank...At about 7 a.m. on May 14, the massacre began in the Salvadoran village of La Arada. Two helicopters, the [Salvadoran] National Guard, soldiers

363 Anderson, Thomas P., *Politics in Central America: Guatemala, El Salvador, Honduras, and Nicaragua*, 144.

364 Schulz, Donald E., and Deborah Sundloff Schulz, 60.

and men from ORDEN began firing at the defenseless people. Women were tortured before being killed; babies were tossed into the air for target practice. Those people lucky enough to cross the river were met by the Honduran soldiers who returned them to the scene of the slaughter. By afternoon the genocide ceased, leaving a minimum of 600 dead.[365]

Later, Salvadorean president Jose Napoleon Duarte would claim that 300 had been killed, all of them "communist guerillas."

The Salvadoreans and Hondurans signed a collaboration agreement, and henceforth the Salvadoreans would regularly cross the border to pursue suspected insurgents. Salvadorean refugees were killed crossing the border, and their camps were regularly invaded resulting in kidnappings and further killings. In retaliation, the FMLN began carrying its guerilla activities into Honduras also.

It was August of 1981 when Duane "Dewey" Clarridge was appointed chief of the CIA operations directorate's Latin American section. Clarridge traveled to Honduras where he told Paz that the U.S. would support the resistance in its efforts to "liberate" Nicaragua. Thus, the Nicaraguan Democratic Force (Fuerza Democratica Nicaraguense – FDN) was born on August 11 with support from Honduras, Argentina, and the CIA. Comprised mainly of members of Somoza's Guardia Nacional, the FDN was headed by Enrique Bermudez as the CIA's point man.

With Honduran cooperation, U.S. and Argentine personnel began training the contras in camps along the Nicaraguan border. Their war, as described in the chapters on Nicaragua was aimed at creating vast economic destruction and forcing the Sandinistas to spend their scarce resources on a military buildup. At the same time, it was hoped that the Sandinistas would become more repressive, thus activating the moderates in the country and winning them over to the contra cause.

To an extent, this did happen. The Sandinistas forcibly relocated some 8,500 Miskito Indians who could not otherwise be defended, and this proved to be a propaganda opportunity for the United States to use against them. The Reagan administration, moreover, insisted that it had proof that the Sandinistas were still supplying arms to the FMLN and domestically depending on Cuban and Soviet advisors.

Then, in 1981, General Gustavo Alvarez, chief of the National Intelligence Department (DNI) and of the Public Security Forces (FUSEP), became head of the Armed Forces Superior Council

---

365 Brett, Donna W., 126.

(COSUFA). Alvarez had already proven his extreme right-wing, anticommunist orientation in campaigns within Honduras against the FMLN, Salvadorean exiles, and Honduran leftists. Now, the appointment of Alvarez, combined with the institutional independence of the military in Honduras, allowed the U.S. to bypass the president and the legislature in setting up base camps in Honduras to aid and support the contras.[366]

The Suazo Era

As the contra war proceeded, the Paz administration promised to return the country to free and fair elections. In April 1980, it held polling for a new Congress, which was to set forth procedures for new Congressional and presidential elections in 1981. The outcome of the April 1980 elections was a victory for the PLH, which won thirty five seats in Congress. The PNH won thirty-three and PINU (the Popular Liberal Alliance–Alianza Liberal del Pueblo) won three.

The drafting of the new constitution and the development of electoral guidelines was such a protracted affair that the elections had to be postponed until November 1981.

The outcome was that the PLH's Suazo Cordova won the presidency, with the PLH also winning a majority of the seats in Congress and a majority of the municipal councils. Suazo was sworn in during January 1982, ending nearly a decade of militarily decided rule.[367]

Suazo was faced, in 1982 with the emergence of the Morazanista Front for the Liberation of Honduras (FMLH), which, in imitation of the FMLN in El Salvador, was comprised of The Honduran Communist Party (PCH); the Honduran branch of the PRTC (part of the FMLN in El Salvador); the Popular Liberation Movement (MPL); and the Popular Revolutionary Front (FPRLZ), as well as other small organizations. The FMLH began conducting low-intensity warfare, including the seizure of a meeting of the San Pedro Sula Chamber of Commerce at which several prominent cabinet

---

366 Mattinson, Sylvia, Sandor Halebsky, James Sacouman, Henry Veltmeyer, John M. Kirk, and George W. Schuyler, eds., *Central America: Democracy, Development, and Change* (New York: Praeger Publishers, 1988) 51.

367 "Honduras: The Return to Civilian Rule, 1978-82" Library of Congress, http://workmall.com/wfb2001/honduras/honduras_history_the_return_to_civilan_rule_1978_82.html.

---

members were present. They demanded, among other things, the release of FMLN prisoners, but did not succeed with their demands beyond guaranteeing their own safety. Their resistance was largely broken in August of 1983, when the Honduran army hunted down the guerrillas in the region of Olancho.

To undercut the rebels, the Suazo administration also renewed efforts toward agrarian reform. During the first three years, approximately 146,000 acres were distributed, benefiting about 36,000 rural families.[368] This progress, nevertheless, was only one-sixth of that projected by the actual agrarian laws. Moreover, much of the land granted was in extremely remote areas and the USAID funds of $12 million for the project were difficult, if not impossible, to acquire. Thus, many of the small farms were abandoned at the same time that peasant unrest and land seizures continued to pose a problem.

By July 1983, President Suazo had begun to question his country's close ties to the United States. In a letter to President Reagan, he wrote, "our people are beginning to ask with greater vigor if it is convenient to our own interests to be so intimately linked to the interest of the United States if we receive so little in exchange."[369] U.S. aid was therefore increased, rising from US $16.3 million between 1975 and 1980 to US $169 million between 1981 and 1985. Likewise, the military budget increased from 7 percent in 1980 to 76 percent in 1985.

The Hondurans remained uneasy, believing that Washington would abandon the contras in the event that they lost their war. They believed in that event that the contras would become bandits within their country, unable to assimilate with the people and their culture. Also of concern, was the drain on Honduras' resources. The Hondurans were expected to provide the contras with health care and to suffer the disruption of their military bases. As Charles D. Brockett observes:

> Around 56,000 fighters and their dependents occupied an area of 279 square miles in Honduras with deleterious consequences. As Schulz and Schulz (1994) describe the situation, 'Many communities had become uninhabitable because of fighting between the contras and the Sandinistas...Assassinations, murders, armed robberies, kidnappings, torture, intimidation, prop-

368 Brockett, Charles D., 193.

369 "Honduras: Honduras and the Nicaraguan Conflict," Library of Congress, http://workmall.com/wfb2001/honduras/honduras_history_honduas_and_the_nicaraguan_conflict.html.

erty seizures, and cattle rustling had become a part of everyday life. Land mines were a constant danger...Damage to the local economy was in the tens of millions of dollars.'[370]

In January 1984, it was announced that North American military facilities, including a regional defense center (CREM), would be constructed. This was a deal which General Alvarez had negotiated in secret, but it was ratified by the president and the Congress. In exchange, the U.S. promised more military and economic aid.

However, the forced departure of General Alvarez on March 31, 1984 and his replacement by General Walter Lopez Reyes, warranted a change in thinking. In August 1984, Lopez informed the United States that it would have to pay the future cost of any and all maneuvers. In that regard, a commission was set up to negotiate future terms, through which Honduras announced that it wanted $1.3 billion in economic aid and $400 million in military aid over the next four years. When Washington balked at the figures, Honduras shut down the CREM and discontinued training for Salvadorean soldiers. Finally, Vice-President George Bush was sent to Honduras in 1985 in order to appease the Hondurans and persuade them to accept lesser figures.[371]

Yet, support appeared to be waning regarding the war of the contras. When the Sandinista EPS crossed into Honduran territory in March of 1986 to engage contra forces near the hamlet of Las Vegas, the Reagan administration seized on the event as an international incident meriting U.S. assistance. The Honduran government itself downplayed the event, as it did with further incursions in December 1986 and June 1987.

In the interim, economic and social conditions within Honduras were largely a disaster. Unemployment was gauged to be 20 percent at the same time that inflation had risen to 50 percent, and annual per capita income remained below US $900. The IMF had imposed loan conditions which required Honduras to cut food subsidies in a full forty categories, and per capita consumption had fallen by 20 percent. As for the persecution of the Honduran people, Mattinson et al, have the following to say:

> Much of Honduras' social and economic decline followed the right dominated years of the first Reagan administration (1980–84). Unusually harsh repression characterized these years, including systematic violations of human rights and the unleash-

---

370 Brockett, Charles D., 196.

371 Anderson, Thomas P., *Politics in Central America: Guatemala, El Salvador, Honduras, and Nicaragua*, 159.

ing of a 'dirty war' based on the Argentine model. Military and police personnel engaged in these activities with the support of U.S., Argentine, and reputedly, Contra, Chilean and Cuban exile advisers. They operated with the tacit approval of an organized Honduran right.[372]

By 1985, it also became apparent that Suazo would resort to political manipulation to maintain his hold on power. He conspired to nominate Oscar Mejia Arellano, a fellow PLH member, to the presidency, and went about promoting his candidacy with all the power at his disposal. When five justices of the Supreme Court of Justice, whom Suazo was counting on to declare a Mejia victory in the event that he was unable to garner a simple majority, were charged with corruption and replaced, Suaza threatened to declare a state of emergency and had the Court surrounded by troops. The military stepped in to arbitrate, with the result that the leaders of Congress rescinded their dismissal of the five justices, and it was agreed that candidates of all political factions could run for president. The winner of the election would be the member of a party who received the most votes within the winning party, thus sidestepping the constitutional requirement that the winner must obtain a simple majority of the vote.[373]

Resolving the Country's Problems

Because the PLH garnered 54 percent of the vote as a party, the winner of the election was declared to be Jose Azcona Hoyo (whose campaign reportedly cost him $3 million lempiras)[374]. Azcona promised "no magic formulas" to solve the country's problems, noting that the country's external debt would have to be renegotiated within the strict guidelines of creditors, and promising to adhere to a foreign policy that was guided by nonintervention.

Increasingly, it became the desire of the Honduran government to seek peace with its neighbors. This coincided with the Contadora process, an initiative that was started on the Panamanian island after which it was named in January 1983. There, the governments of Mexico, Venezuela, Colombia, and Panama tried to mediate peace agreements between the Central American republics. The

---

372 Mattinson, Sylvia, Sandor Halebsky James Sacouman, Henry Veltmeyer, John M. Kirk, and George W. Schuyler, eds., 54.

373 "Honduras: The Struggle of Electoral Democracy: the Elections of 1985," Library of Congress, http://workmall.com/wfb2001/honduras/honduras_history_the_struggle_of_electoral_democracyhtml.

374 Aguilar, Ernesto Paz, 171.

talks continued until 1985, with the main stumbling grounds being that Nicaragua rejected calls for it to democratize and reconcile as interference in its internal affairs, while Nicaragua demanded that aid to the insurgents be halted. Because Washington continued to fund the contras and the parties could not agree to specific terms, largely due to U.S. manipulation of the process, the talks broke down by June 1986.

Then, Costa Rican president Oscar Arias Sanchez announced a new initiative on February 15, 1987. The Arias initiative called for "dialogue between governments and opposition groups, amnesty for political prisoners, cease-fires in ongoing insurgent conflicts, democratization, and free elections in all five regional states. The plan also called for renewed negotiations on arms reductions and an end to outside aid to insurgent forces."[375] The first meeting of the parties took place in Tegucigalpa on July 31, 1987, paving the way for another meeting in Esquipulas on August 6, 1987. Honduras itself had no problem meeting the terms of the proposed treaty as it had no domestic insurgence and was then democratic. Nicaragua had the most trouble with implementing the Esquipulas Agreement and only did so in a limited fashion by late 1988. In fact, the Nicaraguan government backslid on the agreement during the month of July, breaking up a protest demonstration and expelling the U.S. ambassador and seven other diplomats for alleged collaboration, after which it also shut down the newspaper *La Prensa* and the Roman Catholic radio station.

After more summit meetings in 1989, the presidents of the Central American republics agreed on February 14, 1989 that the contras would have ninety days to demobilize in return for free elections. The elections were set for February 1990, but Washington, in the meantime, continued to send the contras nonmilitary aid. The ninety day timetable also proved unfeasible, such that the presidents met again in Tela, Honduras on August 5, 1989. There, they agreed to a new deadline of December 5, 1989 for contra demobilization, with the OAS to supervise the process. This forced Washington to commit to cutting of nonmilitary aid in the event that the contras failed to do so.[376] The Nicaraguans also agreed that they would drop the suit which they had filed against Honduras in the International

---

375 "Honduras: The Arias Plan," Library of Congress, http://workmall.com/wfb2001/honduras/honduras_history_the_arias_plan.html.

376 "Honduras: Accord in Nicaragua," Library of Congress, http://workmall.com/wfb2001/honduras/onduras_history_accord_in_nicaragua.html.

Court of Justice for allowing the contras on their territory if the timetable was met.

When the December 5 deadline proved unworkable, there was a further summit in Costa Rica at which Nicaraguan president Daniel Ortega threatened to continue to press Nicaragua's suit against Honduras. Soon after, Rafael Leonardo Callejas, an opposition candidate of the PNH, won the Honduran presidential polls in November 1989, and Nicaragua's president Daniel Ortega lost the presidency to Violeta Barrios de Chamorro at the February 1990 polls. Thus, the negotiations were concluded with new presidents in office and the war came to an end.

The Honduran Economy

Despite U.S. aid, the 1980s were devastating years for Honduras as it pertained to economic growth. Although the country showed 2.8 percent growth in 1984 and slightly over 3 percent between 1985 and 1986, the simultaneous rise of the population meant that per capita GDP continued to decline and had done so for several years by 1986. Real wages dropped 7.7 percent in 1983 and remained on a downward trend, while unemployment rose from 7–15 percent in 1972–1980 to 26.5 percent in 1986.[377] Much of this was due to a budget shift, which entailed less spending on socioeconomic programs at the same time that two thirds of the budget went to defense spending and debt service. The debt itself doubled between 1980 and 1985 (to rise to $4.675 billion in 2005),[378] causing service charges to absorb almost half of the country's export earnings between 1986 and 1988.[379]

Because of the contra war, capital flight and disinvestment had increased rapidly throughout the 1980s, accounting for anywhere from US $800 million to over US $2 billion in losses. In contrast, U.S. aid from 1980 to 1989 was US $1.15 billion.[380] But U.S. aid alone could not keep the country afloat. The government was faced with either having to adopt an unpopular austerity program that would stimulate public unrest or having to borrow wherever it could, both internationally and domestically. While it chose the latter course,

377 Schulz, Donald E., and Deborah Sundloff Schulz, 190.
378 CIA World Factbook, "Honduras," http://www.cia.gov/cia/publications/factbook/print/ho.html.
379 Schulz, Donald E., and Deborah Sundloff Schulz, 190.
380 Ibid.

its deal with the IMF collapsed by 1983, leaving Honduras to rely increasingly on internal credit to finance its affairs.

> During the Suazo administration, the U.S. had pressed the Honduran government to adopt an IMF-style austerity program. In particular, it had wanted Suazo to devalue the currency, thus passing much of the cost of economic stabilization onto the poor. Suazo had resisted, and the U.S. was forced to be content with Honduran support for the contras as the basis of its continuing relations. But with the election of Azcona, the U.S. began to make progress in forcing through reforms. USAID became the final arbiter of all Honduran affairs, releasing and withholding aid contingent with the country's progress.

While the economy did recover slightly, with GDP rising by 4.2 percent in 1987, Honduras was still plagued with "massive fiscal deficits, an overvalued exchange rate, a shortage of foreign exchange, and declining private-sector confidence."[381] When Rafael Callejas took over in January 1990, he focused on reducing the deficit, reducing the overvalued exchange rate, and other economic reforms, including eliminating structural barriers that stood in the way of foreign investment.[382] Honduras acquired a new Triple A rating with multilateral lending institutions, and aid continued to roll in along with IDB and AID loans of US $110 million and US $17 million respectively. The United States also forgave a total of US $434.6 million of Honduras' foreign debt.

Nonetheless, two thirds of the workforce was either unemployed or under employed, and 170,000 peasant families were landless. Due to the government's Structural Adjustment Program, the National Association of Small and Medium-Sized Industries reported that 255 businesses would declare bankruptcy, while another 1,000 would suspend operations, resulting in the loss of 5,000 jobs.[383] By 1992, poverty grew to 72 percent. And land reform, needless to say, was dead. Outraged campesinos continued with land seizures, and peasant cooperatives, unable to pay the increasingly high costs of credit, were forced to sell out to large landowners and privileged interests to the extent that they became "slaves on their own land."

In the first months of 1992, Honduras received US $52 billion in international assistance, but the status of the poor was no better when Carlos Robert Reina became the next president. Reina initi-

---

381 Schulz, Donald E., and Deborah Sundloff Schulz, 199.
382 "Honduras (12/05)" U.S. State Department, http://www.state.gov/r/pa/ei/bgn/1922.htm.
383 Schulz, Donald E., and Deborah Sundloff Schulz, 293.

ated further austerity measures to bring down the fiscal deficit and also succeeded in generating moderate economic growth. But poverty continued to climb, with 54 percent of the population living in extreme conditions (usually measured by subsistence on less than US $1 per day).[384]

The situation became still more dire when Hurricane Mitch swept the country in October 1998, leaving 5,000 dead and 1.5 million displaced. This occurred under the watch of President Carlos Roberto Flores Facusse, who took office on January 27, 1998.

When the IMF prepared its policy paper on Honduras in 1999 (to cover the period of 1970–97), it recommended the following:

a) privatizing state enterprises (such as those involved in telecommunications and electricity);

b) reducing tax rates on businesses to levels in competitor countries;

c) setting up a framework (including legal safeguards) to encourage foreign investment in new activities such as tourism and infrastructure development; and

d) redirecting public expenditure to activities that complement private investment such as public spending in social areas as education and health.[385]

Of primary concern was the wage and benefit system, which required employers to pay monies into employee-related funds that were said to be wasteful and inefficient. The IMF therefore recommended modernizing the Social Security system and doing away with many of the funds and benefits that made employer relations "inflexible." With downward pressure on wages, it was assumed that employers would be inspired to undertake labor-intensive production, such that it would generate more employment to benefit the poor.

Honduras and the HIPC Initiative

In July 2000, Honduras reached the decision point of the Heavily Indebted Poor Countries (HIPC) initiative, thus qualifying for multilateral debt relief. Until 2004, however, recurrent fiscal deficits derailed the IMF reforms, such that the program was put on hold. As part of putting its house in order, Honduras had to issue

---

384 Brockett, Charles D., 197.

385 Juan-Ramon, V. Hugo, "Honduras's Growth Performance During 1970-97, International Monetary Fund, January 1999.

a progress report on its Poverty Reduction Strategy Paper (PRSP), the details of which are outlined below.

The report notes, firstly, that the percentage of Hondurans living in extreme poverty declined from 49 percent in 1999 to 44.6 percent in 2004 (by approximately one percentage point per year). At the same time, the overall poverty headcount fell less, from 66 percent to 64.2 percent. The PRSP's stated goal is to reduce poverty by a full 24 percentage points by 2015.[386]

Under the HIPC, Honduras received the debt relief equivalent of 0.2 percent of GDP in 2000; 0.9 percent in 2001 and 2002; and 0.8 percent in 2003 and 2004, totaling US $256.8 million at the end of 2004. The total spending on poverty in 2004 was 8.4 percent of GDP, of which 57 percent was invested in human capital, 19 percent was invested in guaranteeing the strategy's sustainability, and 13 percent was invested in reducing poverty in rural zones.[387]

Apart from simple spending, the PRSP lists several other measures that the government has taken to invite further investment and protect vulnerable groups. These are:

1) approval of the Finance System Law and reforms of the law regulating the National Banking and Insurance Commission (CNBS), the BCH and the Insured Deposits Fund (FOSEDE);

2) approval of the Copyright Law and its norms;

3) approval of a work program for the Central American Customs Union, aiding regional integration;

4) conclusion of the CAFTA Agreement;

5) creation of the National Commission on Competitiveness and the National Center to Promote Agro-Business;

6) creation of a Tourism Cabinet and a special Tourism Police Unit;

7) approval of the Financial Support Law for Agricultural Producers, along with the Property Law, which includes the creation of a Property Institute;

8) approval of the Framework Law for Potable Water and Sanitation;

9) approval and initiation of the Education for All (EFA) program for 2003–2015;

10) the strengthening of primary care, primary care for children and women, and better quality health services all around;

---

386 IMF, "Honduras: Poverty reduction Strategy Paper Progress Report," IMF Country Report No. 05/82, March 2005.
387 Ibid.

11) the development of a Plan of Attention for the Most Socially Vulnerable—street children, sexually exploited children, children orphaned by HIV/AIDS, gang members, the disabled, the elderly, and female victims of violence;

12) development of the National Policy on Preventing Disabilities and the Comprehensive Care and Rehabilitation of Disabled Persons and Respecting their Rights and Responsibilities;

13) development of the National Plan of Action for the Disabled;

14) creation of a Commission to Eliminate All Forms of Racial Discrimination;

15) implementation of Preventive Education Programs (managed by the Division of Gang Prevention);

16) implementation of the "Safer Community" program; and

17) implementation of the Strategy to Combat Drug Trafficking.[388]

While this is an ambitious set of programs, they appear to consist mainly of administrative and legal reforms whose object is to make health care and safety more accessible to the public while increasing property rights and promoting the export industry. And just because the government makes these things accessible does not mean that they will be affordable.

We may note, for example, that the government imposed its authority over labor to the extent that the percentage of GDP which was devoted to public sector employees dropped from 10.8 percent in 2002 to 10.2 percent in 2004. This occurred at a time when teachers, in particular, were striking for a 50 percent increase in wages, a thing that was not unreasonable considering that the average teacher earns only US $250 per month and the cost of a minimum food basket in Honduras is US $200.[389] Within the United States, we would consider that poverty, given that it leaves only US $50 to pay for the cost of housing, energy, transportation, and other minimal necessities. The IMF prescription, however, indicates that it would like to see the percentage of GDP that is devoted to public sector employees drop to only 8 percent.

Of course, it should be mentioned that the current measurements for poverty in underdeveloped countries place earnings of $2 dollars a day above the poverty line, which, in realistic terms, is outdated and in need of adjustment. If a teacher cannot make it

---

388 Ibid.

389 Jensen, Soren Kirk, and FOSDEH, "Honduras Pushed to the Edge: Spring Meetings of the IMF and the World Bank, Washington DC, April 2004," Foro Social de Deuda Externa y Desarrollo de Honduras.

on a salary of US $1.60 an hour, imagine what private sector labor-ers earning $2.00 per day can afford to buy in exchange. Thus, the whole conception of poverty reduction is flawed. It is simply not feasible for a nation to support itself on the backs of underpaid and overexploited labor, nor is it exactly accelerated development when we say that we plan to raise 60 percent of the population up to the rate of US $2 per day.

As far as income equality is concerned, the PRSP indicates that 80 percent of households received only 39.8 percent of the nation's total income, whereas 60.2 percent of the nation's income went to the wealthiest 20 percent (May 2003). This structure has remained the same for many years, and only shows that the third and fourth quintiles are slowly losing ground. The percentage of income going to the lowest quintile only appears larger because it has shrunk for slightly higher levels. In sum, people have lost out. Incomes are on a downward, rather than an upward trend overall.

And, like El Salvador, the degree to which Honduras depends on foreign remittances is high. Family remittances from Hondu-rans living abroad rose 19 percent in 2003 to $860 million, thus ac-counting at least in part for the poverty reduction of approximately 5 percent that the government now claims. We can see from the figures, however, that this only boosted 3 percent of the populace above the poverty line, with the remaining 2 percent being elevated to the poor, rather than the desperate. Thus, the results of the gov-ernment's programs have been negligible at best.

Despite its best intentions, the government will have to work within the parameters that the IMF and other multilateral insti-tutions establish as "reasonable" guidelines, meaning that instead of trickling down, as one author puts it, wealth will continue to "bubble up" to the privileged through the reserve army of the un-employed, the country's low wage scale, and the "spiraling race to the bottom," wherein the country's goods are sold in international markets at undervalued prices. The poor, meanwhile, will continue to deal with basic food shortages (because even their bean harvests are shipped abroad for export), landlessness, rising energy prices, and ruthless exploitation.

CHAPTER EIGHTEEN: FAST-FORWARD TO A VOLATILE USA

On January 8, 2011, America was shocked by the shooting of Congresswoman Gabrielle Giffords, Judge John Roll, retiree Dorwin Stoddard and nine-year-old Christina Green by Jared Lee Loughner,[390] a disturbed young man, who left a legacy of strangeness on You Tube and Facebook before he committed his crimes.

Witnesses at the site blamed the sharpshooter's crosshairs pictured on Sarah Palin's web site above Giffords' district as a goad that was taken literally to produce the assassination attempt and the Tea Party was named as Giffords' greatest threat.[391] Sheriff Clarence Dupnik declared that Arizona was more than a dangerous place; in his capacity as a law man with thirty years of experience, he called it the "Mecca of hate and bigotry," invoking a firestorm of rebuke.[392]

---

390 "Arizona Shooting Victims: Judge John Roll, Christina Green, and More," *The Daily Beast*, http://www.thedailybeast.com/blogs-and-stories/2011-01-09/arizona-shooting-victims-christina-green-judge-john-roll-and-more/

391 Fitz, Timothy, "AZ Shooter Jared Lee Loughner: Charged With Shooting Gabrielle Giffords, Killing Others, Inspired by Sarah Palin Tea Party?" http://www.chicagonewsreport.com/2011/01/az-shooter-jared-lee-loughner-charged.html

392 Video, http://vodpod.com/watch/5306571-sheriff-dupnik-on-giffords-shooting-az-is-the-mecca-of-hate-bigotry-the-tombstone-of-the-u-s-

---

Fox News cut away from a mourner once Palin's name was said[393] and all manner of Internet buzz, from fear of the rightwing being implicated to a concerted counterassault featuring unverified Facebook posts[394] and photos of leftwing protests involving nudity and threats, were used to blame the left. It was claimed that Mr. Loughner could be diagnosed as schizophrenic without ever having met him and, instead of leading to reasonable dialogue, measures for gun-control and a modicum of contrition, conservatives warned that blame-mongers[395] and President Obama were attempting to end free speech.[396] The right clung tighter to its gun rights and prepared to ruin Sheriff Dupnik for daring to speak his piece.[397]

Choosing not to confront resistance, the government made an end-run around the issue with a new federal hotline to call if anyone fears someone is mentally ill and in need of crisis intervention. Presumably, this will help state Fusion Centers, which were formed in the 9/11 aftermath, to sift through the millions of names in the law enforcement database and isolate possible dangers more speedily and accurately, now that it only takes one mention of your name in connection with vague (and even unfounded) suspicions to guarantee its inclusion.[398]

393 Christopher, Tommy, "Fox News Briefly Airs Giffords Vigil, Mourner Says, 'And I say to you, Sarah Palin...'" http://www.mediaite.com/online/fox-news-abruptly-cuts-away-from-giffords-vigil-as-mourner-says-%E2%80%98and-i-say-to-you-sarah-palin%E2%80%99/

394 Dimiero, Ben, "Shameless: Jim Hoft Falls for Fake Facebook Profile in Attempt to Link Loughner to Obama," *Media Matters for America*, January 10, 2011, http://mediamatters.org/blog/201101100010. For deceptive Facebook pages supposedly posted by the left, see: http://www.facebook.com/topic.php?uid=15704546335&topic=46928

395 "Bernie Goldberg on Far Left Blaming Conservatives After Arizona Shooting," *O'Reilly Factor*, http://www.foxnews.com/on-air/oreilly/transcript/bernie-goldberg-far-left-blaming-conservatives-after-arizona-shooting

396 Eddlam, Thomas R., "Arizona Shooting: Pretense for an Attack on Free Speech?" New American, January 28, 2011, http://www.thenewamerican.com/index.php/usnews/crime/6086-a-pretense-for-attack-on-free-speech

397 "Bill O'Reilly Wants Investigation Into Sheriff Dupnik's *Responsibility For* Tucson Massacre," http://digg.com/news/politics/bill_o_reilly_wants_investigation_into_sheriff_dupnik_s_responsibility_for_tucson_massacre

398 An example of what was strangely perceived as a "terrorist threat" in Chattanooga, Tennessee can be found in the December 22, 2010 edition of the *Chattanooga Times Free Press*. The Tennessee ACLU was accused of identifiable terrorist activity for writing to the Superintendents of

Something Deeper at Work than Blame

Bloggers and journalists (on both the right and the left) pointed out the indecency of finger-pointing at a time when our nation was hurting, shocked, and appalled by what took place.[399] But what Loughner attacked wasn't just people; he also struck at belief systems, the power to implement policies that were inimical to his views and the right to interact with the citizenry as a fundamental aspect of the American political process, without fear of harassment or violence.[400]

Long before this, reports of the Tea Party's strategy for interfering with town hall meetings uncovered an email directing recipients to intersperse evenly with the crowds (so as to appear more numerous and representative of the groups). The speaking Democrats were to be interrupted frequently by Tea Party members standing up and shouting out, then immediately sitting down, to prevent being removed for harassment. The plan was to "rattle" the Democrats and disrupt their agendas. It was not to debate the speakers or engage in substantive dialogue.[401] By denying the speakers a voice, the Tea Party drove the Democrats to organize "Congress on Your Corner" as a spontaneous alternate venue, which also made them more vulnerable.[402]

Schools to request that they make the Christmas holiday religiously inclusive. When questioned on it, Mike Browning of the Department of Homeland Security indicated that the label had been a mistake, but: "I don't believe that it's outrageous that we're basically taking information that was published in an open service media source and ... making sure it gets to the appropriate law enforcement." http://www.timesfreepress.com/news/2010/dec/22/aclu-bristles-over-terror-list/

399 Pye, Jason, "Absurd finger-pointing continues in wake of Arizona shooting," *United Liberty*, January 11, 2011, http://www.unitedliberty.org/articles/7622-absurd-fingerpointing-continues-in-wake-of-arizona-shooting

400 Swedberg, Nick, "Hultgren Condemns Deadly Arizona Attack; Suspect Stands Accused of Attempted Assassination," *GenevaPatch*, January 10, 2011, http://geneva.patch.com/articles/hultgren-condemns-deadly-arizona-attack-suspect-stands-accused-of-attempted-assassination

401 Beutler, Brian, "Tea Party Town Hall Strategy: 'Rattle Them,' 'Stand Up and Shout,'" *TPM*, August 3, 2009, http://tpmdc.talkingpointsmemo.com/2009/08/tea-party-town-hall-strategy-rattle-them-stand-up-and-shout.php

402 Sonmez, Felicia, "Sarah Palin on Tucson shooting rampage: 'Acts of monstrous criminality stand on their own," *Washington Post*, January 12,

---

A Recipe for Violence

In forming the Tea Party,[403] Dick Armey made a conscious choice to build a populist movement that is armed, revolutionary, and hostile, claiming that politicians in Washington "forgot about Americans."[404] Armey used gun rights and anti-government sentiment of all kinds to bind disparate groups, from the mainstream N.R.A. to the paranoid rightwing fringe, into a force for change that, by its very nature, bullies, threatens and offers no compromise.[405] More binding still is fear, whether it is based on the concept of a New World Order[406] (abbreviated as NWO in conspiracy parlance), a millenarian worldview,[407] a shadow government of bankers, Illuminati, Freemasons and Jews,[408] or a Seventh Day Adventist interpretation of Biblical Revelation that casts the American government in the role of the "Beast"[409] or Antichrist in a unifying call for Christians to commence fighting the good fight from fear for their very souls as we careen toward the end of the world.

New World Order

There are millions of Internet pages dedicated to exposing a sinister New World Order that has its roots in the United Nations as the precursor to one-world Soviet-style collectivism and socialism. Frequently posted by religious groups and rightwing political activists, many cite UN documents that are readily available on the Internet, particularly with respect to the topics of depopulation, a

2011, http://voices.washingtonpost.com/44/2011/01/reports-arizona-rep-gabrielle.html

403 Good, Chris, "The Tea Party Movement: Who's in Charge?" *The Atlantic*, April 13, 2009, http://www.theatlantic.com/politics/archive/2009/04/the-tea-party-movement-whos-in-charge/13041/

404 Gillman, Todd J., "Dick Armey says Tea Party is here to stay," *dallasnews.com*, March 16, 2010, http://www.dallasnews.com/news/politics/national-politics/20100316-Dick-Armey-says-Tea-Party-is-9515.ece

405 Reinstein, Ted, "Dear Tea Party: Don't tread on Me, either (Compares us to the Confederacy)" *Free Republic*, October 29, 2010, http://www.freerepublic.com/focus/f-backroom/2617308/posts

406 New World Order (conspiracy theory), *Wikipedia*, http://en.wikipedia.org/wiki/New_World_Order_%28conspiracy_theory%29

407 Millenarianism, *Wikipedia*, http://en.wikipedia.org/wiki/Millenarianism

408 Radical Right, *Wikipedia*, http://en.wikipedia.org/wiki/Radical_Right

409 "Seventh Day Adventism," *Catholic Answers*, http://www.catholic.com/library/Seventh_Day_Adventism.asp

one-world police force, and a one-world totalitarian government. As a throwback to the Cold War when Communism and socialism were the enemies of religion and capitalism, conspiracy theorists appear to believe that President Obama is the tool of such contro-versial groups as the Bilderbergers and Trilateralists. This may or may not be true, but since their agendas are no different from what we've seen in Central America, what conspiracists are reacting to is mostly a fear of secrecy.

The Bilderbergers are mainly members of royalty, top govern-ment officials, and people who are privileged in wealth and politics. Unlike the United Nations, which holds its proceedings in public, as do international summits on everything from global warming to economics, the Bilderbergers prefer, and are accustomed to, pri-vacy as a matter of their station and meet semi-covertly to discuss matters of mutual importance, especially as they impact trade and global security. These meetings allow face-to-face deliberations and alignment on decisions that are not directly implemented, but in-stead pursued as policies, whether it is through the United Nations, the IMF and World Bank, or other institutions.

The Trilateral Commission is a similar elitist group that formu-lates public policies and approaches to common problems through government officials, members of defense and intelligence agen-cies, and members of corporate industry. Their focus is on national agendas and managing public perception, so that opponents and dissidents are marginalized and discredited. They have a mission to deepen capitalism and neutralize resistance, particularly as eco-nomic stratification produces more deprivation and the repression of the poor becomes necessary.

Just as nation states are controlled through Western indebted-ness, so does private indebtedness create a frantic scenario where families work two, three, and even four jobs to stay ahead of their bills and mortgages. However, these people are not dangerous. They have no time to fight the system while they cling to status and own-ership by the skin of their bitten fingernails, unlike those who are less desperate, with the potential to join insurgencies. Because the latter are potentially dangerous, they are co-opted by politicians who play to their fears and prejudices, even though the process is launched, led, and financed by the very same beneficiaries of the agendas that so frighten them.

Careening Toward Confrontation

When conspiracy is joined with pre-destiny, confrontation becomes inevitable. It's an organizational tactic deliberately designed to radicalize, mobilize and overtly militarize. To that end, Tea Party targets have also been moderate Republicans,[410] including those in Arizona who announced they were stepping down in the wake of Loughner's rampage because they didn't sign on to the job to "take a bullet for anyone."[411] The Tea Party is challenging experienced and respected Republicans, like Indiana's Senator Richard Lugar,[412] to prove they're "real" conservatives while simultaneously launching campaigns to remove them from office.[413]

Funded substantially by the Koch brothers[414] and now eligible for anonymous contributions of the kind that were legalized[415] before the Congressional turnover that brought the Tea Party to power,[416] the radicalized right doesn't lack money or influence. It has aggressively attacked spending and taxation while pursuing a

410 Lewison, Jed, "ME-Sen: Snowe Removal: Tea Party Express targets Olympia Snowe," *Daily Kos*, February 10, 2011, http://www.dailykos.com/story/2011/2/10/942667/-ME-Sen:-Snowe-removal:-Tea-Party-Express-targets-Olympia-Snowe

411 Camia, Catalina, "Ariz. GOP official resigns: 'Won't take a bullet,'" *USA Today*, January 12, 2011, http://content.usatoday.com/communities/onpolitics/post/2011/01/gabrielle-giffords-arizona-tea-party-bullet-/1

412 Blake, Aaron, "Hatch and Lugar blaze different paths as Tea Party stalks," *Washington Post*, February 8, 2011, http://voices.washingtonpost.com/thefix/republican-party/lugar-hatch-tea-party.html

413 The Tea Party has opposed Senator Lugar's endorsement of the START Treaty on the grounds that it threatens national security, when the ostensible point of the Treaty is to decommission weapons that are outdated and costly in favor of updating our arsenal at a time when cash-strapped Russia will be unable to upgrade. The Tea Party has likewise forced the Pentagon to reinstate an abandoned missile project.

414 "The Koch Empire and Americans For Prosperity," October 20, 2010, *No Cure For That*, http://nocureforthat.wordpress.com/2010/10/20/the-koch-empire-and-americans-for-prosperity/

415 Gandelman, Joe, "Could Undisclosed Campaign Contributions Impact 2012 Republican Primaries?" *The Moderate Voice*, November 12, 2011, http://themoderatevoice.com/92250/could-undisclosed-campaign-contributions-impact-2012-republican-primaries/

416 Rucker, Philip, Crites, Alice, and Shackelford, Lucy, "Huge midterm turnover makes House more of an everyman's roost," *Washington Post*, November 4, 2010, http://www.washingtonpost.com/wp-dyn/content/article/2010/11/03/AR2010110308373.html

redefinition and limitation of rights for women,[417] gays,[418] illegal im-migrants[419] and anyone who is not specifically a heterosexual white male Christian.[420]

With a fallback position of violence,[421] the Tea Party's agenda is aimed at worse than intimidation of gays, women, nonwhites and non-Christians. They don't just oppose the 36 percent of America's 308 million citizens self-defined as politically moderate and the 20 percent who are liberal. They despise more than half the nation.[422]

Fitting the Victim Profile

In terms of who they are, or were, we can't overlook what Loughner's victims represent.

Congresswoman Giffords is a Democrat, one who supports healthcare reform and the President's proposed DREAM Act (which would legalize immigrant children through military service or completion of a college degree).[423] She is also pro-choice and has a history of pragmatism on gun rights. Immediately after the shooting, Congresswoman Giffords was labeled a "good dame" by a blogger on Twitter, who misaligned her with pro-life politics and later

---

417 "Scalia to talk about Constitution to House Members," *zimbio*, January 5, 2011, http://www.zimbio.com/Justice+Antonin+Scalia/articles/ xOoKEWYlSCk/Scalia+Talk+Constitution+House+Members (Under Scalia's interpretation, the Fourth Amendment does not protect women.)

418 Bolcer, Julie, "Republicans Reject Gay Rights in Poll," *Advocate.com*, February 3, 2011, http://www.advocate.com/News/Daily_News/ 2010/02/03/Republicans_Reject_Gay_Rights_in_Poll/

419 "Republican legislators target 'anchor babies' with 14th Amendment challenge," *Southern California Public Radio*, January 5, 2011, http://www. scpr.org/programs/madeleine-brand/2011/01/05/14th_ammendment/

420 Hawkins, John, "Fight Back Against the Tolerance Fascists," *Right Wing News*, January 27, 2009, http://rightwingnews.com/mt331/2009/01/my_ latest_townhall_column_figh.php

421 "Fearing Tea Party violence, four Arizona Republicans resign," *The Raw Story*, January 12, 2011, http://www.rawstory.com/rs/2011/01/12/ fearing-tea-party-violence-arizona-republicans-resign/

422 Saad, Lydia, "Conservatives Maintain Edge as Top Ideological Group," *Gallup*, February 14, 2011, http://www.gallup.com/poll/123854/conser- vatives-maintain-edge-top-ideological-group.aspx

423 "Arizona Democrat Shot," *DAP Forum*, January 9, 2011, http://dreamact. info/forum/showthread.php?t=19671&page=6

apologized to his followers for making a hasty assessment based on a Google search.[424]

The death of Judge John Roll, whose controversial decision conveying rights to Arizona illegals placed him on a precarious footing with anti-immigrant groups,[425] was initially seen as collateral damage or random victimization. Most reporters claimed that Loughner shouted incoherently during the shooting. It was clarified only later that he shouted the names of his victims, Judge Roll's among them.[426]

According to the minister of his church, Dorwin Stoddard was a retired construction worker and vitally active church member.[427] From story to story, Mr. Stoddard was later defined as a pastor (a non-ordained spiritual leader) and then a full-fledged Pastor,[428] undoubtedly from respect, but also as an example of how Christians claimed their own icon, consciously or not.

For her part, young Christina Green had just recently engaged in student government with the aspiration of becoming a politician.[429] She was also one of the babies born on 9/11 and featured in the book "Faces of Hope."[430]

The people who reacted most strongly to leftwing blame of Sarah Palin and the Tea Party even stooped to speculation that Loughner may have been brainwashed or mind-controlled (citing declassified information[431] on CIA experiments conducted under

424 "News broken on Twitter by @Markos," *The Huffington Post*, February 14, 2011, http://www.huffingtonpost.com/t/shes-prochoice-prodream-a_24009886572482560.html

425 Cassens Weiss, Debra, "Judge Killed in Ariz. Shooting Spree Had Issued Several High-Profile Decisions," *ABA Journal*, January 10, 2011, http://www.abajournal.com/news/article/judge_killed_in_ariz._shooting_spree_had_issued_several_controversial_decis/

426 "White Terrorism: Jared Lee Loughner Shoots Rep. Gabrielle Giffords," *PakPassion*, January 10, 2011, http://www.pakpassion.net/ppforum/showthread.php?p=3323688

427 McClay, Bob, "'Pastor: Man who died in shooting spree saved wife," *KTAR.com*, January 9, 2011, http://www.ktar.com/category/local-news-articles/20110109/Pastor:-Man-who-died-in-shooting-spree-saved-wife/

428 "Two more victims of deadly shooting identified," KVOA.com, January 9, 2011, http://www.kvoa.com/news/two-more-victims-of-deadly-shooting-identified/

429 "9-year-old Christina Green killed in Tucson shooting," *ABC15.com*, January 8, 2011, http://www.abc15.com/dpp/news/region_central_southern_az/tucson/9-year-old-killed-in-tucson-shooting-identified

430 Berger, Joseph, "Born on Sept. 11, Claimed by a New Horror," *New York Times*, January 9, 2011, http://www.nytimes.com/2011/01/10/us/10green.html

431 Project MKULTRA, http://en.wikipedia.org/wiki/Project_MKULTRA

MKULTRA)[432] to target specific people whose deaths would most *benefit* President Obama in terms of political fallout.[433]

In fact, the mix of victims ensured that people of all beliefs and loyalties were equally brutalized. It was also grieving Christians who defended the Catholic funeral service of Christina Green from an opportunistic protest by the hate-mongering church that regularly organizes at the funerals of gay soldiers.[434]

For some, the shock of the experience translated into an outpouring of solidarity, soul-searching and human decency. Others viewed the incident as a potential political setback, or the means by which they'd lose ground in the radicalization of America, and clearly Loughner's intent was to claim a place for himself as a martyr.

He posted a farewell on Facebook, expecting to be killed for his actions or at least taken into custody. Law enforcement officials revealed that Loughner's web searches, performed before the shooting, centered on death by lethal injection and history's famous assassins.[435]

One possible deconstruction of what inspired Loughner's worldview, offered by Victor Thorn, can be found at Kevin Barrett's TRUTHJIHAD.COM.[436]

Perpetuation of the Real Threat

The idea that violent symbolism and insurrectionist rhetoric might have repercussions is, of course, why leaders employ it.[437] Not

432 Xeno, "Jared Loughner: Mind-controlled Assassin?" *Xenophilia (True Strange Stuff)*, January 13, 2011, http://xenophilius.wordpress.com/2011/01/13/jared-loughner-mind-controlled-assassin/

433 Further criticism centered on the so-called "pep rally" atmosphere generated by reaction to the news that Congresswoman Giffords had finally opened her eyes during President Obama's speech. Accusations of political opportunism on blogs and comment venues were steeped in racial epithets, insults, and even threats, (often reposted verbatim and outweighing positive contributions by a visibly wide margin).

434 Tadlock, Caitlin, "Westboro Baptist Church Banned From Christina Green's Funeral," *ALLVOICES*, January 12, 2011, http://www.allvoices.com/contributed-news/7864923-westboro-baptist-church-banned-today-from-christina-greens-funeral

435 Orfanides, Effie, "Loughner did web search before rampage," *news.gather.com*, January 27, 2011, http://news.gather.com/viewArticle.action?articleId=281474978991552

436 "Victor Thorn on Accused Arizona Shooter Jared Loughner," TRUTHJIHAD.COM, http://www.truthjihad.com/thorn.htm

437 "Violent Political Rhetoric Fuels Violent Attitudes," PHYSORG.COM, http://www.physorg.com/news/2011-01-violent-political-rhetoric-fuels-attitudes.html

to accuse Sarah Palin of cupidity, but if the fact that Giffords' district was really marked by a crosshairs somehow eluded the viewer, let me emphasize that Palin was pictured directly above it, sighting down an assault rifle. The target was taken down after the shooting and a spokesperson for Palin claimed that the crosshairs were actually a surveyor's symbol.[438] When this was greeted with derision, Palin's defenders performed an Internet search to expose instances where the left employed bulls-eyes and also pandered to violence.[439]

Palin's successful ploy to preempt the President and claim the spotlight for herself ensured that attention would be diverted from insurrectionist rightwing rallies, featuring such cries as "If ballots don't work, then bullets will"[440] (from Allen West's Chief of Staff, Sharron Angle and Michele Bachmann) and "It's time to water the tree of liberty," a reference to revolution and especially committing bloodshed. These were consistent with a billboard that read, "There's a revolution coming from Texas," and another with the headline, "A Citizen's Guide to Revolution of a Corrupt Government," which listed three recommendations:

1) Starve the Beast, save your money

2) Vote out incumbents

3) If Steps 1 & 2 Fail? PREPARE FOR WAR – LIVE FREE OR DIE.[441]

The issue with Palin's speech and its politically-loaded (if confused)[442] "blood libel" is that it allowed a more sinister threat to persist by simply shifting the public focus. The presumption of a

---

438 Poe, Bob, "Words Matter – Even When Sarah Palin Says Them," January 10, 2011, http://alaskadispatch.com/voices/tundra-talk/8209-words-matter-even-when-sarah-palin-says-them

439 Malkin, Michelle, "The Progressive 'climate of hate': An illustrated primer, 2000-2010" January 10, 2011 http://michellemalkin.com/2011/01/10/the-progressive-climate-of-hate-an-illustrated-primer-2000-2010

440 "'And if ballots don't work, bullets will,' says West's Chief of Staff," *Atlas Forum*, http://www.uselectionatlas.org/FORUM/index.php?topic=127798.0

441 http://bearcreekledger.com/2010/03/21/a-citizens-guide-to-revolution-of-a-corrupt-government-billboard/

442 In historical terms, "blood libel" referred to the false belief that Jews sacrificed Christian children. Palin, according to a commentator at *The Nation*, appears to have intended the meaning supplied by New Right leader Jon Henke, who wrote on Twitter that he began using "blood libel" in connection with the accusations against Palin on the Saturday after the Arizona shootings and "thought it meant the Jews killed Jesus."

right to overthrow the government in the name of "real" American-ism is what she preserved, whatever the arbitrary characteristics of this particular "ism" may be.

To judge by the leaked document that purports to be "The Con-servative Constitution of Real America" in the January 6, 2011 edi-tion of the *Washington Post*, the attack on principles of democracy, moderation, inclusiveness, and tolerance, which embrace America's true historical greatness, is not limited to Tea Party rallies and should be seen for what it is—insurrection from within, along the lines of a legislative putsch by an illegitimate rival government in-sofar as its representatives were not elected to enact a new consti-tution, prepared secretly in advance—in hopes that it need not be achieved by violence from without.

However, rightwing impatience with President Obama's so-called Camelot (perhaps deliberately linking him to an assassinated president) predictably increases the stakes of the next presiden-tial election and makes insurrection from without in the event of Obama's second term a very real possibility.

Washington Post contributor David Cole claims to have ac-cessed "The Conservative Constitution of Real America" through WikiLeaks,[443] but the date of execution coincides with the news-paper leak (they are both January 6, 2011, well after the onset of Wiki-mania). Nor would WikiLeaks have received it on the coin-ciding date because employees of the site shut down and hijacked the WikiLeaks server in conflict with Assange well before 2011. Presumably, the "leak" was a trial balloon to elicit support and momentum.

Here is the text:

> We, the Real Americans, in order to form a more God-Fearing Union, establish Justice as we see it, Defeat Health-Care Reform, and Preserve and Protect our Property, our Guns and our Right Not to Pay Taxes, do ordain and establish

---

443 Quoted from David Cole: "House members opened the 112th Congress on Thursday by reading aloud the Constitution, presumably as a first step toward fulfilling the tea party's goal of "restoring" our nation's founding document. However, an alternative text, obtained by this au-thor, David Cole, via WikiLeaks, has reportedly begun circulating in secret among incoming GOP lawmakers, representing the Constitution they hope to read aloud when the 113th Congress begins. Here, revealed in public for the first time, is the Conservative Constitution of the United States of Real America." https://www.washingtonpost.com/wp-dyn/content/article/2011/01/06/AR2011010602485_pf.html

this Conservative Constitution for the United States of Real America.

Article I. Congress shall have only the powers literally, specifically and expressly granted herein, and no others. That means definitely, without question, absolutely, no regulation of the Health Insurance or Financial Services industries. The Senate of the United States shall be composed of two Senators from each State, elected not directly by the People, but by other people whom the People have elected to better represent the People. Any law enacted by Congress and signed by the President may be overturned by the vote of three or more States if they find it burdensome, offensive, annoying or in any way touching on Health Insurance, Property Rights or Guns. Congress shall have no power to raise Taxes except on February 29, and then only if all the People of the United States approve such a measure unanimously, in writing and in English.

Congress shall balance the Federal Budget, preferably by eliminating the Departments of Labor, Energy, Education and State. The preceding provision shall not apply to spending for the Department of Defense, appropriations for which shall increase three times as quickly as the growth in gross domestic product and upon the approval of House leadership in conference with Boeing, Halliburton, the Ashcroft Group and Kissinger Associates. Arizona shall have the power to regulate Immigration.

Article II. No person except a natural-born Citizen who can produce video, photographic or eyewitness evidence of birth in a non-island American State shall be eligible to the Office of President. The President shall faithfully execute the laws, except when, as Commander in Chief, he decides he'd really rather not. The President shall not negotiate any Treaty without first receiving a signed and notarized note granting him permission, personally executed by every member of the Senate and the House, all 50 Governors and the editorial board of the Weekly Standard.

Article III. Judges shall strictly construe this Constitution, and we mean strictly, and shall under no circumstances cite, refer to, read or mention at cocktail parties or cookouts any principle or provision of International Law. Suspected Terrorists shall be taken to Guantanamo and drawn and quartered in a public ceremony. Trials are optional, but if they occur, must be conducted in a Military Tribunal in which coerced statements are admissible so long as they support a Guilty verdict.

AMENDMENTS:

1. Congress shall make no law abridging the Freedom of Speech, except where citizens desecrate the Flag of the United States; respecting an establishment of Religion, except to support Christian schools, religious apparitions in food products and the display of crosses and creches in public places; or abridging the free exercise of Religion, except to block the construction of mosques in sensitive areas as determined by Florida Pastors or the Fox News Channel.

2. The right to bear Semi-Automatic Weapons, AK-47s or Bazookas shall not be infringed by background checks, safety locks, age limits or common sense.

3. The right of Corporations, Hedge Funds, Business Leaders and Lobbyists to spend endless cash on campaigns and influence-purchasing shall not be infringed. The so-called right of Unions to associate shall be denied as fundamentally un-American and contrary to the agenda of the Chamber of Commerce.

4. Marriage and the benefits thereof shall be restricted to the Union of a Man and a Woman, consecrated in a Christian house of worship, with vows to expose any and all progeny to daily viewings of Bill O'Reilly.

5. All persons born or naturalized in the United States are Citizens of the United States of Real America only if their parents, grandparents and great-grandparents were Citizens, and only if they pledge opposition to Health Insurance Reform or New Taxation. Any Citizen convicted of providing material support to Terrorist organizations, wearing clothing bearing images created by Shepard Fairey, or displaying Nancy Pelosi bumper stickers shall be stripped of Citizenship.

6. Aliens, of this world or another, shall have none of the rights guaranteed herein to Citizens.

7. Corporations shall have all of the rights guaranteed herein to Citizens, and then some.

8. No White Male shall be denied equal protection of the law through Affirmative Action or otherwise. In keeping with the intent of the Framers, as discerned by the Honorable Justice Antonin Scalia, distinctions on the basis of sex shall not be deemed to deny equal protection.

9. The right to be uninsured and make other people pay the costs of one's Health Care shall not be infringed under any circumstances.

10. Congress shall make no law limiting Americans' right to warm the Planet by using all the energy they darn well please.

11. The Unborn shall have the rights to life, to vote, to bear arms, to practice Religion except in a mosque in Lower Manhattan (see First Amendment) and to make campaign contributions, but once the child is born, it shall have no rights if it is an Alien (see Sixth Amendment).

12. No one may be required to do anything He or She does not want to do. Ever.

Done in Convention by the Unanimous Consent of the Members present the Sixth Day of January in the Year of our Lord Two Thousand and Eleven.

In witness whereof We have hereunto subscribed our names,

[REDACTED] [444]

With its blunt racist, nativist, bigoted and inconceivably backward approach to government, it's difficult to tell whether this document is intended to be taken seriously, but it's important that it should be in light of subsequent actions. The Republicans first sponsored the reading of a "revised" Constitution at the 112th Congress that eliminated mentions of Prohibition and the status of black persons under slavery. [445] Republicans also truncated the name of the U.S. House Judicial Subcommittee on the Constitution, Civil Rights, and Civil Liberties to the Subcommittee on the Constitution, [446] thereby removing civil rights and civil liberties from the purview of the original subcommittee, without designating their assignment to a new or different subcommittee and, in effect, denying their existence. The Chairman of the subcommittee, Representative Trent Franks (R-AZ), has claimed that blacks were "better off under slavery." [447]

This type of revisionism is not limited to Congress. Some states, like Florida, have made constitutional reform ongoing. Others,

---

444 *Washington Post*, January 6, 2011, https://www.washingtonpost.com/wp-dyn/content/article/2011/01/06/AR2011010602485_pf.html

445 NPR, January 6, 2011, http://www.npr.org/2011/01/06/132713950/Constitution-Reading-Sparks-Political-Wrangling

446 Zafar, Walid, "House Republicans Change Committee Names to De-Emphasize Civil Rights, Civil Liberties and Labor," *Political Correction*, January 11, 2011, http://politicalcorrection.org/blog/201101100006

447 Zafar, Walid, "Blacks Better Off Under Slavery," *Political Correction*, February 26, 2010, http://politicalcorrection.org/blog/201002260004

such as Michigan,[448] Arizona, and Texas,[449] have deliberated more recently whether to rewrite their constitutions and, in the case of Arizona, a new immigration law became effective in July, 2010.[450]

While state and federal legislators are making it their business to prevent certain groups from receiving rights and benefits, it's equally important that political parties, communities, counties and even states are openly discussing secession, secession within states, and secession within secession, and have been for some time.[451]

Secession Movements

People who welcome the conservative vision for a dictatorship of virtue and feel that a Christian takeover or relocation of Christian communities (as espoused by the movement Christian Exodus)[452] will guarantee better representation have their committed counterparts in people who are repulsed by the idea of forcible Christian conversion, fundamentalist violence, and dismayed by the corruption in Washington.[453]

The Middlebury Institute, based in Cold Spring, N.Y., met with the League of the South in October 2007 in the second annual North American Secessionist Convention, aimed at peacefully and legally seceding from the union.

In that regard, *Right Truth* reported:

> Dr. Michael Hill of the League of the South said, "From a political standpoint we all agree that the whole political system has been compromised by big money. The candidates are bought and paid for and they work in the interest of those who pay them. They don't work for the interest of the common people."

---

448 "The pros, cons of revising the Michigan Constitution," November 1, 2010, http://www.pressandguide.com/articles/2010/11/01/opinion/doc4ccd8c121b113711447308.txt

449 *Texas Politics*, http://texaspolitics.laits.utexas.edu/7_6_2.html

450 Newton, Casey and Rough, Ginger, "Arizona governor signs bill revising new immigration law," *Arizona Politics*, May 1, 2010, http://www.azcentral.com/news/election/azelections/articles/2010/04/30/20100430arizona-immigration-law-governor-signs-revised-bill.html

451 Secession in the United States, *Wikipedia*, http://en.wikipedia.org/wiki/Secession_in_the_United_States

452 "Forsake the Empire, Seek the Kingdom!" *Christian Exodus*, http://www.christianexodus.org/index.php?option=com_content&view=article&id=9&Itemid=37

453 "States Want to Secede From the United States," *Right Truth*, http://righttruth.typepad.com/right_truth/2007/10/a.html

"Congress, like the presidency, is corporate run and owned. You can't make any headway there so you have to absent yourself from it," according to Kirkpatrick Sale who leads The Middlebury Institute.

WAIT! Hold the presses, I AGREE with the above...

But not so fast. While the group claims to be from all ends of the political spectrum, read this:

Can you imagine being able to move to a state where the right-wing Christians had no voice? Neo-conservatives would relocate to the states that were pro-Bush, and the radical Christians and Neo-conservatives would be able to impose their will on anyone in the state they chose to — and the rest of us could live in freedom and peace...

Imagine the individual states building their own economies, and if corporate America wanted a piece of the pie, they would have to reinvest in that state rather than outsourcing everything to countries that will work for peanuts that are breaking the American economy. It's ironic, but if we allowed all of the right-wing warmongers and fundamentalists to have their own states, when terrorists struck — it would probably be in those areas inhabited by the hate-mongers rather than bombing innocent Americans...

Slate in November 2004 asked, "Could the Blue States Secede? Is there a legal way to opt out of the Union?" *Daily Kos* talked about Liberals and/or Christians breaking off from the rest of the U.S. in 2005.[454]

Conservative counties in California have advocated internal secession and, in August of 2009, thousands of Texans demanded that their state deliver an ultimatum to Washington — either sovereignty or secession.[455]

The problems here are many.

Constitutional changes that render any groups or ethnic denominations unprivileged minorities will invoke retaliation. The question becomes, "Why should I be a minority in your state when you can be one in mine?"

---

454 Ibid.

455 Moon, Robert, "'Sovereignty or secession' movement sweeps Texas capital," *Macon County Conservative Examiner*, August 30, 2009, http://www.examiner.com/macon-county-conservative-in-springfield/sovereignty-or-secession-movement-sweeps-texas-capitol

Randi Shannon Has the Answer

If there is any doubt that "The Conservative Constitution of Real America," signals the rise of an illegitimate rival government, former Republican Senate contender Randi Shannon has just withdrawn from the race with the following message on behalf of the so-called "Republic for Iowa in union with The Republic of the United States of America":

> "Let me now announce to everyone in Iowa, I have become aware of the existence of the Original Republic for the United States of America. 'We the People' re-inhabited our lawful de-jure (*de jure* —"by right of lawful establishment") government on March 30th, 2010. This is the Republic founded in 1787 and then abandoned during the Civil War in the 1860s. It was then replaced in 1871 by the UNITED STATES CORPORATION (de facto — without law)."[456]

Once I got over the shock of Randi Shannon's pronouncement, I took some time to analyze it and here is what I think. Every militant movement has a tightly controlled center of hard-core believers and, in order to keep it pure, the center is kept minimized to those who will sacrifice anything in support of those beliefs. From the center to the outer periphery will be a number of concentric rings, consisting of like-minded people to lessening degrees.

The manifesto of such a movement may downplay the role of violence to attract as many followers as possible, but must be presented in such a way that it appeals to those who thrive on conspiracy, secrecy, exclusivity, and intrigue, and this is what we saw with the "Conservative Constitution of Real America," "leaked" in 2011 by the Washington Post. The idea that it was "leaked" is farcical; in fact, it was launched. As a conservative trial balloon that was written in "blunt-speak," it embraced iconic conservatives and particularly their media entities, while threatening retribution for support of symbolic liberals with derision, hate, and contempt.

This took place two years after the vote of no-confidence on Obama's presidency, when people of means tanked the economy between 2008–2009 via massive capital flight. And, even after the President resorted to public means to recapitalize the banks, they remained in lock-step with conservatives, refusing to lend new funds.

---

456 Talking Points Memo, 2012, http://2012.talkingpointsmemo.com/2012/07/republic-of-the-united-states-of-america-united-states-corporation-randi-johnson.php?ref=fpnewsfeed

Now fast-forward to Talking Points Memo, which published Randi Shannon's pronouncement, complete with all the absurdity of the "UNITED STATES CORPORATION," and notice it does three things. It rolls back the end of slavery, but also rolls back the date on which "We the people" supposedly re-inhabited their "true" government in 2010. "We the people" implies massive support and momentum, as does the date of 2010. It also uses the word "corporation" in a way that is neatly deceptive, with "corporation" used as a key to co-opt frustrated Americans for whom the word corporation equates to corruption, control, and greed.

Then "The Republic for Iowa in Union with the Republic of the United States" implies that Iowa, as a satellite, is loyal to the core believers, as a matter of conditionality on which such union is based.

Of course, timing is everything. Four months from the November election, an "alternative" has to be put in place for the movement to gather momentum under the pressure of political attack ads and shifting political polls, possibly in an attempt to delegitimize, postpone, complicate, or foreclose on the coming election and/or survive it as a movement capable of government overthrow and the usurpation of power if conservatives should lose. Even if they don't, it may be Mitt Romney whom they oppose.

Run a simple Internet search for the words "martial law" and see how many millions of hits are meant to make people believe that such will be the case if Obama wins again. It doesn't matter if a single conspiracist has overloaded the Internet with every one of these hits; in the current political climate some people would rather believe that it represents this movement in which they are included, which surely must be huge, such that joining implies no risk.

The Yugoslavian Meltdown

The fate of Yugoslavia is by no means a template for the future of America. The reason it merits comparison is because of the threat to the social contract under proposed economic reforms, the cooptation of conspiracists who may readily embrace violence, and a potential new constitution that would completely disenfranchise more than half the nation.

In this context, the following excerpts are relevant, cited from my 2006 publication, "Bosnia and Beyond: the 'Quiet' Revolution That Wouldn't Go Quietly":

While no one questions that borrowed money must eventually be repaid, it was the terms of financial restructuring that devastated Yugoslavia. The harshness of economic reform resulted in 17 percent unemployment by the end of the 1980s, while those who were employed were subjected to wage cuts and freezes. The situation was so terrible that it forced people to rely on family, kin, and their extended ethnic communities in order to survive. Nor was there an end in sight.[457]

Political liberalization coupled with economic reform was supposed to bring about regime change. And this did happen. Elections were held in the different republics in the year 1990, and ethno-nationalist leaders were swept to victory. What the elections did not produce was a series of moderate leaders who could allay the fears of the people and hold the country together... The situation when most of the leaders came to power was one of serious unrest, such that they either had to put down strikes and organized mass protests or try to co-opt the people in the name of other causes.[458]

We've already discussed cooptation; now, let's look at an excerpt pertaining to potential resistance and retaliatory violence, should the "Conservative Constitution of Real America" make good on all its provisions:

In modern day Croatia, Serbs could point to their expulsion from their jobs, the confiscation and/or destruction of their property, the new description of Serbs as an unprotected minority in Croatia's revised constitution, and the replacement of their local police forces with men of Croatian heritage, as the beginning of a pogrom... And at no time did Croatia take steps to reassure the Serbs, but rather invited the self-defensive uprisings that were to follow.[459]

Divide and Conquer

When the underlying logic of capitalist competition is to ensure that the same pools of assets cycle in and out of possession, only the wealthiest of Americans really benefit from the fallout. As one person loses a home to foreclosure, it becomes another's bargain. Both buyers can say they once had, or now have, the American dream, but due to negative attribution, there won't be empathy between them.

At the heart of America's outrage is an inability to lash out and demand redemption from the source of its distress because it stems,

457 Haskin, Jeanne M., *Bosnia and Beyond: the 'Quiet' Revolution that Wouldn't Go Quietly*, (New York: Algora Publishers, 2006), 1.
458 Haskin, 1-2.
459 Haskin, 33-34.

not from hatred, but from the fundamental lack of stability built into our way of life.

By the second half of 2012, a fifth of the U.S. population has suffered job loss, foreclosures, and is ineligible for employment due to prejudice, poor credit, a lack of skills or education, a glut of competition and insufficient opportunity, the failure of the system to provide for a helpless majority means the system is at an impasse. Because it can't—or won't—perform, the Tea Party's rise turns out to have been preemptive—with all its overt hatred and "real" American theater—as the means to co-opt potential insurgents and, if necessary, spur them to violence.

Consistent with this goal, Maine Governor, Paul LePage, just recently employed incendiary language, equating the IRS to the Gestapo with the potential to kill millions,[460] in order to project gross (albeit untrue) victimization common to anti-government groups and, in particular, conspiracy theorists. By claiming the IRS has the potential to kill as many as the Holocaust (which we fought against as The Good Fight, seventeen million souls too late), he also fed the impression that insurrection is valid and needed. The IRS and its agents are already the most frequent targets of militant hatred and death threats. But, for historical reconstructionists intent on proving taxation is predatory, even Adam Smith said that taxes should be paid in proportion to what one earns. This is a form of hate speech. In the interest of protecting this nation and its legitimate civil servants, such hysterical accusations cannot stand unchallenged. Death threats, violent rhetoric, and insubordination are notably ratcheting up as the November election approaches. No one should be so complacent as to think they don't have power.

Conclusion

Economic elitists deferred expectations for people all over the world through decades of education that allowed hard-line conservative governments to deepen stratification, consolidate industries, depress wages, and export jobs. And because today's citizens perceive no opportunity in the increasingly hard-line atmosphere favored by rightwing radicals, there are bound to be scapegoats and an escalation of conflict aimed at producing crises.

---

460 Shen, Aviva, *Think Progress*, July 12, 2012, http://thinkprogress.org/health/2012/07/12/515784/maine-governor-irs-is-headed-in-the-direction-of-killing-a-lot-of-people/?mobile=nc

Conservatives aren't just biding their time while Obama remains in office. They're using every opportunity to attack women, gays, Veterans, immigrants, nonwhites, the disabled, the elderly, unions, moderates, liberals and non-Christians in order to render them powerless to block more harmful agendas.

Ideally, rational leaders will heed the indicators and counter the trends while reasonable means remain.

BIBLIOGRAPHY

Albin, Peter S., *Progress without Poverty: Socially Responsible Economic Growth* (New York: Basic Books, 1978).

Alonso, Irma Tirado de, ed., *Trade, Industrialization and Integration in Twentieth-Century Central America* (Westport, CT: Praeger Publishers, 1994).

Anderson, Thomas P., *The War of the Dispossessed: Honduras and El Salvador, 1969* (Lincoln, NE: University of Nebraska Press, 1981).

_____, *Politics in Central America: Guatemala, El Salvador, Honduras, and Nicaragua* (New York: Praeger, 1988).

_____, *Matanza: The 1932 "Slaughter" That Traumatized a Nation, Shaping US–Salvadoran Policy to This Day* (Willimantic, CT: Curbstone Press, 1992).

Andreski, Stanislav, *Parasitism and Subversion: The Case of Latin America* (New York: Pantheon Books, 1967).

Armony, Ariel C., *Argentina, the United States, and the Anti-Communist Crusade in Central America 1977-1984* (Athens, OH: Ohio University Press, 1997).

Arnson, Cynthia J., *Crossroads: Congress, the President, and Central America, 1976-1993* (University Park, PA: Pennsylvania State University Press, 1993).

Atkins, G. Pope, *Latin America and the Caribbean in the International System* (Boulder, CO: Westview Press, 1999).

Attwood, Donald W., Thomas C. Bruneau, and John G. Galaty, eds., *Power and Poverty: Development and Development Projects in the Third World* (Boulder: Westview Press, 1988).

Bahl, Roy, Jorge Martinez-Vazquez, and Sally Wallace, *The Guatemalan Tax Reform* (Boulder, CO: Westview Press, 1996).

Baloyra, Enrique A., *El Salvador in Transition* (Chapel Hill, NC: University of North Carolina Press, 1982).

Barba Navaretti, Giorgio, Riccardo Faini, and Giovanni Zanalda, eds., *Labour Markets, Poverty, and Development* (Oxford: Clarendon Press, 1999).

Bell, David E. and Michael R. Reich, eds., *Health, Nutrition, and Economic Crises: Approaches to Policy in the Third World* (Dover, MA: Auburn House, 1988).

Beneria, Lourdes and Shelley Feldman, eds., *Unequal Burden: Economic Crises, Persistent Poverty, and Women's Work* (Boulder, CO: Westview Press, 1992).

Bhalla, Surjit S., Gabriel Siri, Luis Dominguez Raul, R.C.L. Robles Chander, and K.P. The *World, Inflation and Developing Countries* (Washington, DC: Brookings Institution, 1981).

Biersteker, Thomas J., ed., *Dealing with Debt: International Financial Negotiations and Adjustment Bargaining* (Boulder, CO: Westview Press, 1993).

Bird, Graham, *IMF Lending to Developing Countries: Issues and Evidence* (New York: Routledge, 1995).

Birdsall, Nancy, Carol Graham, and Richard H. Sabot, eds., *Beyond Tradeoffs: Market Reforms and Equitable Growth in Latin America* (Washington, DC: The Brookings Institution, 1998).

Black, Jan Knippers, *Sentinels of Empire: The United States and Latin American Militarism* (New York: Greenwood Press, 1986.

Black, Stanley W., Anne O. Krueger, Carlos F. Diaz-Alejandro, Montek S. Ahluwalia, Frank J. Lysy, Alejandro Foxley, Irving S. Friedman, James H. Weaver, Arne Anderson, Stephen E. Guisinger, Roger D. Norton, Seung Yoon Rhee, and Lance Taylor, *Economic Stabilization in Developing Countries*, Eds. Willian R. Cline and Sidney Weintraub (Washington, DC: The Brookings Institution, 1981).

Blanchard, William H., *Neocolonialism American Style 1960-2000* (Westport, CT: Greenwood Press, 1996).

Blustein, Paul, *The Chastening: Inside the Crisis That Rocked the Global Financial System and Humbled the IMF* (New York: Public Affairs, 2001).

Boas, Morten and Desmond Mcneill, eds., *Global Institutions and Development: Framing the World?* (New York: Routledge, 2003).

Bolland, O. Nigel, *Colonialism and Resistance in Belize: Essays in Historical Sociology* (Barbados: University of the West Indies Press, 2003).

Booth, John A., *Costa Rica: Quest for Democracy* (Boulder, CO: Westview Press, 1998).

Booth, John A. and Mitchell A. Seligson, eds., *Elections and Democracy in Central America* (Chapel Hill, NC: University of North Carolina Press, 1989).

Booth, John A. and Thomas W. Walker, *Understanding Central America* (Boulder, CO: Westview Press, 1999).

Borge, Tomas, *The Patient Impatience: From Boyhood to Guerilla: a Personal Narrative of Nicaragua's Struggle for Liberation* (Willimantic, CT: Curbstone Press, 1992).

Bouchet, Michel Henri, *The Political Economy of International Debt: What, Who, How Much, and Why?* (New York: Quorum Books, 1987).

Bouvier, Virginia M., ed., *The Globalization of U.S.-Latin American Relations: Democracy, Intervention, and Human Rights* (Westport, CT: Praeger, 2002).

Bracamonte, Jose Angel Moroni, and David E. Spencer, *Strategy and Tactics of the Salvadoran FMLN Guerrillas: Last Battle of the Cold War, Blueprint for Future Conflicts* (Westport, CT: Praeger Publishers, 1995).

Brecher, Jeremy, and Tim Costello, *Global Village or Global Pillage: Economic Reconstruction from the Bottom Up* (Cambridge, MA: South End Press, 1998).

Brockett, Charles D., *Land, Power, and Poverty: Agrarian Transformation and Political Conflict in Central America* (Boulder, CO: Westview Press, 1998.

Brookings Institution, *International Monetary Reform and the Developing Countries* (Washington, DC: The Brookings Institution, 1976).

Browder, John O., ed., *Fragile Lands of Latin America: Strategies for Sustainable Development* (Boulder, CO: Westview Press, 1989).

Buckley, Peter J., and Mark Casson, *The Future of the Multinational Enterprise* (New York: Holmes & Meier, 1976).

Bugajski, Janusz, *Sandinista Communism and Rural Nicaragua* (New York: Praeger Book, 1990).

Bulmer-Thomas, Victor, *The Economic History of Latin America since Independence* (Cambridge, England: Cambridge University Press, 2003).

Byrne, Hugh, *El Salvador's Civil War: A Study of Revolution* (Boulder, CO: Lynne Reinner, 1996).

Canak, William L., ed., *Lost Promises: Debt, Austerity, and Development in Latin America* (Boulder, CO: Westview Press, 1989).

Carter, William P., Yassin El-Ayouty, Kevin J. Ford, and Mark Davies, eds., *Government Ethics and Law Enforcement: Toward Global Guidelines* (Westport, CT: Praeger Publishers, 2000).

Carvounis, Brinda Z., *United States Trade and Investment in Latin America: Opportunities for Business in the 1990s* (Westport, CT: Quorum Books, 1992).

Carvounis, Chris C., *The Foreign Debt/National Development Conflict: External Adjustment and Internal Disorder in the Developing Nations* (New York: Quorum Books, 1986).

Chasteen, John Charles, ed., *The Contemporary History of Latin America* (Durham, NC: Duke University Press, 1993).

Child, Jack, *The Central American Peace Process, 1983-1991: Sheathing Swords, Building Confidence* (Boulder, CO: Lynne Reinner, 1992).

Chomsky, Noam, *Turning the Tide: U.S. Intervention in Central America and the Struggle for Peace* (Boston: South End Press, 1985).

Clark, Gerald, *The Coming Explosion in Latin America* (New York: D. McKay Co., 1963).

Cling, Jean-Pierre, Mireille Razafindrakoto, and Francois Rubaud, eds., *New International Poverty Reduction Strategies* (New York: Routledge, 2003).

Close, David, *Nicaragua: The Chamorro Years* (Boulder, CO: Lynne Reinner, 1999).

Cohen, Benjamin J., *The Question of Imperialism: The Political Economy of Dominance and Dependence* (New York: Basic Books, 1973).

Colclough, Christopher, ed., *Marketizing Education and Health in Developing Countries: Miracle or Mirage?* (Oxford: Clarendon Press, 1997.

Condon, Bradly J., *NAFTA, WTO, and Global Business Strategy: How Aids, Trade, and Terrorism Affect Our Economic Future* (Westport, CT: Quorum Books, 2002).

Connolly, Michael and Claudio Gonzalez-Vega, eds., *Economic Reform and Stabilization in Latin America* (New York: Praeger Publishers, 1987).

Considine, John J., *New Horizons in Latin America* (New York: Dodd Mead, 1958).

Corea, Gamani, *Development Policy and Planning: A Third World Perspective*, Ed. Pradip K. Ghosh (Westport, CT: Greenwood Press, 1984).

_____, *Economic Integration and Third World Development*, Ed. Pradip K. Ghosh (Westport, CT: Greenwood Press, 1984).

Cox, Isaac Joslin, *Nicaragua and the United States 1909-1927* (Boston: World Peace Foundation, 1927).

Cox, Ronald W., and Daniel Skidmore-Hess, *U.S. Politics and the Global Economy: Corporate Power, Conservative Shift* (Boulder, CO: Lynne Reinner, 1999).

Crawford, Neta C., *Argument and Change in World Politics: Ethics, Decolonization, and Humanitarian Intervention* (Cambridge, England: Cambridge University Press, 2002).

Cruz, Arturo J., *Nicaragua's Conservative Republic 1858-93* (New York: Palgrave, 2002).

Cuenca, Alejandro Martinez, *Sandinista Economics in Practice: An Insider's Critical Reflections* (Boston: South End Press, 1992).

Cullather, Nick, *Secret History: The CIA's Classified Account of Its Operations in Guatemala, 1952-1954* (Stanford, CA: Stanford University Press, 1999).

Cunneen, Chris, *Conflict, Politics and Crime: Aboriginal Communities and the Police* (Crows Nest, N.S.W.: Allen & Unwin, 2001).

Danaher, Kevind, ed., *50 Years is Enough: The Case Against the World Bank and the International Monetary Fund* (Boston: South End Press, 1994).

Das, Dilip K., *Financial Globalization and the Emerging Market Economies* (New York: Routledge, 2004).

De Pauw, John Whylen and George A. Luz, eds., *Winning the Peace: The Strategic Implications of Military Civic Action* (New York: Praeger Publishers, 1992).

Defilippis, James, *Unmaking Goliath: Community Control in the Face of Global Capital* (New York: Routledge, 2004).

Del Testa, David W., ed., *Government Leaders, Military Rulers, and Political Activists* (Westport, CT: Oryx Press, 2001).

Demartino, George, *Global Economy, Global Justice: Theoretical Objections and Policy Alternatives to Neoliberalism* (London: Routledge, 2000).

Dent, David W., ed., *Handbook of Political Science Research on Latin America: Trends from the 1960s to the 1990s* (New York: Greenwood Press, 1990).

Dent, David W., *The Legacy of the Monroe Doctrine: A Reference Guide to U.S. Involvement in Latin America and the Caribbean* (Westport, CT: Greenwood Press, 1999).

Derman, William and Scott Whiteford, eds., *Social Impact Analysis and Development Planning in the Third World* (Boulder, CO: Westview Press, 1985).

Derose, Laurie, Ellen Messer, and Sandra Millman, *Who's Hungry? And How Do We Know? Food Shortage, Poverty and Deprivation* (New York: United Nations University Press, 1998).

Desai, Meghnad and Yahia Said, eds., *Global Governance and Financial Crises* (New York: Routledge, 2003).

DeSouza, Patrick J., ed., *Economic Strategy and National Security: A Next Generation Approach* (Boulder, CO: Westview Press, 2000).

Deutsch, Klaus Gunter and Bernhard Speyer, eds., *The World Trade Organization Millennium Round: Freer Trade in the Twenty-First Century* (London: Routledge, 2001).

Dichter, Thomas W., *Despite Good Intentions: Why Development Assistance to the Third World Has Failed* (Amherst, MA: University of Massachusetts Press, 2003).

Dirlik, Arif, *The Postcolonial Aura: Third World Criticism in the Age of Global Capitalism* (Boulder, CO: Westview Press, 1997).

Dixon, C.J.D. Drakakis-Smith, and H.D. Watts, eds., *Multinational Corporations and the Third World* (Boulder, CO: Westview Press, 1986).

Dominguez, Jorge I. and Marc Lindenberg, eds., *Democratic Transitions in Central America* (Gainesville, FL: University Press of Florida, 1997).

Donohoe, William Arlington, *A History of British Honduras* (Montreal: Provincial Publishing Co., 1946).

Dosal, Paul J., *Power in Transition: The Rise of Guatemala's Industrial Oligarchy, 1971-1994* (Westport, CT: Praeger Publishers, 1995).

Dovring, Folke, *Inequality: The Political Economy of Income Distribution* (New York: Praeger Publishers, 1991).

Dowd, Douglas, *U.S. Capitalist Development since 1776: Of, By, and for Which People?* (Armonk, NY: M.E. Sharpe, 1993).

Dozer, Donald Marquand, *Are We Good Neighbors?* (Gainseville, FL: University of Florida Press, 1959).

Drache, Daniel, ed., *The Market or the Public Domain? Global Governance and the Asymmetry of Power* (New York: Routledge, 2001).

Draper, Theodore, *A Very Thin Line The Iran-Contra Affairs* (New York: Hill and Wang, 1991).

Dunkerley, James, *The Long War: Dictatorship and Revolution in El Salvador* (London: Junction Books, 1982).

_____, *Political Suicide in Latin America and Other Essays* (London: Verso, 1992).

Eckstein, Susan Eva and Timothy P. Wickham-Crowley, eds., *What Justice? Whose Justice? Fighting for Fairness in Latin America* (Berkeley, CA: University of California Press, 2003).

Edelman, Marc., *The Logic of the Latifundio: The Large Estates of Northwestern Costa Rica since the Late Nineteenth Century* (Stanford, CA: Stanford University, 1992).

_____, *Peasants Against Globalization: Rural Social Movements in Costa Rica* (Stanford, CA: Stanford University Press, 1999).

Edie, Carlene J., *Democracy in the Caribbean: Myths and Realities* (Westport, CT: Praeger Publishers, 1994).

Edmisten, Patricia Taylor, *Nicaragua Divided: La Prensa and the Chamorro Legacy* (Pensacola, FL: University of West Florida Press, 1990).

Enders, Thomas O., *Latin America: The Crisis of Debt and Growth* (Washington, DC: The Brookings Institution, 1984).

Enriquez, Laura J., *Harvesting Change: Labor and Agrarian Reform in Nicaragua, 1979-1990* (Chapel Hill, NC: University of North Carolina Press).

_____, *Agrarian Reform and Class consciousness in Nicaragua* (Gainesville: University Press of Florida, 1997).

Eriksson, John, Alcira Kreimer, and Margaret Arnold *Post-Conflict Reconstruction: Country Case Evaluation* (Washington, DC: World Bank, 2000).

Escobar, Arturo, *Encountering Development: The Making and Unmaking of the Third World* (Princeton, NJ: Princeton University Press, 1995).

Euraque, Daraio, *Reinterpreting the Banana Republic: Region and State in Honduras, 1970-1972* (Chapel Hill, NC: University of North Carolina Press, 1996).

Falk, Richard, *Human Rights and State Sovereignty* (New York: Holmes & Meier Publishers, 1981).

Falla, Ricardo, *Massacres in the Jungle: Ixcan, Guatemala, 1975-1982*, Translated by Howland, Julia (Boulder, CO: Westview Press, 1994).

Feinberg, Richard E., ed., *Central America, International Dimensions of the Crisis* (New York: Holmes and Meier, 1982).

Fincher, Ruth and Peter Saunders, eds., *Creating Unequal Futures?: Rethinking Poverty, Inequality and Disadvantage* (Crows Nest, N.S.W.: Allen & Unwin, 2001).

Findling, John E., *Close Neighbors, Distant Friends: United States-Central American Relations* (New York: Greenwood Press, 1987).

Fine, Ben, Costas Lapavistas, and Jonathan Pincus, eds., *Development Policy in the Twenty-First Century: Beyond the Post-Washington Consensus* (London: Routledge, 2001).

Fishel, John T., *Civil Military Operations in the New World* (Westport, CT: Praeger, 1997).

_____, *The Savage Wars of Peace: Toward a New Paradigm of Peace Operations* (Boulder, CO: Westview Press, 1998).

Fisher, Julie, *The Road from Rio: Sustainable Development and the Nongovernmental Movement in the Third World* (Westport, CT: Praeger Publishers, 1993).

_____, *Nongovernments: NGOs and the Political Development of the Third World* (West Hartford, Ct: Kumarian Press, 1998).

Ford, Katherine Morrow, and James Ford, *The Abolition of Poverty* (New York: The Macmillan Company, 1937).

Forman, Shepard and Stewart Patrick, eds., *Good Intentions: Pledges of Aid for Postconflict Recovery* (Boulder, CO: Lynne Reinner, 2000).

Forrin, Miguel and John D. Martz, *Latin-American Political Thought and Ideology* (Chapel Hill, NC: University of North Carolina Press, 1970).

Frank, Andre Gunder, *Crisis in the Third World* (New York: Holmes & Meier Publishers, 1981).

Frundt, Henry J., *Refreshing Pauses: Coca-Cola and Human Rights in Guatemala* (New York: Praeger Publishers, 1987).

Fry, Maxwell J., Charles A.E. Goodhart, and Alvaro Almeida, *Central Banking in Developing Countries: Objectives, Activities and Independence* (New York: Routledge, 1996).

Galal, Ahmed and Mary Shirley, eds., *Highlights From a World Bank Conference* (Washington, DC: World Bank, 1994).

Gambone, Michael D., *Eisenhower, Somoza, and the Cold War in Nicaragua, 1953-1961* (Westport, CT: Greenwood, 1997).

_____, *Capturing the Revolution: The United States, Central America, and Nicaragua, 1961-1972* (Westport, CT: Praeger, 2001).

Gareau, Frederick H., *State Terrorism and the United States: From Counterinsurgency to the War on Terrorism* (Atlanta: Clarity Press, 2004).

Garst, Rachel, and Tom Barry, *Feeding the Crisis: U.S. Food Aid and Farm Policy in Central America* (Lincoln, NE: University of Nebraska Press, 1990).

Gates, Jeff, and Stephan Schmidheiny, *The Ownership Solution: Toward a Shared Capitalism for the Twenty-First Century* (Reading, MA: Perseus Publishing, 1999).

Gates, Marilyn, *In Default: Peasants, the Debt Crisis, and the Agricultural Challenge in Mexico* (Boulder, CO: Westview Press, 1993).

Gedicks, Al, *The New Resource Wars: Native and Environmental Struggles Against Multinational Corporations* (Cambridge, MA: South End Press, 1993).

Gelbspan, Ross, *Break-Ins, Death Threats, and the FBI: The Covert War against the Central American Movement* (Boston: South End Press, 1991).

Gentry, Bradford S., *Private Capital Flows and the Environment: Lessons from Latin America* (Cheltenham, England: Edward Elgar, 1998).

George, Susan, *The Debt Boomerang: How Third World Debt Harms Us All* (Boulder, CO: Westview Press, 1992).

George, Susan, and Fabrizio Sabelli, *Faith and Credit: The World Bank's Secular Empire* (Boulder, CO: Westview Press, 1994).

Ghorayshi, Parvin and Claire Belanger, eds., *Women, Work, and Gender Relations in Developing Countries: A Global Perspective* (Westport, CT: Greenwood Press, 1996).

Ghosh, B.N., ed., *Contemporary Issues in Development Economics* (London: Routledge, 2001).

Ghosh, Dilip and Pradip K. Ghosh, eds., *International Trade and Third World Development* (Westport, CT: Greenwood Press, 1984).

Ghosh, Pradip K., ed., *Developing Latin America: A Modernization Perspective* (Westport, CT: Greenwood Press, 1984).

_____, *Development Co-Operation and Third World Development* (Westport, CT: Greenwood Press, 1984).

_____, *Economic Policy and Planning in Third World Development* (Westport, CT: Greenwood Press, 1984).

_____, *Energy Policy and Third World Development* (Westport, CT: Greenwood Press, 1984).

_____, *Foreign Aid and Third World Development* (Westport, CT: Greenwood Press, 1984).

_____, *Health, Food, and Nutrition in Third World Development* (Westport, CT: Greenwood Press, 1984).

_____, *Multi-National Corporations and Third World Development* (Westport, CT: Greenwood Press, 1984).

_____, *New International Economic Order: A Third World Perspective* (Westport, CT: Greenwood Press, 1984).

_____, *Population, Environment and Resources, and Third World Development* (Westport, CT: Greenwood Press, 1984).

_____, *A Third World Perspective* (Westport, CT: Greenwood Press, 1984).

_____, *Third World Development: A Basic Needs Approach* (Westport, CT: Greenwood Press, 1984).

Gill, Lesley, *Teetering on the Rim: Global Restructuring, Daily Life, and the Armed Retreat of the Bolivian State* (New York: Columbia University Press, 2000).

Gillis, Malcolm, ed., *Tax Reform in Developing Countries* (Durham: Duke University Press, 1989).

Gilpin, Robert, *U.S. Power and the Multinational Corporation: The Political Economy of Foreign Direct Investment* (New York: Basic Books, 1975).

Girot, Pascal O., *The Americas* (New York: Routledge, 1994).

Goldberg, Ellen S., and Dan Haendel, *On Edge: International Banking and Country Risk* (New York: Praeger Publishers, 1987).

Gonzalez, Alfonso and Jim Norwine, eds., *The New Third World* (Boulder, CO: Westview Press, 1998).

Goode, Richard, *Economic Assistance to Developing Countries through the IMF* (Washington, DC: The Brookings Institution, 1985).

Goodman, David and Michael Watts, eds., *Globalising Food: Agrarian Questions and Global Restructuring* (London: Routledge, 1997).

Goodman, Louis W., William M. LeoGrande, and Johanna Mendelson Forman, eds., *Political Parties and Democracy in Central America* (Boulder, CO: Westview Press, 1992).

Gordon, Andrew, Daniel James, and Alexander Keyssar, eds., *Identity and Struggle at the Margins of the Nation-State: The Laboring Peoples of Central America and the Hispanic Caribbean* (Durham, NC: Duke University Press, 1998).

Gordon, Sara L., *The United States and Global Capital Shortages: The Problem and Possible Solutions* (Westport, CT: Quorum Books, 1995).

Gordon, Wendell C., *The Economy of Latin America* (New York: Columbia University Press, 1950).

Gorman, Robert F., *Refugee Aid and Development: Theory and Practice* (Westport, CT: Greenwood Press, 1993).

Gould, Jeffrey L., *To Lead as Equals: Rural Protest and Political Consciousness in Chinandega, Nicaragua, 1912-1979* (Chapel Hill, NC: University of North Carolina Press, 1990).

Grabendorff, Wolf, Heinrich-W. Krumwiede, and Jorg Todt, eds., *Political Change in Central America: Internal and External Dimensions* (Boulder, CO: Westview Press, 1984).

Grandin, Greg, *The Blood of Guatemala: A History of Race and Nation* (Durham, NC: Duke University Press, 2000).

Green, Linda, *Fear as a Way of Life: Mayan Widows in Rural Guatemala* (New York: Columbia University Press, 1999).

Greenfield, Gerald Michael and Sheldon L. Maram, eds., *Latin American Labor Organizations* (New York: Greenwood Press, 1987).

Greenleaf, Richard E., and Samuel Z. Stone, *Ruling Classes in Central America from the Conquest to the Sandinistas* (Lincoln, NE: University of Nebraska Press, 1990).

Griffin, Keith, *International Inequality and National Poverty* (New York: Holmes & Meier, 1978).

_____, *World Hunger and World Economy: And Other Essays in Development Economics* (New York: Holmes & Meier, 1987).

Gross, Liza, *Handbook of Leftist Guerrilla Groups in Latin America and the Caribbean* (Boulder, CO: Westview Press, 1995).

Gruber, Lloyd, *Ruling the World: Power Politics and the Rise of Supranational Institutions* (Princeton, NJ: Princeton University Press, 2000).

Gudmundson, Lowell, and Hector Lindo-Fuentes, *Liberalism before Liberal Reform* (Tuscaloosa, AL: University of Alabama Press, 1995).

Gugelberger, Georg M., ed., *The Real Thing: Testimonial Discourse and Latin America* (Durham: Duke University Press, 1996).

Gupta, Dipak K., *The Economics of Political Violence: The Effect of Political Instability on Economic Growth* (New York: Praeger Publishers, 1990).

Gwynne, Robert N. and Cristobal Kay, eds., *Latin America Transformed: Globalization and Modernity* (London: Arnold, 1999).

Haggard, Stephan, *Developing Nations and the Politics of Global Integration* (Washington, DC: Brookings Institution, 1995).

Haldane, Andrew G., *Fixing Financial Crises in the 21ˢᵗ Century* (New York: Routledge, 2004).

Hale, Charles R., *Resistance and Contradiction: Miskitu Indians and the Nicaragua State, 1894-1987* (Stanford, CA: Stanford University, 1994).

Halebsky, Sandor and Richard L. Harris, eds., *Capital, Power, and Inequality in Latin America* (Boulder, CO: Westview Press, 1995).

Hamouda, Omar F., Robin Rowley, and Bernard M. Wolf, eds., *Change, Coordination or Instability?* (Armonk, NY: M.E. Sharpe, 1989).

Handelman, Howard and Werner Baer, eds., *Paying the Costs of Austerity in Latin America* (Boulder, CO: Westview Press, 1989).

Handy, Jim, *Revolution in the Countryside: Rural Conflict and Agrarian Reform in Guatemala, 1944-1954* (Chapel Hill, NC: University of North Carolina Press, 1994).

Harris, David J. and Stephen Livingstone, eds., *The Inter-American System of Human Rights* (Oxford: Clarendon Press, 1998).

Harriss, John, Janet Hunter, and Colin M. Lewis, eds., *The New Institutional Economics and Third World Development* (London: Routledge, 1997).

Hartlyn, Jonathan, Lars Schoultz, and Augusto Varas, eds., *The United States and Latin America in the 1990s: Beyond the Cold War* (Chapel Hill, NC: University of North Carolina Press, 1992).

Hedrick, Basil C., and Anne K. Hedrick, *Historical Dictionary of Panama* (Metuchen, NJ: Scarecrow Press, 1970).

Herman, Edward S., and Frank Brodhead, *Demonstration Elections: U.S.-Staged Elections in the Dominican Republic, Vietnam, and El Salvador* (Boston: South End Press, 1984).

Hoekman, Bernard M. and Michel M. Kostecki, *The Political Economy of the World Trading System: From GATT to WTO* (Oxford: Oxford University Press, 1995).

Hoeven, Rolph Van Der and Anthony Shorrocks, eds., *Perspectives on Growth and Poverty* (New York: United Nations University Press, 2003).

Holden, Robert H., *Armies without Nations: Public Violence and State Formation in Central America, 1821-1960* (New York: Oxford University Press, 2004).

Hollander, Jack M., *The Real Environmental Crisis: Why Poverty, Not Affluence, Is the Environment's Number One Enemy* (Berkeley, CA: University of California Press, 2003).

Holm, Hans-Henrik, and Geog Sorenson, *Whose World Order? Uneven Globalization and the End of the Cold War* (Boulder, CO: Westview Press, 1995).

Honey, Martha, *Hostile Acts: U.S. Policy in Costa Rica in the 1980s* (Gainesville, FL: University Presses of Florida, 1994).

Hope, Kempe Ronald, *Development in the Third World: From Policy Failure to Policy Reform* (Armonk, NY: M.E. Sharpe, 1996).

Houston, John A., and Ricardo J. Alfaro, *Latin America in the United Nations* (New York: Carnegie Endowment for International Peace, 1956).

Howard, Michael, *Public Sector Economics for Developing Countries* (Barbados: University Press of the West Indies, 2001).

Hoy, Paula, *Players and Issues in International Aid* (West Hartford, CT: Kumarian Press, 1998).

Huglett, Lloyd J., ed., *Industrialization of Latin America* (New York: McGraw-Hill Book Company, Inc., 1946).

Hurrell, Andrew and Ngaire Woods, eds., *Inequality, Globalization, and World Politics* (Oxford: Oxford University Press, 1999).

International Bank for Reconstruction and Development, *The World Bank in Latin America: A Summary of Activities* (Washington, DC: World Bank, 1960).

Jackson, John H., and Alan O. Sykes, *Implementing the Uruguay Round* (Oxford: Oxford University, 1997).

James, Herman G., and Percy A. Martin, *The Republics of Latin America: Their History, Governments, and Economic Conditions* (New York: Harper & Brothers, 1923).

James, Valentine Udoh, ed., *Sustainable Development in Third World Countries Applied and Theoretical Perspectives* (Westport, CT: Praeger Publishers, 1996).

Jauberth, H. Rodrigo, *The Difficult Triangle: Mexico, Central America, and the United States* (Boulder, CO: Westview Press, 1992).

Jeffries, Ian, *A Guide to the Economies in Transition* (New York: Routledge, 1996).

Jha, Raghbendra, *Macroeconomics for Developing Countries* (New York: Routledge, 2003).

Jilberto, Alex E. Fernandez and Andre Mommen, eds., *Liberalization in the Developing World: Institutional and Economic Changes in Latin America, Africa, and Asia* (New York: Routledge, 1996).

Joes, Anthony James, ed., *Saving Democracies: U.S. Intervention in Threatened Democratic States* (Westport, CT: Praeger Publishers, 1999).

Johns, Christina Jacqueline, and P. Ward Johnson, *State Crime, the Media, and the Invasion of Panama* (Westport, CT: Praeger Publishers, 1994).

Jonas, Susanne, *Of Centaurs and Doves: Guatemala's Peace Process* (Boulder, CO: Westview Press, 2000).

Jonas, Susanne and Edward J. Mccaughan, eds., *Latin America Faces the Twenty-First Century: Reconstructing a Social Justice Agenda* (Boulder, CO: Westview Press, 1994).

Jonas, Susanne and Nancy Stein, eds., *Democracy in Latin America: Visions and Realities* (New York: Bergin & Garvey Publishers, 1990).

Jonas, Susanne, and Edelberto Rivas Torres, *The Battle for Guatemala: Rebels, Death Squads, and U.S. Power* (Boulder, CO: Westview Press, 1991).

Jones, Phillip W., *World Bank Financing of Education: Lending, Learning, and Development* (New York: Routledge, 1992).

Jorge, Antonio and Jorge Salazar-Carrillo, eds., *Price Policies and Economic Growth* (Westport, CT: Praeger, 1997).

Kantor, Harry, *The Continuing Struggle for Democracy in Latin America*, Howard J. Wiarda, ed., (Boulder, CO: Westview Press, 1980).

Kaplan, Temma, *Taking Back the Streets: Women, Youth, and Direct Democracy* (Berkeley, CA: University of California Press, 2004).

Karnes, Thomas L., *The Failure of Union: Central America, 1824-1960* (Chapel Hill: University of North Carolina Press, 1961).

Karns, Margaret P. and Karen A. Mingst, eds., *The United States and Multilateral Institutions: Patterns of Changing Instrumentality and Influence* (London: Routledge, 1992).

Kaul, Chandrika and Valerie Tomaselli-Moschovitis, eds., *Statistical Handbook on Poverty in the Developing World* (Phoenix: Oryx Press, 1999).

Kenworthy, Eldon, *Myth in the Making of U.S. Policy toward Latin America* (University Park, PA: Pennsylvania State University Press, 1995).

Khoury, Sarkis J., *The Deregulation of the World Financial Markets: Myths, Realities, and Impact* (New York: Quorum Books, 1990).

Kiggundu, Moses N., *Managing Globalization in Developing Countries and Transition Economies: Building Capacities for a Changing World* (Westport, CT: Praeger, 2002).

Killick, Tony, *IMF Programs in Developing Countries: Design and Impact* (New York: Routledge, 1995).

Klaren, Peter F. and Thomas J. Bossert, eds., *Promise of Development: Theories of Change in Latin America* (Boulder, CO: Westview Press, 1986).

Kleymeyer, Charles David, ed., *Cultural Expression and Grassroots Development: Cases from Latin America and the Caribbean* (Boulder, CO: Lynne Reinner, 1994).

Klitgaard, Robert, *Tropical Gangsters* (New York: Basic Books, 1990).

Kohli, Atul, Chung-In Moon, and George Sorensen, eds., *States, Markets, and Just Growth: Development in the Twenty-First Century* (New York: United Nations University Press, 2003).

Korzeniewicz, Roberto Patricio and William C. Smith, eds., *Latin America in the World-Economy* (Westport: Praeger Paperback, 1996).

Kramer, Wendy, *Encomienda Politics in Early Colonial Guatemala, 1524-1544: Dividing the Spoils* (Boulder, CO: Westview Press, 1994).

Krueger, Anne O., *Economic Policies at Cross-Purposes: The United States and Developing Countries* (Washington, DC: The Brookings Institution, 1993).

Kryzanek, Michael J., *U.S.-Latin American Relations* (Westport, CT: Praeger Publishers, 1996).

Kumar, Krishna, ed., *Transnational Enterprises: Their Impact on Third World Societies and Cultures* (Boulder, CO: Westview Press, 1980).

Kumar, Nagesh, John H. Dunning, Robert E. Lipsey, Jamuna P. Agarwal, and Shujiro Urata, *Globalization, Foreign Direct Investment, and Technology Transfers: Impacts on and Prospects for Developing Countries* (London: Routledge, 1998).

Lafeber, Walter, *United States Foreign Policy at Home and Abroad since 1750* (New York: Norton, 1994).

Lal, Deepak, and H. Myint, *The Political Economy of Poverty, Equity, and Growth: a Comparative Study* (Oxford: Clarendon Press, 1998).

Lee, Boon-Chye, *TheEconomics of International Debt Renegotiation: The Role of Bargaining and Information* (Boulder, CO: Westview Press, 1993).

Lehoucq, Fabrice E., and IvAn Molina, *Stuffing the Ballot Box: Fraud, Electoral Reform, and Democratization in Costa Rica* (New York: Cambridge University Press, 2002).

Lentner, Howard H., *State Formation in Central America: The Struggle for Autonomy, Development, and Democracy* (Westport, CT: Greenwood Press, 1993).

LeoGrande, William M., *The United States in Central America, 1977-1992* (Chapel Hill, NC: University of North Carolina Press, 1998).

Leonard H. Jeffrey, ed., *Divesting Nature's Capital: The Political Economy of Environmental Abuse in the Third World* (New York: Holmes & Meier, 1985).

Leonard, Thomas M., *The United States and Central America, 1944-1949: Perceptions of Political Dynamics* (Alabama: University of Alabama, 1984).

Lincoln, Jennie K. and Elizabeth G. Ferris, eds., *The Dynamics of Latin American Foreign Policies: Challenges for the 1980s* (Boulder, CO: Westview Press, 1984).

Lissakers, Karin, *Banks, Borrowers, and the Establishment: A Revisionist Account of the International Debt Crisis* (New York: Basic Books, 1991).

Lockey, Joseph Byrne, *Pan-Americanism: Its Beginnings* (New York: Macmillan, 1920).

Loker, William M., ed., *Globalization and the Rural Poor in Latin America* (Boulder, CO: Lynne Reinner, 1999).

Lopez, George A. and Michael Stohl, eds., *Dependence, Development, and State Repression* (New York: Greenwood Press, 1989).

Lowenthal, Abraham F. and J. Samuel Fitch, eds., *Armies and Politics in Latin America* (New York: Holmes & Meier, 1986).

Lutz, Mark A., *Economics for the Common Good: Two Centuries of Social Economic Thought in the Humanistic Tradition* (London: Routledge, 1999).

Macarov, David, *What the Market Does to People: Privatization, Globalization, and Poverty* (Atlanta: Clarity Press, 2003).

Macesich, George, *World Debt and Stability* (New York: Praeger Publishers, 1991).

Mainwaring, Scott and Arturo Valenzuela, eds., *Politics, Society, and Democracy: Latin America* (Boulder, CO: Westview Press, 1998).

Manz, Beatriz, *Paradise in Ashes: A Guatemalan Journey of Courage, Terror, and Hope* (Berkeley, CA: University of California Press, 2004).

Marber, Peter, *From Third World to World Class: The Future of Emerging Markets in the Global Economy* (Reading, MA: Perseus Books, 1998).

Mares, David R., *Violent Peace: Militarized Interstate Bargaining in Latin America* (New York: Columbia University Press, 2001).

Martin, William G. and Immanuel Wallerstein, eds., *Semiperipheral States in the World-Economy* (New York: Greenwood Press, 1990).

Martz, John D., ed., *United States Policy in Latin America: A Decade of Crisis and Challenge* (Lincoln, NE: University of Nebraska Press, 1995).

Mattinson, Sylvia, Sandor Halebsky, James Sacouman, Henry Veltmeyer, John M. Kirk, and George W. Schuler, eds., *Central America: Democracy, Development, and Change* (New York: Praeger Publishers, 1988).

Mawby, R.I., *Policing across the World: Issues for the Twenty-First Century* (London: UCL Press, 1999).

May, Stacy, Just Faaland, Albert R. Koch, Howard L. Parsons, Clarence Senior, and Woodrow Wilson International Center for Scholars, *Costa Rica: A Study in Economic Development* (London: G.Allen & Unwin, 1952).

May, Stacy, and Galo Plaza, *The United Fruit Company in Latin America* (Washington, DC: National Planning Association, 1958).

McCain, William D., *The United States and the Republic of Panama* (Durham, NC: Duke University Press, 1937).

McClaurin, Irma, *Women of Belize: Gender and Change in Central America* (New Brunswick, NJ: Rutgers University Press, 1996).

Mccombie, J.S.L., and A.P. Thirlwall, *Essays on Balance of Payments Constrained Growth: Theory and Evidence* (New York: Routledge, 2004).

Mecham, J. Lloyd, *The United States and Inter-American Security 1889-1960* (Austin: University of Texas Press, 1961).

Meeks, Brian, *Caribbean Revolutions and Revolutionary Theory: An Assessment of Cuba, Nicaragua and Grenada* (Kingston, Jamaica: University of the West Indies Press, 2001).

Mehmet, Ozay, Errol Mendes, and Robert Sinding, *Towards a Fair Global Labour Market: Avoiding the New Slave Trade* (New York: Routledge, 1998).

Melmed-Sanjak, Jolyne, Carlos E. Santiago, and Alvin Magid, *Recovery or Relapse in the Global Economy: Comparative Perspectives on Restructuring in Central America* (Westport, CT: Praeger Publishers, 1993).

Metoyer, Cynthia Chavez, *Women and the State in Post-Sandinista Nicaragua* (Boulder, CO: Lynne Reinner, 2000).

Meyer, Carrie A., *The Economics and Politics of NGOs in Latin America* (Westport, CT: Praeger Publishers, 1999).

Michie, Jonathan and John Grieve Smith, eds., *Global Instability: The Political Economy of World Economic Governance* (London: Routledge, 1999).

Mikdashi, Zuhayr, ed., *Financial Intermediation in the 21st Century* (New York: Palgrave, 2001).

Mikesell, Raymond F., *Foreign Exchange in the Postwar World* (New York: Twentieth Century Fund, 1954).

Miller, Marian A.L., *The Third World In Global Environmental Politics* (Boulder, CO: Lynne Reinner, 1995).

Miller, Russell R., *Doing Business in Newly Privatized Markets: Global Opportunities and Challenges* (Westport, CT: Quorum Books, 2000).

Miller-Adams, Michelle, *The World Bank: New Agendas in a Changing World* (London: Routledge, 1999).

Millington, Thomas, *Debt Politics after Independence: The Funding Conflict in Bolivia* (Gainesville, FL: University Presses of Florida, 1992).

Mohan, Brij, *Eclipse of Freedom: The World of Oppression* (Westport, CT: Praeger Publishers, 1993).

Molle, Willem, *Global Economic Institutions* (New York: Routledge, 2003).

Montejo, Victor, *Testimony: Death of a Guatemalan Village*, Translated by Perera, Victor (Willimantic, CT: Curbstone Press, 1987).

Montgomery, Tommie Sue, *Revolution in El Salvador: From Civil Strife to Civil Peace* (Boulder, CO: Westview Press, 1995).

Moore, John Norton, *The Secret War in Central America: Sandinista Assault on World Order* (Frederick, MD: University Publications of America, 1987).

Moore-Gilbert, Bart, Gareth Stanton, and Willy Maley, eds., *Postcolonial Criticism* (London: Longman, 1997).

Moreno, Dario, *The Struggle for Peace in Central America* (Gainesville, FL: University Press of Florida, 1994).

Morss, Elliott R. and David D. Gow, eds., *Implementing Rural Development Projects: Lessons from Aid and World Bank Experience* (Boulder, CO: Westview Press, 1985).

Moser, Caroline O.N., and Cathy Mcilwaine, *Encounters with Daily Violence in Latin America: Urban Poor Perceptions from Columbia and Guatemala* (New York: Routledge, 2004).

Mosler, David and Bob Catley, *Global America: Imposing Liberalism on a Recalcitrant World* (Westport, CT: Praeger, 2000).

Mosley, Paul and Elizabeth Dowler, eds., *Poverty and Social Exclusion in North and South: Essays on Social Policy and Global Poverty Reduction* (New York: Routledge, 2003).

Mourdoukoutas, Panos, *The Global Corporation: The Decolonization of International Business* (Westport, CT: Quorum Books, 1999).

Mower, A. Glenn, *Regional Human Rights: a Comparative Study of the West European and Inter-American Systems* (New York: Greenwood Press, 1991).

Mowforth, Martin and Ian Munt, *Tourism & Sustainability: Development and Tourism in the Third World* (New York: Routledge, 2003).

Munro, Dana G., *The Five Republics of Central America: Their Political and Economic Development and Their Relation with the United States*, David Kinley, ed., (New York: Oxford University Press, 1918).

Muravchik, Joshua, *News Coverage of the Sandinista Revolution* (Washington, DC: American Enterprise Institute, 1988).

Munoz, Heraldo, and Joseph S. Tulchin, *Latin American Nations in World Politics* (Boulder, CO: Westview Press, 1996).

Nanda, Ved P., George W. Shepherd, and Eileen McCarthy-Arnolds, eds., *World Debt and the Human Condition: Structural Adjustment and the Right to Development* (Westport, CT: Greenwood Press, 1993).

Nazer, Hisham M., *Power of a Third Kind: The Western Attempt to Colonize the Global Village* (Westport, CT: Praeger, 1999).

Needler, Martin, *Latin American Politics in Perspective* (Princeton, NJ: Van Nostrand, 1967).

Needler, Martin C., *The Problem of Democracy in Latin America* (Lexington, MA: Lexington Books, 1987).

Nelson, Michael, *The Development of Tropical Lands: Policy Issues in Latin America* (Baltimore, MD: Resources for the Future, 1973).

Nevaer, Louis E.V., *New Business Opportunities in Latin America: Trade and Investment After the Mexican Meltdown* (Westport, CT: Quorum Books, 1996).

Nickson, R. Andrew, *Local Government in Latin America* (Boulder, CO: L. Reinner Publishers, 1995).

Nolan, Brian and Christopher T. Whelan, *Resources, Deprivation, and Poverty* (Oxford: Clarendon Press, 1996).

Norberg, Johan, *In Defense of Global Capitalism* (Washington, DC: Cato Institute, 2003).

North, Liisa L. and Alan B. Simmons, eds., *Refugee Return and National Transformation in Guatemala* (Montreal: MCGill-Queen's University Press, 2000).

O'Brien, Robert, Anne Marie Goetz, Jan Aart Scholte, and Marc Williams, *Contesting Global Governance: Multilateral Economic Institutions and Global Social Movements* (Cambridge, England: Cambridge University Press, 2000.

O'Cleireacain, Seamus, *Third World Debt and International Public Policy* (New York: Praeger Publishers, 1990).

Olson, Paul R. and C. Addison Hickman, *Pan American Economics* (New York: John Wiley & Sons, Inc., 1943).

Olson, Robert K., *U.S. Foreign Policy and the New International Economic Order: Negotiating Global Problems, 1974-1981* (Boulder, CO: Westview Press, 1981).

O'Neill, Bard E., William R. Heaton, and Donald J. Alberts, eds., *Insurgency in the Modern World* (Boulder: Westview Press, 1980).

Orford, Anne, *Reading Humanitarian Intervention: Human Rights and the Use of Force in International Law* (Cambridge, England: Cambridge University Press, 2003).

Osberg, Lars, ed., *Economic Inequality and Poverty: International Perspectives* (Armonk, NY: M.E. Sharpe, Inc., 1991).

Overbeek, Henk, ed., *Restructuring Hegemony in the Global Political Economy: The Rise of Transnational Neo-Liberalism in the 1980s* (New York: Routledge, 1993).

Owen, Richard, *The Times Guide to World Organisations: Their Role and Reach in the New World Order* (London: Westview Press, 1996).

Palmer, Ransford W., ed., *The Repositioning of U.S.-Caribbean Relations in the New World Order* (Westport, CT: Praeger, 1997).

Pardo-Maurer, R., Edward N. Luttwak, and Center for Strategic and International Studies *The Contras, 1980-1989: A Special Kind of Politics* (New York: Praeger, 1990).

Parsa, Misagh, *States, Ideologies, and Social Revolutions: A Comparative Analysis of Iran, Nicaragua, and the Philippines* (Cambridge, England: Cambridge University Press, 2000).

Pastor, Manuel, *The International Monetary Fund and Latin America: Economic Stabilization and Class Conflict* (Boulder, CO: Westview Press, 1987).

Pastor, Robert, *Exiting the Whirlpool: U.S. Foreign Policy toward Latin Ameirca and the Caribbean* (Boulder, CO: Westview Press, 2001).

Pauly, Louis W., *Who Elected the Bankers? Surveillance and Control in the World Economy* (Ithaca, NY: Cornell University Press, 1997).

Peeler, John A., *Latin American Democracies: Colombia, Costa Rica, Venezuela* (Chapel Hill, NC: University of North Carolina Press, 1985).

Pendergrast, Mark, *Uncommon Grounds: The History of Coffee and How it Transformed Our World* (New York: Basic Books, 1999).

Perdue, William D., *Terrorism and the State: A Critique of Domination through Fear* (New York: Praeger, 1989).

Pierre, Andrew J., ed., *Third World Instability: Central America as a European-American Issue* (New York, NY: Council on Foreign Relations Press, 1985).

Pike, Frederick B., *Freedom and Reform in Latin America* (Notre Dame, IN: University of Notre Dame Press, 1959).

Pirages, Dennis C., ed., *Building Sustainable Societies: A Blueprint for a Post-Industrial World* (Armonk, NY: M.E. Sharpe, 1996).

Poitras, Guy, *The Ordeal of Hegemony: The United States and Latin America* (Boulder, CO: Westview Press, 1990).

Porter, Charles O., and Robert J. Alexander, *The Struggle for Democracy in Latin America* (New York: Macmillan, 1961).

Puiggros, Adriana, *Neoliberalism and Education in the Americas*, Translated by Fischman, Gustavo and Julie Thompson (Boulder, CO: Westview Press, 1999).

Purcell, Randall B., ed., *The Newly Industrializing Countries in the World Economy: Challenges for U.S. Policy* (Boulder, CO: Lynne Reinner Publications, 1989).

Rao, P.K., *The World Trade Organization and the Environment* (New York: St. Martin's Press, 2000).

Ray, Edward John, *U.S. Protectionism and the World Debt Crisis* (New York: Quorum Books, 1989).

Reardon, John J., *America and the Multinational Corporation: The History of a Troubled Partnership* (Westport, CT: Praeger, 1992).

Reinicke, Wolfgang H., *Global Public Policy: Governing without Government?* (Washington, DC: Brookings Institution, 1998).

Rhoodie, Eschel M., *Discrimination Against Women A Global Survey of the Economic, Educational, Social and Political Status of Women* (Jefferson, North Carolina: McFarland & Company, Inc., 1989).

Rippy, J. Fred, *Globe and Hemisphere: Latin America's Place in the Post-war Foreign Relations of the United States* (Chicago: Henry Regnery, 1958).

———, *Latin America: A Modern History* (Ann Arbor, MI: University of Michigan Press, 1958).

Ritter, Archibald R.M., *Latin America to the Year 2000: Reactivating Growth, Improving Equity, Sustaining Democracy*, Maxwell A.

Cameron and David H. Pollock eds., (New York: Praeger Publishers, 1992).

Rivage-Seul, Marguerite K. and D. Michael Rivage-Seul, *A Kinder and Gentler Tyranny: Illusions of a New World Order* (Westport, CT: Praeger Publishers, 1995).

Roberts, Paul Craig, and Karen LaFollette Araujo, *The Capitalist Revolution in Latin America* (New York: Oxford University Press, 1997).

Robinson, William I., *A Faustian Bargain: U.S. Intervention in the Nicaraguan Elections and American Foreign Policy in the Post-Cold War Era* (Boulder, CO: Westview Press, 1992).

Rondinelli, Dennis A., John Middleton, and Adriaan M. Verspoor, *Planning Education Reforms in Developing Countries: The Contingency Approach* (Durham, NC: Duke University Press, 1990).

Ross, Robert J.S., and Kent C. Trachte, *Global Capitalism: The New Leviathan* (Albany, NY: State University of New York Press, 1990).

Ryan, Phil, *The Fall and Rise of the Market in Sandinista Nicaragua* (Montreal: McGill-Queens University Press, 1995).

Salvatore, Dominick, James W. Dean, and Thomas D. Willett, eds., *The Dollarization Debate* (New York: Oxford University Press, 2003).

Sampson, Gary P., ed., *The Role of the World Trade Organization in Global Governance* (New York: United Nations University Press, 2001).

Sands, William Franklin, and Joseph M. Lalley, *Our Jungle Diplomacy* (Chapel Hill, NC: The University of North Carolina Press, 1944).

Schapiro, J. Salwyn, *The World in Crisis: Political and Social Movements in the Twentieth Century* (New York: McGraw-Hill, 1950).

Schechter, Henry B., *The Global Economic Mismatch: High Technology and Low Pay* (Westport, CT: Praeger Publishers, 1993).

Schmertz, Eric J., Natalie Datlof, and Alexej Ugrinsky, eds., *President Reagan and the World* (Westport, CT: Greenwood Press, 1997).

Schmidt, Johannes Dragsbaek and Jacques Hersh, eds., *Globalization and Social Change* (London: Routledge, 2000).

Schneider, Ronald M., *Communism in Guatemala, 1944-1954* (New York: Praeger, 1959).

Schoonover, Thomas D., *The United States in Central America, 1860-1911: Episodes of Social Imperialism and Imperial Rivalry in the World System* (Durham, NC: Duke University Press, 1991).

Schulz, Donald E., and Deborah Sundloff Schulz, *The United States, Honduras, and the Crisis in Central America* (Boulder, CO: Westview Press, 1994).

Schulz, Donald E. and Douglas H. Graham, eds., *Revolution and Counterrevolution in Central America and the Caribbean* (Boulder, CO: Westview Press, 1984).

Seligson, Mithcell A. and John A. Booth, eds., *Election and Democracy in Central America, Revisited* (Chapel Hill: University of North Carolina Press, 1995).

Setzekorn, William David, *Formerly British Honduras: A Profile of the New Nation of Belize* (Chicago: Ohio University Press, 1981).

Sewell, James Patrick, *Functionalism and World Politics: A Study Based on United Nations Programs Financing Economic Development* (Princeton, NJ: Princeton University Press, 1966).

Shafer, D. Michael, *Winners and Losers: How Sectors Shape the Developmental Prospects of States* (Ithaca, NY: Cornell University Press, 1994).

Shavit, David, *The United States in Latin America: A Historical Dictionary* (New York: Greenwood Press, 1992).

Shaw, D. John, *The UN World Food Program and the Development of Food Aid* (New York: Palgrave, 2001).

Shepherd, George W. and Ved P. Nanda, eds., *Human Rights and Third World Development* (Westport, CT: Greenwood Press, 1985).

Shepherd, William R., *Latin America* (New York: H. Holt and Company, 1914).

Sherman, John W., *Latin America in Crisis* (Boulder, CO: Westview Press, 2000).

Sherman, William L., *Forced Native Labor in Sixteenth-Century Central America* (Lincoln, NE: University of Nebraska Press, 1979).

Silverman, Milton, Mia Lydecker, and Philip R. Lee, *The Prescription Drug Industry in the Third World* (Stanford, CA: Stanford University, 1992).

Simon, Paul, and Arthur Simon, *The Politics of World Hunger: Grass-Roots Politics and World Poverty* (New York: Harper's Magazine Press, 1973).

Singer, Hans W., *Economic Liberalization and Labor Markets*, Parvis Dabir-Alai and Mehmet Odekon, eds., (Westport, CT: Greenwood Press, 1998).

Sklar, Holly, ed., *Trilateralism: the Trilateral Commission and Elite Planning for World Management* (Boston, MA: South End Press, 1980).

Sklar, Holly, *Washington's War on Nicaragua* (Boston: South End Press, 1988).

Smillie, Ian, *Mastering the Machine: Poverty, Aid, and Technology* (Boulder, CO: Westview Press, 1991).

Smith, Alan G., *Human Rights and Choice in Poverty: Food Insecurity, Dependency, and Human Rights-Based Development Aid for the Third World Rural Poor* (Westport, CT: Praeger, 1997).

Smith, David A., Dorothy J. Solinger, and Steven C. Topik, *States and Sovereignty in the Global Economy* (London: Routledge, 1999).

Smith, Jackie, Charles Chatfield, and Ron Pagnucco, eds., *Transnational Social Movements and Global Politics: Solidarity Beyond the State* (Syracuse, NY: Syracuse University Press, 1997).

Snider, Lewis W., *Growth, Debt, and Politics: Economic Adjustment and the Political Performance of Developing Countries* (Boulder, CO: Westview Press, 1996).

Snooks, Graeme Donald, *The Global Crisis Makers: An End to Progress and Liberty?* (New York: Palgrave, 2000).

Solberg, Ronald L., ed., *Country-Risk Analysis: A Handbook* (New York: Routledge, 1992).

Solomon, Robert, *Money on the Move: The Revolution in International Finance since 1980* (Princeton, NJ: Princeton University Press, 1999).

Soros, George, *Open Society: Reforming Global Capitalism* (New York: Public Affairs, 2000).

_____, *The Crisis of Global Capitalism: Open Society Endangered* (New York: Public Affairs, 1998).

Spalding, Rose J., *Capitalists and Revolution in Nicaragua: Opposition and Accommodation, 1979-1993* (Chapel Hill: University of North Carolina Press, 1994).

Spencer, David E., *From Vietnam to El Salvador: The Saga of the FMLN Sappers and Other Guerrilla Special Forces in Latin America* (Westport, CT: Praeger Publishers, 1996).

Stanley, William Deane, *The Protection Racket State: Elite Politics, Military Extortion, and Civil War in El Salvador* (Philadelphia: Temple University Press, 1996).

Steinberg, Michael K., Joseph J. Hobbs, and Kent Mathewson, eds., *Dangerous Harvest: Drug Plants and the Transformation of Indigenous Landscapes* (New York: Oxford University Press, 2004).

Stohl, Michael and George A. Lopez, eds., *The State as Terrorist: The Dynamics of Governmental Violence and Repression* (Westport, CT: Greenwood Press, 1984).

--*Terrible Beyond Endurance?: The Foreign Policy of State Terrorism* (New York: Greenwood Press, 1988).

Stokes, William S., *Honduras: an Area Study in Government* (Westport, CT: Greenwood Press, 1974).

Stoll, David, *Rigoberta Menchu and the Story of All Poor Guatemalans* (Boulder, CO: Westview Press, 1999).

Stonich, Susan C., *I Am Destroying the Land! The Political Ecology of Poverty and Environmental Destruction in Honduras* (Boulder, CO: Westview Press, 1993).

Suter, Christian, *Debt Cycles in the World Economy: Foreign Loans, Financial Crises, and Debt Settlements, 1820-1990* (Boulder, CO: Westview Press, 1992).

Sainz, Juan Pablo Perez, *From the Finca to the Maquila: Labor and Capitalist Development in Central America* (Boulder, CO: Westview Press, 1999).

Tapinos, G.A. Mason, and J. Bravo, eds., *Demographic Responses to Economic Adjustment in Latin America* (New York: Oxford University, 1997).

Taylor, Alonzo, *The New Deal and Foreign Trade* (New York: The Macmillan Co., 1935).

Taetreault, Mary Ann and Charles Frederick Abel, eds., *Dependency Theory and the Return of High Politics* (New York: Greenwood Press, 1986).

Thorp, Rosemary, ed., *Inflation and Stabilization in Latin America* (New York: Holmes & Meier, 1979).

Timmer, C. Peter, ed., *Agriculture and the State: Growth, Employment, and Poverty in Developing Countries* (Ithaca, NY: Cornell University Press, 1991).

Torres-Rivas, Edelberto, *Repression and Resistance: The Struggle for Democracy in Central America* (Boulder, CO: Westview Press, 1989).

Trevorton, Gregory F., and Lee Mizell, *The Future of the Information Revolution in Latin America: Proceedings of an International Conference* (Santa Monica, CA: Rand, 2001).

Troncoso, Moisaes Poblete, and Ben G. Burnett, *The Rise of the Latin American Labor Movement* (New Haven, CT: College & University Press, 1962).

Tsuchiya, Kenzaburo, *Protecting Workers' Health in the Third World: National and International Strategies*, Michael R. Reich and Toshiteru Okubo, eds., (New York: Auburn House, 1992).

Tucker, Richard P., *Insatiable Appetite: The United States and the Ecological Degradation of the Tropical World* (Berkeley, CA: University of California Press, 2000).

Tula, Maria Teresa, *Hear My Testimony: Maraia Teresa Tula, Human Rights Activist of El Salvador*, Translated by Stephen, Lynn (Boston: South End Press, 1994).

Tulchin, Joseph S., Gary Bland, eds., *Is There a Transition to Democracy in El Salvador?* (Boulder, CO: L. Reinner Publishers, 1992).

Tussing, A. Dale, *Poverty is a Dual Economy* (New York: St. Martin's Press, 1975).

Twomey, Michael J. and Ann Helwage, eds., *Modernization and Stagnation: Latin American Agriculture into the 1990s* (New York: Greenwood Press, 1991).

Tetreault, Mary Ann, Robert A. Denemark, Kenneth P. Thomas, and Kurt Burch, eds., *Rethinking Global Political Economy: Emerging Issues, Unfolding Odysseys* (New York: Routledge, 2003).

Ucles, Mario Lungo, *El Salvador in the Eighties: Counterinsurgency and Revolution*, Translated by Shogan, Amelia F., Arthur Schmidt, ed., (Philadelphia: Temple University Press, 1996).

Uzan, Marc, *The Financial System Under Stress: An Architecture for the New World Economy* (New York: Routledge, 1996).

Veeser, Cyrus, *A World Safe for Capitalism: Dollar Diplomacy and America's Rise to Global Power* (New York: Columbia University Press, 2002).

Vogelgesang, Sandy, *American Dream, Global Nightmare: The Dilemma of U.S. Human Rights Policy* (New York: Norton, 1980).

Von Hippel, Karin, *Democracy by Force: U.S. Military Intervention in the Post-Cold War World* (Cambridge, England: Cambridge University Press, 2000).

W. Jr., Thomas Palmer, *Search for a Latin American Policy* (Gainesville, FL: University of Florida Press, 1962).

Waddell, D.A., *British Honduras: A Historical and Contemporary Survey* (London: Oxford University Press, 1961).

Waggoner, George R., and Barbara Ashton Waggoner, *Education in Central America* (Lawrence, KS: University Press of Kansas, 1971).

Walker, Thomas W., ed., *Reagan Versus the Sandinistas: The Undeclared War on Nicaragua* (Boulder, CO: Westview Press, 1987).

Wallerstein, Immanuel, *Emerging Issues in the 21st Century World-System: Crises and Resistance in the 21st Century World-System*, Wilma A. Dunaway, ed., (Westport, CT: Praeger, 2003).

Walsh, Lawrence E., *The Iran-Contra Conspiracy and Cover-Up* (New York: W.W. Norton, 1997).

Walton, John, *Reluctant Rebels: Comparative Studies of Revolution and Underdevelopment* (New York: Columbia University Press, 1984).

Weaver, Frederick Stirton, *Inside the Volcano: The History and Political Economy of Central America* (Boulder, CO: Westview Press, 1994).

_____, *Latin America in the World Economy: Mercantile Colonialism to Global Capitalism* (Boulder, CO: Westview Press, 2000).

Weeks, John, *The Economies of Central America* (New York: Holmes & Meier, 1985).

Wennergren, E. Boyd, Donald L. Plucknett, Nigel J.H. Smith, William L. Furlong, and Joan H. Joshi, *The United States and World Poverty* (Cabin John, MD: Seven Locks Press, 1989).

Wesson, Robert, ed., *Coping with the Latin American Debt* (New York: Praeger Publishers, 1988).

Westra, Laura and Peter S. Wenz, eds., *Faces of Environmental Racism: Confronting Issues of Global Justice* (Lanham, MD: Rowman & Littlefield, 1995).

Wiarda, Howard J., ed., *Rift and Revolution: The Central American Imbroglio* (Washington, DC: American Enterprise Institute, 1984).

_____, *The Democratic Revolution in Latin America: History, Politics, and U.S. Policy* (New York: Holmes & Meier, 1990).

Wiarda, Howard J. and Harvey F. Kline, eds., *Latin American Politics and Development* (Boulder, CO: Westview Press, 1996).

_____, *An Introduction to Latin American Politics and Development* (Boulder, CO: Westview Press, 2001).

Wilkinson, Richard, *Unhealthy Societies: The Afflictions of Inequality* (New York: Routledge, 1996).

Willetts, Peter, ed., *The Conscience of the World: The Influence of Non-Governmental Organisations in the UN System* (Washington, DC: Brookings Institution Press, 1996).

Williamson, Robert C., *Latin American Societies in Transition* (Westport, CT: Praeger, 1997).

Wilson, Charles Morrow, *Challenge and Opportunity: Central America* (New York: H. Holt and Company, 1941).

Wolff, Robert Paul, *The Poverty of Liberalism* (Boston: Beacon Press, 1968).

Woodward, Ralph Lee, ed., *Central America: Historical Perspectives on the Contemporary Crises* (New York: Greenwood Press, 1988).

World Bank, *The World Bank and Ida in the Americas: A Summary of Activities* (Washington, DC: World Bank, 1962).

Yashar, Deborah J., *Demanding Democracy: Reform and Reaction in Costa Rica and Guatemala, 1870s-1950s* (Stanford, CA: Stanford University Press, 1997).

Yeager, Timothy J., *Institutions, Transition Economies, and Economic Development* (Boulder, CO: Westview Press, 1998).

Yeung, Ophelia M. and John A. Mathieson, *Global Benchmarks: Comprehensive Measures of Development* (Washington, DC: The Brookings Institution, 1998).

Yunker, James A., *Common Progress: The Case for a World Economic Equalization Program* (Westport, CT: Praeger Publishers, 2000).

INDEX

.